To Gaylene:
How bout a little
Texas food? Dawn
and I hope you'll
enjoy this taste of
Texas!
Betsy

The
Mystique of Entertaining

Texas Tuxedos to Tacos

New Expanded Edition

By
Tricia Henry & Betsy Nozick

EAKIN PRESS WACO, TEXAS

FIRST EDITION
Copyright © 2007
By Tricia Henry and Betsy Nozick
Published in the United States of America
By Eakin Press
A Division of Sunbelt Media, Inc.
P.O. Drawer 90159 ⓓ Austin, Texas 78709-0159
email: sales@eakinpress.com
🖥 website: www.eakinpress.com 🖥
ALL RIGHTS RESERVED.
1 2 3 4 5 6 7 8 9
ISBN 978-1-57168-893-4
ISBN 1-57168-893-5
Library of Congress Control Number 2006925924

To our husbands, Mike and Robert, who not only put up with the hours we spent away from home while we catered, helped out in the frequent pinches and willingly ate leftovers without complaining, but who also lovingly listened to our tales while they rubbed our weary backs. This book, and our years of catering together, would not have been possible with out their constant support and love.

About the Authors

Tricia Henry was raised in Wilmette, Illinois, a North Shore suburb of Chicago. Her interest in foods and entertaining was inspired by her mother-in-law, a gourmet Swedish cook extraordinaire. As the mother of four and the wife of a marketing executive, Tricia had many opportunities to develop creative and interesting recipes, and to home her shills as a party-giver. The Henrys have lived in various parts of the United States, and have traveled extensively, allowing Tricia to draw inspiration from regional and international cuisines and to expand her culinary knowledge. When the Henry family moved to Austin, Tricia met Betsy, and soon joined her young Gourmet Gals Catering team.

Betsy Nozick was born and raised in Dallas and is a fourth generation Texan. She began her business, Gourmet Gals Catering, in Amarillo. A few months later the Nozick family moved to Austin, and the saga of Gourmet Gals and Guys, as it exists today, began. Under Betsy's direction and dedication to fine foods and the art of presentation, the business has thrived in Austin for 30 years. She credits her loyal staff with the continuing creative success of the company. Betsy believes her culinary skills are a direct influence from her mother, "although my late father told anyone who listend that I couldn't boil water before being married."

Texas Tuxedos to Tacos is the result of 30 years of catering together at Gourmet Gals and Guys, where each event is the "only" event. This paired them with clients who have become family, and for more than two decades Tricia and Betsy have helped them celebrate their births, birthdays, weddings, and other grand affairs. This book is a voyage through Texas partying, featuring stories about the dignitaries that Tricia and Betsy have been privileged to serve, including presidents, senators, authors, and even His Royal Highness, Prince Charles. Here are chronicled memories, the menus, and kitchen-tested recipes which can now serve 10 guests instead of 500. Like their years of catering, this book combines two personalities that complement each other, and describes the culinary magic they created.

Contents

Foreword

There is a special mystique to Texas. Texans represent many things to the uninitiated: We are bigger than life in our boots and Stetsons, rugged individualists whose two-steppin' has achieved worldwide acclaim, and we were the first to define hospitality. Our imitators strive to be like us, but one thing will elude them because they may never understand *The Texas State of Mind* — that mysterious secret which also supports our remarkable individualism.

Tricia Henry and Betsy Nozick have captured the essence of Texas hospitality in their recollection of some of their most interesting culinary moments created by Gourmet Gals and Guys. They have beautifully shared some of their finest efforts, both casual and elegant, while also providing that all-important information necessary for the discerning hostess to produce the perfect party. What we Texans have known for years now belongs to the rest of you.

All that will be left for you, the reader, is the guest list and the exciting anticipation of producing your very own special event — with the emphasis on your own individualism and creativity. So, ENJOY! And read on — the secret to the *Mystique of Entertaining* awaits you. . .

Former Texas Governor The Late Ann Richards

Acknowledgments

Contributors

Mr. and Mrs. Ed Auler (Susan and Ed)
Ms. Diane Goforth Bray
Mrs. Allen Childs (Brenda)
Ms. Anne DeBois
Ms. Carol Felauer
Mr. and Mrs. Gary Edminston
Mrs. Lyndon Baines Johnson (Lady Bird)
Mr. Joey Lopez
Mrs. Eugene McDermott (Margaret)
Mrs. Buddy Michelson (Abbi)
Mrs. Charles Morrison (Mary Lou)
Ms. Marsha Kruger

Mrs. Ralph Novin (Roz)
Mr. Terry Nowell
Mrs. Joe Payne (Nancy)
Ms. Norma Reeves
Ms. Ann W. Richards
Mrs. Bob Richardson (Susan)
Mrs. Jim Schnell (Ardis)
Mrs. Milton Smith (Helen)
Texas Beef Council
Mrs. Mark White (Linda Gale)
Mr. Craig Zrubek

Testers

Michele Henry Beltz
Mary Bryant
Debbie Henry
Karen Henry
Robin Nozick Krumme

Hatsie Meloy
Sharon Myers
Erin Henry Price
Marci Nozick Santiago

Tasters

Erik Beltz
Ernie Beltz, Jr.
Nikki Beltz
David Biedermann
Sheila Biedermann
Jolene and Alan Frank
Brandon Henry
Caitlin Henry
Debbie Norvell Henry
Michael Henry
Mike Henry
Peter Henry
Ryan Henry

Gregg Krumme
Kendall Krumme
Kyle Krumme
Cindy and Robert Mitchell
Robert Nozick
Tara Price
Tony Price
Trisha Price
Hector Santiago
Taryn Santiago
Zachary Santiago
Carla and Brandon Sharp
Jenny Silverman

Introduction

his book takes a "look back" at 30 years of experience with Gourmet Gals & Guys Catering and Events. It is a celebration of our catering memories. We hope you will enjoy reminiscing with us as we recount the triumphs of serving future kings, presidents, celebrities, and the many other special people who included us in their celebrations. We never dreamed we would have these incredible opportunities, all of which translated into awesome responsibilities.

Gourmet Gals & Guys' location in Austin, Texas, has given us a considerable advantage. Texas is a big place, and Austin is its capital. We've been able to entertain a number of guests who came to the Lone Star State expecting tumbleweed and sagebrush, black-eyed peas and barbecue, but instead went home with pleasant memories of sophisticated service, fine caviar, and sublime food spreads.

Catering is in many ways a theatrical production, with the caterer playing the rather overwhelming roles of director and producer, set and prop manager, costume designer, and the show's ultimate star — the chef! Yes, putting on a successful party is truly a *"Lights! Camera! Action!"* affair, but without the benefit of a dress rehearsal. Each event is a much-anticipated opening night, and the guests make up both the attentive audience and willing pool of critics. Our goal, or course, has always been to make every event, great or small, a perfectly orchestrated production.

The following chapters are but a sampling of our catering escapades. We reveal some tricks of the trade as well as divulge fabulous recipes that were closely guarded secrets for many years.

Every cookbook has a personality all its own. To better understand ours, take note of these practical guides and reminders:

- If there is an asterisk on a menu item, you will not find a recipe for it in the book. Such foods are generally ones that can be bought at a store, do not need to be cooked, or are simple vegetables that should be served in large quantity.

- The guest lists of the parties we catered often included 200 to 2,500 names. For your sake (assuming you don't cook for such large crowds), we have tested every recipe in our own kitchens and scaled them down to more manageable numbers, with the number of servings specified for almost every recipe.

- Many of the meats are seasoned and refrigerated overnight — it's a personal style. If you are pressed for time, do as far ahead as possible. When cooking most meats, we bring them to room temperature so that they cook faster.

- Garlic is a mainstay in our cooking.

(Another personal favorite is vanilla — but usually not in a recipe that uses garlic!) Please note that granulated garlic is *not* garlic salt. Do not substitute!

- A quick-read meat thermometer is a must for ensuring the correct temperature and quality. Buy one and hide it so that you alone will know where it is (they disappear).

- We have included several of our favorite bread and sweetbread recipes. However, we have asterisks on some breads listed on menus. It is sometimes easier to put those items on your grocery list if you have a favorite bakery.

- Seasoning food is truly in the mouth of the one doing the cooking. Suit your tastebuds.

- This cookbook is intended as a guide. Be your own caterer; mix and match these menus to meet your own tastes. Why not plan a "Mystique Dinner Party," and have your guests bring a dish to complete an entire menu?

We hope that *Texas Tuxedos to Tacos* will help your own entertaining, wherever you live, to be easier and more enjoyable. Our tips will save you some of the inevitable frustration and cut the time-consuming preparation of party giving. We learned the short cuts the hard way — through trial, error, and necessity. Most of all, it is our hope that *Texas Tuxedos to Tacos* will supply you with a few chuckles as we share some of our most impossible situations (like the time we prepared for a guaranteed 2,000 guests, only to have 3,500 hungry people appear!).

Have fun, and *BON APPETIT!*

Chapter 1

"What Are You Doing About the Weather?"
. . . and Other Stories

he original title for this book was *"And What Are You Doing About the Weather?"* because all too often a gourmet caterer's top priority — serving a memorable meal — ends up of secondary concern to a host or hostess, upstaged by the caterer's assumed ability to control the weather. Don't be misled: Hours of culinary preparation do go into the planning of any event. It's just that fickle Mother Nature, with little respect for our hard work, often has ideas of her own about a party, and well-meaning clients count on us not only to feed them but to tame her.

Blessed with a temperate climate, Texans love to entertain outdoors. Though the odds are generally on our side when it comes to staging an outside affair, all true Texans know nonetheless that the only sure thing about Texas weather is that it changes quickly, unexpectedly, and violently. As you might expect, we've had our fair share of wrangles with the weather, and we've included some of the most memorable tales here along with other stories.

August in Austin is characterized traditionally by the three "H's": hazy, hot, and humid. Therefore, we hope most of our parties are planned indoors with the benefit of air conditioning. When we first discussed an August wedding with the parents of a future bride, it was no surprise to learn that they favored a formal, seated buffet dinner reception in the thermostat-regulated ballroom of Austin's finest hotel.

But, as everyone knows, weddings are emotionally charged events and the father-of-the-bride can get awfully worked up when it comes to "giving away" his pride and joy. As this particular father began to wax sentimental, he forsook reason, becoming firmly convinced that the only appropriate backdrop for his daughter's wedding reception was his own lovingly tended yard, replete with stately trees and trim flower gardens. Forget the gleaming, climate-controlled ballroom. Nothing could compare to his lawn — a manicured masterpiece! Besides, he added, the weather would pose no problem. Everyone knows it rarely rains in Central Texas in early August. . .

Try as we did, there was no discouraging this proud father. So we acquiesced, turning our attention to menu planning. Flowers were ordered, embroidered tablecloths were sent from New York, and all the heirloom silver polished. Everything was in place. Almost. The only hitch in our well-laid plans was that Mother Nature was uncharacteristically out of sorts, and for three weeks, Austin had been the object of her aggression. Rainfall exceeded the monthly average by some six inches. Flash floods had become commonplace. The wedding was fast approaching, but

1

this dad held firm, rejecting our suggestions to erect a large, graceful, air-conditioned white tent. No, in his opinion, the tent would mar the beauty of his emerald showplace, and he was positive it wouldn't rain. Such faith!

A week before the event, on yet another rainy morning, we received the obligatory call from the mother-of-the-bride. Much to our amazement, there was not the slightest waver in her voice as she finalized the last-minute details for setting up on her lawn. Then, with admirable contained hysteria, she asked pleadingly, "And what are you doing about the weather?"

Though not entirely to our credit, the reception turned out beautifully. Mother Nature continued to rage until just twelve hours prior to the guests' arrival, but her gift to all was a bright sunrise on the morning of the nuptials that transformed the rain-soaked lawn into a sparkling, dry showplace. The sun continued to shine on the picture-perfect setting until the newlyweds stole off together. As the last guests departed, the skies opened in a deluge that drenched the tables, drowned the remaining food, flooded the precious yard, and, of course, soaked the catering staff. When the bride's mother came over to thank us for making dreams come true, she seemed convinced that we really could control the weather. It was then that we knew we had to write a book!

While weddings make up a number of the parties we handle, a multitude of other events are equally important. Just as every host or hostess is unique, so is the occasion planned in cooperation with him or her. Our golden rule of party planning is that each party's menu and decor reflect the personality of its host.

Banks are frequent clients, and with the recent reorganization, restructuring and re-opening trend, bank parties have been plentiful. Of course, each institution expects its ribbon-cutting event to be more memorable than the last. One such party particularly challenged our creativity. Some 100 guests had been invited to enjoy cocktails and hors d'oeuvres in the bank's newly unveiled boardroom, which was dominated by an oversized, custom-made conference table. The organizers had requested light foods, beverages, and appropriate music, but they had ruled out decorating with flowers, which left the massive conference table looking far too empty.

Our solution? The centerpiece would double as the entertainment. A harpist gowned beautifully in black graced the center of the table and strummed angelic chords as the guests mingled and helped themselves to food offerings artfully arranged around her—truly gourmet with a wink!

Another memorable party was a small affair aboard a boat chartered on Austin's nearby Lake Travis. Cosmetic giant Estee Lauder had specified it wanted "something different" to entertain area sales reps. We took that as a cue to pamper the honored female guests! Shortly after a light, leisurely lunch served on the boat's deck, the women were invited to relax atop floats on the lake's glistening waters. The day was a scorcher, but before the bright sun could take its toll on the guests, a handsome prince of sorts (Gourmet Gals & Guys' own Jerry Doran) came to the rescue, swimming cautiously among the women, a silver platter balanced precariously overhead laden with chilled champagne and light refreshments. The women were charmed, and the ever-resourceful Jerry had a quick, cooling dip.

Even a rare ice storm didn't keep

2

guests away from a sumptuous black-tie fashion show fund-raiser featuring top New York designer Bill Blass. A makeshift kitchen was set up on the loading dock of the luxury department store where the party was held, and a showstopping buffet was created. It ran the length of the display cases and was topped magnificently by two 50-pound rounds of aged cheddar, carved with the designer's "BB" insignia. Even more dazzling was our dessert selection. Spread throughout the store's glimmering showcases of emeralds, rubies, and sapphires was a lavish assortment of sinfully rich sweets — precious jewels themselves — accompanied by scattered, hand-dipped chocolate strawberries and winter-white chocolate branches glinting with silver and gold.

There were many other memorable occasions, among them building openings for which we were commissioned not only to cater the food but to make thousands of square feet of empty corporate space come alive. One such party for prominent developers Phil Capron and Bob Shepherd found us transforming 8,000 echoing square feet into an antique wonderland. A full orchestra set up near a 25-foot antique bar serenaded the crowd, luxurious chandeliers hung overhead, and an astounding array of food was served to guests seated in authentic Queen Anne chairs atop imported Oriental rugs.

Another exceptional event, for a well-known real estate company, was the opening of a giant industrial business park in Austin. We received 2,000 acceptances from the businesses that had recently opened in the complex. We greeted the guests to a ragin' Cajun celebration beginning at 4:00 P.M. The outdoor party site, covered by a huge, white tent, had been completely trans-formed into the rollicking French Quarter, and 2,000 Hurricane glasses etched with the client's logo were lined up alongside pots of sizzling jambalaya and Cajun gumbo. A Dixieland band enhanced the Bourbon Street mood, as did masks and wrought iron fixtures. But what indelibly marked the party in our memories was that word of the big event had traveled through the office grapevines, and 1,500 unexpected guests descended upon us, eager to join the fun and partake in the New Orleans buffet.

Our catering collaboration began during one particularly hectic holiday season. A gala Christmas party for more than 300 guests was hosted by a prominent Austin couple at their home. The event was a caterer's dream in that the hosts had enthusiastically embraced every menu item and decorating idea we suggested. It must be said that Christmas in Austin is generally mild. In fact, many a winter we have turned on the air-conditioning in order to enjoy a crackling holiday fire. So our plans to create a winter wonderland complete with "icicles" and "snow" inside a huge, white tent were especially well received.

Four days before the party, on a balmy December day, we began to set up the tent and its corresponding canopy, creating the entrance into our winter wonderland. Enter the weatherman! Word was that a "norther" was due to arrive within a few days, making it necessary to enclose our makeshift Ice Castle, to keep the real arctic air outside.

After hours of calls, we arranged to have practically every portable heater in Austin delivered to the tent. We also blanketed the structure with isinglass curtains we could roll right down to enclose the tent with plastic walls, in order to protect the buffets and guests from the elements. As we stepped back to admire the splendid outcome, we felt the first signs of Jack Frost's arrival, adding real dimension to the party decor.

The guests spent the evening in a kind of virtual reality. Santa Claus escorted them into his Ice Castle, while outside, Mother Nature whipped up freezing sleet, causing actual icicles to form on the tent's edges.

The Christmas party marked the beginning of a successful partnership dedicated to mastering the mystique of Texas entertaining. For us, "mystique" is best defined as that unexpected, fleeting magic that occurs when everything about a party — food, drink, and ambiance — falls perfectly into place. Guests feel it, as do their hosts. As caterers, we do our best to make it happen.

Chapter 2

Political Feats and Feasts

atering is a nonpartisan occupation, and at formal, seated dinner parties it's of little consequence to us whether the guests of honor are Democrats, Republicans, or Independents. Our aim is to capture votes of approval for the food and service.

Preparation for these polished events typically begins the day prior to the dinner, as setting the tables with fine china, crystal, and silver alone demands hours of work. The day of the party is especially intense, with as much attention paid to the perfect napkin fold and balanced lighting as to the quality of the food.

When serving within the time constraints of a formal dinner, even the basics —keeping the "hots" hot and "colds" cold —can become a logistical feat. Beautifully arranged plates must arrive at each table in a timely fashion after the guests have been seated. Stress levels of the caterers run high because every second counts! But when the plates are returned to us with "tongue tracks," we know our hard work was worth it.

Austin and the beautiful surrounding Hill Country can boast of having been home to the country's 36th president, Lyndon Baines Johnson. The LBJ Presidential Library and Museum is located on the sprawling University of Texas campus, and former First Lady Lady Bird Johnson retained an Austin home in addition to the family's ranch in nearby Stonewall. On numerous occasions, we have had the privilege of serving the Johnson family, friends, and associates at the Library, in town, and at the ranch.

It's a thrill to stage parties at the LBJ Library, and we have organized varied events in several different parts of the building. Mrs. Johnson's private quarters include a beautifully appointed dining room with a view of the Austin skyline. Intimate dinners and smaller formal affairs have been served there. An atrium area on the same floor is the perfect setting for formal and informal celebrations. But the most magnificent area of the Library is its second floor, appropriately named "The Great Hall." There, an imposing marble staircase ascends to five floors of immaculately preserved presidential files. The red and gold bound archives, rising over the 50-foot-long electro-copperplated mural of Presidents Franklin D. Roosevelt, Harry S. Truman, Dwight D. Eisenhower, John F. Kennedy and Lyndon Baines Johnson, provides a magnificent backdrop for our parties. Harry Middleton was the director of the LBJ Library and Museum; however, our contact and liaison was Dorothy Territo, the former acting assistant director of the LBJ Library and Museum and formerly one of President Johnson's staff assistants. Relying on her impeccable expertise in party planning and inevitable crossfire, we planned and carried through many successful events and built a lasting friendship along the way. Dorothy once told us that one of President Johnson's favorite sayings was, "If you're not being challenged, you're not growing."

Challenged we were, and grow we did, with each event presenting its own logistical tasks. Sometimes the Great Hall was dressed in Mexican finery to complement our popular Tex-Mex buffet. Other times the room was draped in a more understated black and gold for elegant black-tie affairs. Occasionally, bright red tables splendidly set off the rows of stately archives looming overhead. But the LBJ Library was at its most superb when decorated regally for dinner in honor of a special guest, His Royal Highness, The Prince of Wales. (See Chapter 10 for details.)

What follows in this chapter are a number of the menus we served to dignitaries, including former President and First Lady Mr. and Mrs. Gerald Ford, Israeli Prime Minister Benjamin Netanyahu, David and Julie Nixon Eisenhower, former Senator and one-time presidential candidate Barry Goldwater, Senator Daniel Patrick Moynihan, Representative Patricia Schroeder, former U.S. Ambassador to Russia Bob Strauss, John Kenneth Galbraith, and luminaries Jack Valenti, president of the Motion Picture Association of America, Bill Moyers, Walter Cronkite, and columnists Ann Landers and Art Buchwald.

For all the recipes included, the votes were overwhelmingly in favor of seconds!

An Evening With the President

Hors d'oeuvres:
Oregano Pesto Torta
Smoked Salmon and Cream Cheese Pate

Starter:
Orange Glazed Leeks

Entree:
Grilled Pork Medallions
with Basil Sauce and Texas Goat Cheese Sauce

Fresh Asparagus
in Garlic Butter

Petite Caramelized Onions

French Bread Rounds
with Oregano Butter

Dessert:
Bavarian Berry Chocolate Cake Roll
with seasonally fresh berries and Regal Whipping Cream

OREGANO PESTO TORTA

Pesto:

2-3	bunches oregano, finely minced	1	poblano pepper
½	cup roasted pine nuts	1½	lbs. cream cheese, softened
½	cup grated Parmesan cheese	1	lb. provolone cheese, thinly sliced
2	cloves garlic		
¾	cup olive oil	1	cup toasted sliced almonds
1	red bell pepper		

Combine first five ingredients in food processor and process thoroughly to make pesto. Set aside. Roast the bell pepper and poblano pepper until they are black on all sides. Place the peppers in a bowl and seal bowl with plastic wrap (this will allow the peppers to steam and therefore be easier to peel); cool. Peel and cut into thin strips and set aside. Place cream cheese in a medium bowl and beat until creamy. Add pesto to taste. Line an 8-inch cake pan with plastic wrap. Cover the bottom and sides of cake pan with sliced provolone cheese, allowing some cheese to hang over the edges. Spread a thin layer of the cream cheese/pesto mixture over the cheese; then layer strips of peppers and sliced almonds.

(Having thin layers assures that the layers will not separate.) Repeat layering process, pressing as you go to seal well. When pan is filled, complete the Torta with a layer of provolone. Refigerate overnight. Serve with assorted crackers and breads. Torta can be made in advance and will keep, refrigerated, for one week. Serves 20.

SMOKED SALMON AND CREAM CHEESE PATE

1 ½	oz. sliced smoked salmon	½	tsp. granulated garlic (optional)
8	oz. cream cheese		
1	T. sour cream	¼	tsp. Worcestershire
1/8	tsp. salt	1	bunch chopped green onions, greens only
1/8	tsp. ground white pepper		

Dice smoked salmon by hand. Reserve a few pieces for garnish. Set salmon aside. In a food processor, blend the cream cheese, sour cream, salt, pepper, granulated garlic, and Worcestershire until smooth. Add smoked salmon and blend. Mold into desired serving piece and chill.

Before serving, allow pate to come to room temperature. Garnish with chopped green onions and extra salmon pieces, and serve with cocktail rye bread. If you prefer passed hors d'oeuvres, this pate can be spread on party rye or crackers, and garnished with slivers of smoked salmon and chopped green onions.

ORANGE GLAZED LEEKS

10	small to medium leeks	1	cup orange marmalade
4	quarts water with 2 T. white wine vinegar added	1	cup chicken broth
		2	T. fresh grated ginger
½	cup (1 stick) butter	1	T. grated orange zest
1	T. oil	1	cup chopped green onions
1	garlic clove, crushed		Dijon mustard and white wine to taste
1	cup freshly squeezed orange juice	1	cup chopped fresh parsley

Trim tops and bottoms of leeks, discarding any tough or discolored outer leaves. Cut leeks into 6-inch lengths. Combine 4 quarts water and 2 T. vinegar and soak leeks for 10 minutes. Rinse well with cold water, removing all traces of dirt. Drain on paper towels.

Melt butter and oil together in large skillet. Add garlic and cook until soft. Add leeks, and cook until barely tender, turning continuously to coat the vegetables with butter mixture. (Approximately 5 minutes.) Remove leeks, placing them on an ovenproof platter, and keep warm in oven on low heat. Using same skillet, add all remaining ingredients except mustard and parsley and bring to boil. Reduce heat and simmer until sauce thickens. Add white wine and Dijon mustard to taste. Add parsley. Blend well, and pour over leeks. Can be held in warm oven for no longer than 10 minutes. Serves 8.

GRILLED PORK MEDALLIONS
with Basil and Texas Goat Cheese Sauces

Basil Sauce:

3 lbs. pork tenderloin
2 T. granulated garlic
1 tsp. white pepper
1 T. dried basil

1 cup chopped spinach (approx. 4 oz.)
1 cup fresh basil
4 oz. pine nuts, lightly toasted
4 T. olive oil
½ tsp. balsamic vinegar
¼ tsp. ground black pepper

Texas Goat Cheese Sauce:

4 oz. Texas Goat Cheese
4 ½ oz. sun-dried tomatoes
2 cups sour cream

4 large garlic cloves, minced
½ tsp. salt
¼ tsp. white pepper

Pork Medallions:

Rinse pork and pat dry. Roll tenderloin in combined garlic, pepper, and basil. Cover and refrigerate for 6 hours. Remove from refrigerator and allow to come to room temperature 1 hour before grilling. Place on grill over hot coals, turning once, for approximately 10 minutes. Cut into ½-inch thick medallions and serve on sauces — one medallion on the Basil Sauce, and one medallion on the Texas Goat Cheese Sauce. Garnish each medallion with chopped parsley.

Basil Sauce:

Combine all ingredients in a food processor and purée. (This can be made several days ahead and refrigerated.) Bring to room temperature before reheating over low heat. Add a little milk, if necessary, to thin sauce.

Texas Goat Cheese Sauce:

Combine all ingredients in food processor and blend until smooth. Heat on low, adding milk if sauce appears too thick. Serve immediately. Serves 6.

FRESH ASPARAGUS
in Garlic Butter

1 ½ lbs. fresh asparagus,
      or 4 oz. per person
½ cup melted butter

4 garlic cloves, minced
Juice of one whole lemon

Wash and trim asparagus, cutting stems at an angle, and steam for approximately 5 minutes. Drain, then run under cold water, to stop the cooking. Melt butter. Add garlic and cook until soft. Remove mixture from heat and add lemon juice. Pour over asparagus. Ten minutes before serving place asparagus in 375-degree oven. Serves 6.

PETITE CARAMELIZED ONIONS

3 dozen petite white onions	¼ cup honey
1 T. olive oil	½ tsp. salt
4 oz. melted butter	1/8 tsp. nutmeg
1 garlic clove, minced	¼ tsp. white pepper
1 T. dark brown sugar	¼ cup wine

Cook onions in boiling water, skins on, for 2 minutes, allowing the skin to slip off easily. In a heavy skillet, heat olive oil and butter. Add garlic and cook until soft. Add remaining ingredients. Taste and adjust seasonings, if necessary. Add onions, tossing to coat well. Reduce heat to medium low. Tossing frequently, cook for approximately 45 minutes, or until the onions are nicely browned. Again, taste and adjust seasonings, if necessary. Serves 6.

FRENCH BREAD ROUNDS
with Oregano Butter

2 French baguettes	2 T. drained green chiles
1 cup unsalted butter	1 T. mayonnaise
1 T. oregano	Salt and white pepper to taste
1 cup Parmesan cheese, freshly grated	(optional)
	Hot pepper sauce to taste (optional)

Slice French bread into rounds. Place remaining ingredients in food processor and process until smooth and creamy. Salt and pepper and season with hot pepper sauce to taste. Spread butter mixture on bread rounds. Bake in 350-degree oven for 10 to 12 minutes. Serve hot. (Butter mixture can be made several days ahead and stored in refrigerator. You might want to make extra, because the butter is wonderful in baked potatoes!) Serves 6.

BAVARIAN BERRY CHOCOLATE CAKE ROLL

Chocolate Cake:

3 oz. semisweet chocolate, chopped	6 egg yolks
2 T. unsalted butter	½ cup sugar, divided
1 T. water	4 egg whites, room temperature
6 T. flour	¼ tsp. cream of tartar
3 T. cornstarch	

Preheat oven to 375 degrees. Line a 17" x 11" rimmed baking sheet with foil. (If necessary overlap sheets of foil, making sure the bottom and sides are covered.) Butter the foil. Combine chocolate, butter, and water in a double boiler. Melt over low heat, stirring occasionally until smooth. Remove chocolate from hot water and cool. Sift flour and cornstarch into a medium bowl. In a separate large bowl, beat egg yolks lightly. Add 6 T. sugar and continue mixing on high about 5 minutes, or until thick and pale. Fold chocolate mixture into yolk mixture.

In a large bowl, beat egg whites and cream of tartar at medium speed, until soft peaks form. Beat in remaining 2 T. sugar on high until whites are stiff, but not dry. Gently fold about 1/3 of the whites into chocolate mixture. Fold ½ of flour mixture into chocolate mixture. Repeat until all flour is used and blended. Pour batter into prepared baking sheet, spreading evenly. Bake about 6 minutes or until cake is just firm and springs slightly back from edges. Cake will be very thin. Transfer cake with foil to rack and cool.

Berry Filling:

2½	cups chilled whipping cream		1¼	cups sliced strawberries
3	T. plus 1 tsp. sugar		¾	cup raspberries
2	T. brandy		¾	cup blackberries
6	T. clear raspberry brandy			

Chill large bowl and beaters for whipping cream. Whip cream with sugar until stiff. Add brandy and raspberry brandy and beat on low speed until blended. Reserve 3 cups of cream for filling. Fold berries into remaining cream.

Assembly:

Move cake on foil to a large board or tray. Spread gently with filling, using a metal spatula, being careful not to bruise berries. Beginning with the long edge and holding on to the foil, gently roll the cake into a "log." Using the foil, turn cake over onto serving platter, seam side down. Do not worry if the cake cracks during rolling, as the cream will cover it. Spread cake with remaining cream and refrigerate at least 30 minutes before serving. (Completed cake can be held in the refrigerator up to 8 hours.) Serves 10.

Garnish:

Whole strawberries   **Blackberries**
Raspberries

Filibuster Filet

Starter:
French Salad
Bibb lettuce, red romaine, and oak leaf lettuces
dressed with Roquefort cheese and Sherried French Dressing

Entree:
Tenderloin of Beef
with Sauce Robert

Parmesan Zucchini Fans

Potato Trio
Tri-colored miniature potatoes in parslied butter

Reba's Dinner Rolls and Butter

Dessert:
Fruit Gazpacho

FRENCH SALAD

2 heads bibb lettuce	1 red pepper, sliced into strips
2 heads red romaine lettuce	1 green pepper, sliced into strips
1 head oak leaf lettuce	2 oz. Roquefort or bleu cheese
1 pkg. Enoki mushrooms	

Wash, dry, tear and combine lettuces. When ready to serve, mound evenly on individual salad plates; garnish with mushrooms, pepper slices and crumbled cheese. Lightly toss with Sherried French Dressing. Serves 6.

Sherried French Dressing:

1 tsp. sugar	3 cups garlic olive oil
1 tsp. salt	½ cup balsamic vinegar
1 tsp. black pepper	½ cup sherry
1 cup walnut oil	2 garlic cloves

Combine sugar, salt, and black pepper in blender or food processor. Alternately and slowly add oils, vinegar and sherry, until well blended. Store the 2 cloves of garlic in the dressing jar for added flavor. This dressing can be made ahead and stores well. Yields 5 cups.

TENDERLOIN OF BEEF
with Sauce Robert

1   3-lb. beef tenderloin, peeled   Coarse black pepper
Granulated garlic   Olive oil

One day prior to serving, generously season beef tenderloin with garlic and pepper. Wrap in plastic wrap and refrigerate.

One hour before cooking, remove the meat from the refrigerator, allowing it to come to room temperature. Brush with oil. Preheat the oven to 375 degrees and cook meat 25 to 30 minutes for rare. Use a meat thermometer for accuracy. Allow tenderloin to "rest" for 5 minutes before slicing. Serves 8.

Sauce Robert:

2   T. butter
2   garlic cloves, minced
2   medium onions, finely chopped
2   T. flour
1   cup dry white wine
1   cup Meat Stock (recipe follows)

½   tsp. red wine vinegar
1   tsp. Dijon mustard
1   tsp. English beef tea (can be found in gourmet food section of grocery)

In a heavy-bottomed medium saucepan, melt butter and sauté garlic and onions until soft and golden brown. Remove onions with slotted spoon and set aside. Make a roux by adding flour and cook 3 to 4 minutes, until bubbling. Return onions to pan; add wine, stock, red wine vinegar, mustard, and English beef tea. Bring to a boil, whisking constantly. Reduce heat and simmer, uncovered, for 20 minutes. Keep warm on low until ready to serve.

Meat Stock:

3 to 4 lbs. beef bones with meat
3   quarts water
4   carrots, coarsely chopped
2   celery stalks with leaves, coarsely chopped
2   small turnips, diced, if desired

3   onions, halved
2   garlic cloves
4   whole cloves
1   tsp. salt
14 whole black peppercorns

Place bones with meat in roasting pan and bake at 400 degrees, turning once, until brown. Place the bones and meat in a large kettle with 3 quarts of water. Add all ingredients, except salt and peppercorns. Bring to a boil over medium heat. Add salt and peppercorns. Reduce heat and simmer, uncovered, for 3½ to 4 hours. Skim surface as needed. Strain in a fine sieve and cool. Cover and store in refrigerator for up to 1 week. Can be frozen in 1 cup amounts. As a time saver, Sauce Robert can be made using canned beef broth, reduced by half. If you use beef broth, reduce the amount of salt in sauce. Yields 8 to 10 cups.

PARMESAN ZUCCHINI FANS

½ cup Parmesan cheese
½ tsp. granulated garlic
Salt and pepper to taste

1 T. parsley flakes
4 medium zucchini, approximately 7 inches long

Combine Parmesan cheese, garlic, salt and pepper, and parsley. Set aside.

Cut zucchini in half, crosswise. (Each half should be approximately 3 inches long.) Round off each cut end, removing the skin (approximately ½ inch.) Cut each half in half lengthwise, giving you 16 pieces. Using a sharp paring knife, make sliver cuts to within 1 inch of each stem. Gently flatten with your hand to "fan" the sliced zucchini.

Place the fanned zucchini on a cookie sheet sprayed with cooking spray. Sprinkle evenly with Parmesan blend. Bake for approximately 12 minutes in the upper part of the oven. Do not overcook. Broil for 2 final minutes to brown and serve immediately. Serves 8.

POTATO TRIO

Using purple, red and white miniature potatoes purchased from a gourmet grocery store, this recipe offers a unique look. Plan on using one potato of each color per serving.

Miniature potatoes, 3 per serving
2 T. butter
2 T. olive oil

½ cup chopped fresh parsley
1 tsp. granulated garlic
Salt and pepper to taste

Parboil unpeeled potatoes until almost tender. Drain. Combine butter and oil in a pan over medium heat. Add potatoes and seasonings; cook, turning occasionally until tender and lightly brown.

REBA'S DINNER ROLLS

"Reba Rolls" are a 15-year Gourmet Gals & Guys tradition and have been served at more dinner parties than we can count. They were developed by employee and good friend Reba Frenzel.

1½ cups buttermilk
2 T. dry yeast
2 cups + 2½ to 3 cups flour
1/3 cup sugar

2 tsp. salt
½ tsp. baking soda
½ cup butter, melted

In a small saucepan, heat the buttermilk and add yeast. Allow to sit for 10 minutes until yeast is completely dissolved. In the large mixing bowl, combine 2 cups of flour, sugar, salt, and baking soda. Melt butter in buttermilk; add to flour mixture and blend on lowest speed until moistened. Beat for 2 minutes at medium speed. Remove from mixer. By hand, mix in enough flour to form stiff dough. Cover with a towel and let rise until double in size — about 1 hour.

Preheat oven to 350 degrees. Punch dough down, and divide in half. Roll out one half on floured surface into a 12-inch circle. Using a pastry cutter, cut into 10 pie-shaped wedges. Starting with the wide edge, roll each wedge toward the point. Place point side down on baking sheet. Repeat with second half. Cover and let rise until double in size— about 30 minutes. Bake for 15 to 20 minutes, or until golden brown. Yields 20 rolls.

FRUIT GAZPACHO

This fabulous recipe is especially for our friends who are watching their weight. We know that nothing really substitutes for chocolate, but this is a perfect alternative.

Strawberry Sauce:

1	10-oz. pkg. frozen strawberries in syrup, thawed	2	T. strawberry jam
½	cup frozen strawberry daiquiri concentrate	1	tsp. finely grated orange zest
		1	tsp. finely grated lemon zest
			Rum to taste

In food processor, process the strawberries and strawberry daiquiri concentrate until puréed. Stir in jam, lemon zest, and orange zest. Transfer to a medium saucepan and cook until just boiling. Remove from heat; add rum. Allow to cool. Refrigerate.

Fruit Gazpacho:

1	cup finely chopped, peeled kiwi (approximately 4)	1	cup finely chopped cored pears
1	cup finely chopped cored apples	1	cup pitted royal cherries, drained
1	cup finely chopped canteloupe	1	cup whole fresh raspberries
1	cup finely chopped honeydew melon	½	tsp. cinnamon
		1/3	cup peach schnapps

In a large bowl, combine all the chopped and whole fruit; add cinnamon and peach schnapps. Add the chilled Strawberry Sauce and toss.

Whipped Topping:

1	cup whipping cream	½	tsp. vanilla
2	T. powdered sugar		

Whip cream until slightly thickened. Add powdered sugar and vanilla; beat until soft peaks form.

Assembly:

1 pound cake or angel food cake	Orange slices and mint leaves for garnish

In a clear serving bowl, place a 1-inch slice of pound cake or angel food cake. Spoon Fruit Gazpacho on cake. Top with flavored whipped cream. Garnish with mint leaves and an orange twist. Serves 12.

A "Politically Correct" Dinner

Starter:
Mushroom Vegetable Soup

Entree:
Filet of Beef
with Roquefort Sauce and Mixed Nuts

Salmon en Croute
Served with Cucumber Dill Sauce
in lemon cups on a bed of fresh dill

*Steamed Julienne Carrots
with red, yellow, and green peppers

Soft French Bread Rounds
with Goat Cheese and Butter Spread

Dessert:
Raspberry Mousse
with Raspberry Sauce

* Recipe not included

MUSHROOM VEGETABLE SOUP

1/3 cup olive oil	1½ cups mushrooms
1 large onion, quartered	6½ cups fresh or canned chicken broth
2 garlic cloves	
4 large celery stalks, chopped	2 cups fresh or canned beef broth
4 large carrots, cleaned and cut into chunks	

Heat oil in stock pot and sauté onion and garlic until tender and transparent. Add remaining ingredients. Bring to boil; cover and simmer for an hour, or until all the vegetables are tender. Remove from heat and allow to cool. Mix in blender until smooth. Return it to the stock pot and season with salt and pepper to taste. If you like a richer flavor, add ½ cup sherry. Garnish with croutons or crab meat.

This basic soup also makes a wonderful vegetable broth. After you cool the soup, strain out the vegetables. Taste for seasonings. Again, sherry can be added for richness. Garnish with chopped fresh parsley.

FILET OF BEEF WITH ROQUEFORT SAUCE AND MIXED NUTS

This recipe was contributed to Gourmet Gals & Guys by the Texas Beef Council, a frequent client.

1 centercut piece of beef tenderloin, approximately 2 lbs.	½ cup beef bouillon
½ tsp. salt	2 oz. creamy Roquefort cheese
½ tsp. pepper, freshly ground	4 T. unsalted butter, softened
1 T. vegetable oil	3 T. heavy cream, whipped until stiff
2 tsp. peanut oil, for searing	2 T. pine nuts, lightly toasted
1 tsp. clarified butter	2 T. walnut pieces, lightly toasted
1 T. shallots, minced	2 T. sliced almonds, lightly toasted
3 T. dry Madeira wine	1 T. fresh parsley, chopped

Salt and pepper meat, then rub vegetable oil over the surface. Keep meat refrigerated, loosely covered with plastic wrap, until 1 hour before cooking.

In a large heavy-bottomed skillet, heat peanut oil and clarified butter until very hot. Sear the meat on all sides (about 4 minutes). Transfer meat to a wire rack or grid; let rest a minimum of 20 minutes. Discard cooking fat. Add chopped shallots and Madeira to the skillet; reduce to a glaze. Add the beef bouillon and bring to a boil. Reduce to a syrupy consistency. Scrape into a smaller skillet, if desired. Set aside.

Beat the Roquefort cheese and butter in a small bowl until smooth and refrigerate.

About 30 minutes before serving, preheat oven to 450 degrees. Pat beef dry with paper towels. Finish beef filet on a rack in the oven: 18 minutes for rare; 19 minutes for medium-rare.

Meanwhile, gently reheat the syrupy sauce in the skillet; swirl in cheese and butter mixture one spoonful at a time. Remove from heat and fold in the whipped cream. Spoon sauce onto a heated service platter. Slice the meat and arrange on the sauce, overlapping. Surround the meat with nuts mixed with parsley. Serve immediately. Serves 4-6.

SALMON EN CROUTE

3 T. butter	½ lb. butter, chilled and cut into chunks
1 8-oz. can artichoke bottoms, drained and chopped	8 oz. cream cheese, chilled and cut into chunks
1 onion, chopped	2 cups all-purpose flour
1 lb. fresh mushrooms, coarsely chopped	8 5 oz. salmon fillets, ¾ inches thick
¼ cup Madeira	1 egg yolk, beaten, for glaze
Salt and pepper	

Filling:

Melt butter in skillet and sauté artichokes and onions. Add mushrooms and wine. Cook, stirring, until most of the liquid has evaporated. Season to taste. Place in a bowl and chill. Can be done ahead.

Pastry:

In a food processor, using a metal blade, mix butter and cream cheese until blended. Add flour; process until well blended. Shape into 2 flat balls. Refrigerate for several hours.

Assembly:

Roll ½ of the pastry on a floured board into a rectangle about 14 inches long and 12 inches wide. Cut into 4 rectangles. Repeat with remaining dough. Place fillets on greased baking sheet. (Tuck the thinner part of fillet under, making the fillets all the same thickness.) Divide the artichoke-mushroom filling among the fillets, and spread evenly on top. Cover each fillet with a pastry rectangle, tucking ½ inch under fillets; trim off excess dough. (Do not cover the bottom with pastry.) Brush each fillet with beaten egg yolk for even browning. Use pastry scraps for small decorations, brushing with egg yolk. Refrigerate.

One hour before serving, remove from refrigerator and bring to room temperature. Preheat oven to 425 degrees; bake for 20 to 25 minutes or until golden brown. Serve with Cucumber Dill Sauce (recipe below).

CUCUMBER DILL SAUCE

1	cup sour cream		2	T. fresh dill
1½	T. vinegar		½	cucumber, peeled, seeded
1½	T. Dijon mustard			and finely diced
3	T. brown sugar			

Combine all ingredients and chill. Best if made a day ahead. Yields 1⅓ cups.

GOAT CHEESE AND BUTTER SPREAD

½	cup unsalted butter	1/8	cup dried parsley
½	cup goat cheese		French bread
1/8	tsp. ground black pepper		Parmesan cheese

Process butter and goat cheese until soft. Add pepper and parsley. This will make 1 cup. Cut French bread into 1-inch slices. Spread with cheese mixture. Sprinkle with Parmesan cheese and place under broiler until browned (approximately 3 minutes). Can be served hot or at room temperature. Can be stored, refrigerated, for one week.

RASPBERRY MOUSSE

1	cup milk		1	tsp. white vanilla
4	egg yolks		2	cups frozen raspberries,
3	T. sugar			sugared
1½	T. unflavored gelatin, softened in		2	cups whipping cream, whipped
	¼ cup cold milk		4	egg whites, stiffly beaten

Mix milk, egg yolks, and sugar. Cook in double boiler over hot water until a custard is formed. Remove from heat. Add softened gelatin and vanilla. Blend and chill. Purée raspberries in the blender, then strain. Add the raspberry juice to the custard. Taste for sweetness, adding more sugar if necessary. Refrigerate. When mixture begins to thicken, fold in whipped cream and egg whites. Pour into a 2-quart soufflé dish or ring mold. Refrigerate overnight. Serve with Raspberry Sauce (recipe follows).

Raspberry Sauce:

1	jar seedless raspberry jam	2	T. brandy

Melt jam; add brandy. Place 2 T. of mixture in serving bowl before adding mousse.

Dinner and Book Signing with Art Buchwald

Starter:
Fresh Spinach Salad
With cherry tomato halves and red onion,
fresh ground pepper, tossed with vinaigrette

Entree:
Breast of Chicken Basil
Served with Basil Tomato Sauce
*Steamed Haricot Verts
*Angel Hair Pasta
Garlic Bread Sticks

Dessert:
Double Lemon Dessert
Served in a scalloped half of orange,
with Lemon Wafers

*Recipe not included

FRESH SPINACH SALAD

1	lb. fresh spinach	1	cup grated raw carrots
¼	cup chopped green onions	½	cup fresh grated Parmesan cheese
1	clove garlic, finely minced	8	cherry tomatoes, halved
1	cup black olives, finely chopped	1	red onion, thinly sliced

Wash spinach and tear into bite-sized pieces. Dry well; place in plastic bag and refrigerate. When ready to serve, place onions, garlic, olives, carrots, and Parmesan in salad bowl. Add spinach and toss well. Season with freshly cracked black pepper to taste. Garnish with cherry tomato halves and red onion rounds. Dress with the following:

Spinach Salad Dressing:

½	cup white wine vinegar	¼	tsp. dried basil
1	cup olive oil	½	tsp. Worcestershire sauce
½	tsp. salt	1 garlic clove	
1	T. Dijon mustard		

Put all ingredients in blender and mix until smooth. Serve dressing at room temperature. Serves 6.

BREAST OF CHICKEN BASIL

8 5-oz. breasts of chicken, boneless, skinless	1 cup flour
White pepper to taste	1 tsp. lemon pepper
Granulated garlic to taste	1 tsp. ground oregano
Dried basil to taste	1 T. dried parsley
1½ cups Parmesan cheese	3 egg whites
	Olive oil

Early in the day, rinse chicken and remove membrane. Lightly pound and season breasts with pepper, garlic, and basil. Cover and place in refrigerator.

When ready to serve, remove from refrigerator and pat dry. Combine the Parmesan cheese, flour, lemon pepper, oregano, and parsley. Dip breasts in egg whites and then in Parmesan mixture. Heat olive oil in skillet and sauté chicken until cooked through. Hold in a warm oven until ready to serve. Serve with Basil Tomato Sauce (recipe follows). Serves 8.

Basil Tomato Sauce:

4 T. olive oil	2 T. sugar
4-6 large garlic cloves, minced	1 tsp. ground black pepper
2/3 cup tomato paste	2 tsp. ground basil (or 1 T. fresh, chopped)
4 28-oz. cans Italian tomatoes	
5 T. sun-dried tomatoes, chopped	1 cup dry red wine (optional, to taste)
1 tsp. salt	Red pepper flakes to taste

Cook garlic in oil over medium heat until glazed and fragrant, about 3 minutes. Add tomato paste and cook thoroughly, stirring frequently. Add remaining ingredients and simmer slowly for approximately 20 minutes, stirring occasionally. Sauce should be thick. Add wine, and check seasonings to taste.

Yields approximately 7 cups of sauce. Can be made several days ahead and refrigerated in a nonmetallic container, and frozen.

GARLIC BREAD STICKS

½ lb. butter	8 bread sticks, purchased at grocery
2 large garlic cloves, minced	½ lb. fresh grated Parmesan cheese

Melt butter in skillet. Sauté the minced garlic until tender. Remove from heat. Roll each bread stick in the butter-garlic mixture, then in the Parmesan cheese. Bake in a 350-degree oven, on the upper rack, for 10 minutes. Serve immediately.

DOUBLE LEMON DESSERT

This is a rather simple, palate-cleansing dessert that can be made ahead. The elegance of this dessert is in your choice of serving dish.

1 qt. lemon sherbet (or your favorite ice cream)
4 large oranges, cut in half and scalloped

Four hours before serving, fill the oranges with the lemon sherbet (or ice cream of your choice) and freeze until ready to serve.

LEMON WAFERS

These are client Ron Kessler's favorite lemon cookie and it has always been our pleasure to serve them to him.

1	cup butter, softened	1	T. milk
1	cup granulated sugar	¼	tsp. vanilla
1	egg	2 ¾	cups flour
2	tsp. shredded lemon peel	¼	tsp. baking soda
1	T. fresh lemon juice	¼	tsp. salt

Preheat oven to 375 degrees. Mix butter and sugar together in a bowl until creamy. Beat in the egg, lemon peel, lemon juice, milk, and vanilla and set aside. In a separate bowl, combine the flour, baking soda, and salt. Add dry ingredients to the butter/sugar mixture and mix thoroughly. Shape into two 9-inch rolls and wrap with plastic wrap. Chill overnight.

Cut each roll into ¼ inch slices. Bake round, or cut into petal shapes, using a cookie cutter. Bake on an ungreased cookie sheet for 10 to 12 minutes. Remove the cookies from baking sheets immediately and cool on baking rack. (Allowing the cookies to cool on the baking sheets will continue to cook and harden them.)

Cookies can be sprinkled with sugar before baking, or frosted afterwards with a light lemon frosting (recipe follows). Yields 6 dozen.

Lemon Frosting:

3	cups powdered sugar	¼	cup lemon juice
½	tsp. lemon rind, grated	1	tsp. vanilla extract

Mix ingredients together. Add a touch of cream if the mixture appears too thick. Spoon over each cookie while they are still warm.

Seated Dinner for the Honorable
Patricia Schroeder, U. S. Representative

Starter:
Carrot Vichyssoise

Entree:
Glazed Quail
on crouton spread with Onion Duxelle
*Steamed Broccoli Crowns
*Dinner Rolls and Butter

Dessert:
Cranberry Pecan Pie

*Recipe not included

CARROT VICHYSSOISE

2 T. oil	1 pt. heavy cream
4 cups chopped fresh leeks, white part only	Salt and white pepper to taste
2 garlic cloves, minced	¼ to ½ cup sherry
4 cups carrots, diced	Fresh dill, chopped, to taste
3 cups potatoes, diced	Dash of hot pepper sauce (optional)
6 cups chicken stock	Fresh mint leaves for garnish

Heat oil in large, heavy-bottomed pot. Add leeks and garlic; sauté until soft. Add carrots, potatoes, and chicken stock. Bring to boil, then reduce heat and simmer, covered, for about 45 minutes or until all ingredients are soft. Remove from heat and allow to cool. Purée vegetables in a blender until smooth. Transfer to a large bowl and add heavy cream. (If calories are a concern, skim milk can be substituted for the cream.) If soup is too thick, add additional liquid for a thinner consistency. Add salt, pepper, sherry, dill, and hot pepper sauce. Chill.

Best if made at least one day in advance. Can be held for three days in the refrigerator. Serve cold and garnish with mint leaves. This soup is also delicious served hot, with carrot curl garnishes. Yields approximately 12 cups.

GLAZED QUAIL

Marinade:

¼ cup bourbon
¼ cup red wine vinegar
½ cup molasses
¼ cup olive oil

4 large garlic cloves, crushed
½ cup honey
½ cup sweet soy sauce
Dash of red pepper flakes

Process all ingredients in food processor until completely blended. Can be made up to a week in advance and stored in the refrigerator.

16 Quail:

Cut each quail in half, leaving skin on. Marinate quail for at least 8 hours in the refrigerator. One hour before cooking, bring to room temperature. Remove from marinade and dry well. Bake at 350 degrees, basting frequently, for approximately 30 minutes. While quail is cooking, reduce remaining marinade until thickened. This will be used as a sauce. Serves 8.

Onion Duxelle:

2 T. oil
1½ cups white onions, finely chopped
½ cup green onions, finely chopped
1 cup red onions, finely chopped

1 cup whites of leeks, finely chopped
1 cup dried apple slices, cut into pieces
2 cups white wine

Heat oil in large skillet. Sauté all onions until they are toasty brown. Add apple and white wine. Cook for approximately 45 minutes on low heat. Remove from heat and allow to cool. When cool, purée in food processor. Keep warm until ready to serve. This can be made one day ahead and reheated.

Crouton:

1 large loaf French bread

Cut bread into 1-inch slices and toast lightly. Spread each slice with Onion Duxelle.

Assembly:

Place crouton, with Onion Duxelle, in the middle of each plate. Arrange 4 halves of quail on plate, with leg portion touching the crouton. Ladle the reduced sauce over each quail and arrange steamed broccoli crowns between the quail. Garnish with a cherry tomato for a beautifully finished plate.

CRANBERRY PECAN PIE

½ cup chopped cranberries
½ cup orange juice
9-inch single pie shell, unbaked
3 eggs
2/3 cup sugar

¼ tsp. salt
1/3 cup butter, melted
1 cup dark corn syrup
1 tsp. vanilla
¾ cup pecan pieces

The day before you make the pie, cover the chopped cranberries with orange juice and refrigerate.

Drain the cranberries and set aside. Preheat oven to 375 degrees. Make your favorite 9-inch single pie shell. Do not prick the bottom.

Slightly beat the eggs. Add sugar and salt, mixing well until dissolved. Slowly add the melted butter and corn syrup; add vanilla, mixing well. Stir in pecans and cranberries. Pour mixture into unbaked pie shell and bake for 50 to 55 minutes, or until the filling is set in the center when gently shaken. Allow to cool; store in the refrigerator. Yields 6 to 8 servings.

A Senator's Soiree

Hors d'oeuvres:
Cocktail Cheese Beignets

Starter:
Le Trianon Salad
Bibb and romaine lettuce, radicchio, sprouts,
hearts of palm, button mushrooms and bell pepper strips
dressed with Garlic Vinaigrette and topped with toasted croutons

Entree:
Broiled Lambchops
served with Mint Pesto

Southwestern Yams

*Sautéed Green Beans

*Dinner Rolls and Butter

Dessert:
Lover's Chocolate Cake

'Recipe not included

COCKTAIL CHEESE BEIGNETS

½	cup water	¼	tsp. dry mustard
4	oz. butter	1	oz. Dijon mustard
½	cup all-purpose flour	¼	cup Parmesan cheese
2	eggs	¼	cup Swiss cheese, grated
Pinch of salt		Oil for frying	
Pinch of cayenne pepper		Parmesan cheese, for garnish	

In a heavy saucepan, bring water and butter to a rolling boil. Add flour all at once. Reduce heat, and cook on low, stirring constantly with a wooden spoon until mixture comes away from sides of pan. Put mixture in mixing bowl and beat vigorously for 1 minute or until cool. Beat in eggs one at a time on medium speed, blending completely before adding the next egg. Add salt, pepper, mustards, and both cheeses and continue to beat until well blended. Heat oil in a deep fryer to 350 degrees. Form 2 tsps. batter into a ball and drop each ball into hot oil, a few at a time, frying until golden brown, about 4 to 5 minutes. Turn for even browning. Drain on paper towels. Serve hot, sprinkled with Parmesan. Dough may be refrigerated or frozen. Yields: cocktail serving for 25 guests.

LE TRIANON SALAD

2 heads bibb lettuce	2 yellow bell peppers, cut into
2 heads romaine lettuce	strips
3 heads radicchio	2 red bell peppers, cut into strips
2 14-oz. cans hearts of palm	Croutons (recipe follows)
1 pt. button mushrooms	Garlic Vinaigrette dressing
¼ lb. bean sprouts	(recipe follows)

Chill salad plates and forks. Wash and tear the bibb and romaine lettuce. Dry well and refrigerate to crisp. Separate and wash radicchio leaves. Cut hearts of palm into 1-inch pieces. Brush mushrooms to clean. Line the salad plates with radicchio leaves. Mound the lettuces in the middle of the radicchio. Place a layer of sprouts; arrange pepper strips in a sunburst pattern; place button mushrooms on top, to "crown" your salad. Arrange hearts of palm pieces at the base, surrounding the lettuce. Place a few croutons on top and dress with Garlic Vinaigrette (recipe follows). Serves 6.

Croutons:

1 loaf French bread	1 T. granulated garlic
1 cup butter	¼ tsp. paprika
1 cup Parmesan cheese	

Slice French bread into ½-inch slices. Melt butter. Combine remaining ingredients. Dip each side of the sliced bread first in the butter, then in the cheese mixture. Place on large baking sheet and bake at 250 degrees for approximately 45 minutes, or until bread is dry and slightly browned. Allow to cool. Cut into ½-inch cubes. Save any crumbs and use as a topping for your vegetables.

Garlic Vinaigrette:

6 T. balsamic vinegar	½ tsp. salt
1 T. lemon juice	Dash of white pepper
½ cup garlic olive oil	1 tsp. sugar
2 garlic cloves, crushed	

Combine all ingredients in the food processor and give it a whirl! Bring to room temperature before serving.

BROILED LAMBCHOPS WITH MINT PESTO

8 large loin lambchops, cut at least 1-inch thick
Granulated garlic
Ground black pepper
Mint leaves

Early in the day, season chops and refrigerate. Bring to room temperature one hour before cooking. Grill over coals for about 5 minutes per side for medium rare. Can also be broiled. Place a layer of Mint Pesto (recipe follows) on top of each chop. Garnish with mint leaves and serve immediately.

Mint Pesto:

2 cups mint leaves	½ cup Parmesan cheese
½ cup parsley leaves	¼ cup minced pecans
⅓ cup garlic olive oil	2 heaping T. mint jelly
2 garlic cloves	
Pinch of salt (optional)	

Process mint, parsley, olive oil, garlic, and salt in food processor until well combined. Stir in Parmesan cheese, pecans, and mint jelly. Pesto can be made 4 days in advance.

SOUTHWESTERN YAMS

2 large yams, cooked until just done	Pinch of white pepper
½ cup brown sugar	1/8 tsp. granulated garlic
2 T. yellow mustard	1/8 tsp. cumin

Spray a large baking dish with cooking spray. Peel and slice cooked yams into ½-inch slices; place in single layer in baking dish. Microwave the brown sugar, mustard, white pepper, granulated garlic, and cumin until soft. Spoon ½ tsp. of sugar/mustard mixture on each slice. Bake in a 350-degree oven until mixture has melted. Transfer to serving plate and serve immediately. Serves 6.

LOVER'S CHOCOLATE CAKE

This dessert requires lengthy preparation. It's a bonus that it can be prepared in advance, and it freezes well, too.

Cake:

2 1-oz. squares unsweetened chocolate	1 tsp. vanilla
¼ cup unsalted butter, softened	2 T. Italian hazelnut liqueur
1 cup sugar	¾ cup unsifted all-purpose flour
2 large eggs separated, room temperature	½ tsp. baking powder
¼ cup milk	¼ tsp. salt

Preheat oven to 350 degrees. Grease and flour a 9½-inch springform pan. Melt chocolate in a double boiler over hot but not boiling water. Remove from heat and cool. In a large mixing bowl, beat butter and sugar until light and creamy. Add cooled chocolate and beat. Add egg yolks, one at a time, until blended. Add milk, vanilla, and liqueur and mix. In a separate bowl, combine flour, baking powder, and salt. Stir dry ingredients into chocolate mixture and blend well. Beat egg whites until they form soft peaks and fold into chocolate mixture. Pour into springform pan and bake 25 to 30 minutes, or until cake tester comes out clean. Cool in pan on a wire rack.

Mousse:

1	envelope unflavored gelatin	¾	cup sugar
1/3	cup water	5	large egg yolks
1¼	cups butter	2	T. brandy
1	T. instant espresso coffee powder	1	T. vanilla
12	oz. semisweet chocolate		

Using a heavy, 2-quart saucepan, combine water and gelatin. Allow to stand for 2 minutes, until gelatin has softened. Add butter and espresso. Heat on medium, stirring until mixture is blended. In a food processor, chop the chocolate with the sugar. With the food processor running pour the butter mixture into the chocolate. Process until all the chocolate is melted. Allow to cool slightly. Add egg yolks, brandy, and vanilla; process until smooth. Return to saucepan, stirring over medium heat, until thickened. Transfer to a medium bowl and place inside a larger, ice-filled bowl in order to cool and thicken mousse. Stir often.

Assembly:

1	pkg. Pirouette cookies	1	cup heavy cream, whipped

Pour ½ of the mousse mixture over the cake (still in the springform pan). Cut the cookies in half, crosswise. Insert, cut side down, around the top edge of mousse. Fold whipped cream into remaining mousse mixture. Pour over mousse in springform pan, being careful that cookies remain upright. Refrigerate for at least 4 hours, or until very firm. Remove carefully from springform pan and garnish. When we served this, we garnished each serving with a whipped cream rosette and a strawberry.

A Vote for Veal

Starter:
*Tossed Green Salad
Fresh garden greens, dressed with a light vinaigrette

Entree:
Grilled Veal Chops
with Chateau Sauce

Artichoke Bottoms
filled with Artichoke Florentine Mousse

Mushroom Rice

*Fresh Baguettes
with Texas-shaped butter

Dessert:
Individual English Trifles

*Recipe not included

GRILLED VEAL CHOPS

¼ cup fresh lemon juice	1 garlic clove, minced
¼ cup olive oil	8 1-inch-thick veal chops
2 T. chopped fresh thyme	Salt and pepper to taste
2 T. minced shallots	Sprigs of fresh thyme

Mix the first 5 ingredients in a small bowl. Place veal chops in a shallow dish and pour marinade over them. Turn to coat evenly. Let stand 1 hour at room temperature. Preheat barbecue grill to medium high. Remove veal chops from marinade. Season with salt and pepper. Grill to desired doneness, about 5 minutes per side for medium-rare. Heat plates in warm oven. Serve with Chateau Sauce (recipe follows). Ladle sauce on plate and place chop on top of sauce. Garnish with fresh thyme.

Chateau Sauce:

½ cup unsalted butter	1 T. Dijon mustard
⅓ cup shallots, minced	1 tsp. black pepper
½ cup flour	⅓ cup chopped fresh parsley
3 cups warm beef stock (see p. 13)	½ cup seedless red raspberry jam
1 to 1½ cups Cabernet Sauvignon	

Melt butter in a medium skillet. Sauté shallots until soft. Add flour to make a roux and stir frequently, over medium heat, until roux is browned, approximately 10 minutes. Slowly add the warm stock. Cook until thickened. Add wine, Dijon mustard, spices, and jam to taste. Yields 4½ cups.

OPTIONS: This is a very good basic sauce but can be modified to complement other meats. If used with pork, substitute apple jelly for the jam; for lamb, mint jelly; for chicken, orange marmalade.

ARTICHOKE FLORENTINE MOUSSE
in Artichoke Bottoms

2   T. unsalted butter
½   cup onions, chopped
8   oz. cream cheese, softened
1   10-oz. pkg. frozen spinach,
defrosted and squeezed lightly
Dash of nutmeg

Salt and pepper
1   cup artichoke pieces
12 artichoke bottoms
½   T. fresh parsley, chopped
Gruyere cheese, grated

Melt butter and lightly sauté the onions. Add cream cheese to pan and stir until it melts. Add spinach, nutmeg, salt and pepper. Process artichoke pieces in food processor. Add the spinach-cream cheese mixture to processor and blend. Taste for seasoning. Fill the artichoke bottoms with mousse and heat 12 to 15 minutes in 350-degree oven. Sprinkle with Gruyere cheese. Serves 6.

SERVING HINT: Cut off the underside of the artichoke bottoms to allow them to sit flat on the plate.

MUSHROOM RICE

1   10½-oz. can beef consomme
1   10½-oz. can French onion soup
1   cup rice
4   oz. margarine

1   pt. sliced mushrooms
1   T. dried parsley
Dash of red pepper flakes
¼   tsp. thyme

Preheat oven to 375 degrees. Spray a medium casserole dish with cooking spray and add all the ingredients. Bake for 1 hour, covered for the first half hour and uncovered the last ½ hour. Serves 6.

INDIVIDUAL ENGLISH TRIFLES

1   large pound cake
1   pt. fresh red raspberries
    (any fresh berries can be
    substituted)
Sour cream custard filling
    (recipe follows)

½   cup raspberry liqueur
1   10-oz. jar seedless red
    raspberry jam, melted
1   pt. fresh blackberries
Mint leaves

Cut pound cake lengthwise, into about ¾-inch slices. Cut each piece of cake to fit individual serving pieces. We like the look of a saucer champagne glass, so we cut our cake into rounds to fit inside the glass. (Shrimp icers could also be used. We like to see the layers through the glass.) First, place a layer of berries on the bottom of each serving piece. If the berries are large, cut in half. Carefully place a layer of the sour cream custard on top of the berries. Top with a trimmed piece of cake. Sprinkle cake with 1 T. raspberry liqueur, and pour melted raspberry jam over the cake, allowing it to drip down the sides. Add another layer of custard, also allowing it to drip down the sides of the cake. Repeat layers.

Garnish with assorted berries and mint leaves. Chill until ready to serve. Best if made a day in advance. Serves 8.

Variations of this recipe are many, such as using the basic recipe and substituting mandarin oranges for the berries and French orange brandy for the raspberry liqueur; bananas and chocolate chips with Mexican coffee liqueur; or use your favorite flavors and create your own trifle.

Sour Cream Custard Filling:

1	pkg. vanilla pudding mix	1½ cups milk
1	cup sour cream	¼ tsp. almond extract
1	tsp. vanilla extract	¼ tsp. butter flavor extract

Prepare pudding according to package directions. Let cool in a medium bowl. Whip in the remaining ingredients until creamy. Chill.

Artichokes for an Ambassador

Starter:
Wild Rice Soup

Entree:
Poulet d'Artichauts au Fromage
*Steamed Dilled Baby Carrots
Baby carrots with stems attached

Viennese Peas
*Dinner Rolls and Butter
(see p. 14)

Dessert:
Coeur a la Creme
Served with Peach Sauce

*Recipe not included

WILD RICE SOUP

½ cup wild rice, rinsed and drained
1½ quarts fresh or canned
   chicken stock
1 cup onion, diced
3 celery stalks, diced
1 cup carrot, pared and diced
2 T. oil

2 T. flour
½ tsp. salt
1/8 tsp. white pepper
1 tsp. granulated garlic
½ cup chopped parsley
2 cups light cream
1 cup white wine (or to taste)

Cook rice in chicken stock, covered over medium heat, for about 45 minutes or until tender. While rice is cooking, sauté onion, celery and carrots in oil until onion is transparent. Add flour and cook, stirring frequently, over medium heat for 2 to 3 minutes. Add cooked wild rice and chicken stock while stirring. Simmer for 10 to 15 minutes. Add salt, pepper, granulated garlic, parsley, light cream, and wine. Serve hot.

POULET D'ARTICHAUTS AU FROMAGE

6 5-oz. chicken breast halves, boneless, skinless
White pepper
Granulated garlic
½ cup flour
½ tsp. white pepper
1 tsp. salt

1 T. granulated garlic
2 T. butter
2 T. olive oil
18 cooked or canned artichoke hearts
Artichoke Sauce (recipe follows)

Wash and thoroughly dry the chicken breasts; season with white pepper and granulated garlic. Combine flour, salt, pepper and garlic. Lightly pound the chicken; then coat each piece with seasoned flour. Heat butter and oil in a skillet over moderate heat. Add the chicken breasts and sauté for 5 minutes per side, or until cooked and lightly browned. Remove chicken and keep warm. Place artichoke hearts in the same skillet, adding more oil, if necessary, and cook until browned. When ready to serve, place the chicken on warmed serving plate. Pour ½ to ⅓ cup of Artichoke Sauce over chicken, and top with 3 artichoke hearts. Garnish with cooked fresh artichoke leaves, if available. Serves 6.

Artichoke Sauce:

1 T. olive oil
3 T. butter
1 cup scallions, chopped
2 garlic cloves, minced
2 T. flour
2 cups milk

1 cup Gruyere cheese, grated
1 cup Parmesan cheese
3 tsp. Dijon mustard
3 dashes of hot pepper sauce
1 cup artichoke pieces, chopped
½ cup dry white wine

Heat oil and butter in saucepan. Sauté scallions and garlic. Add flour and cook over low heat, stirring frequently, for 3 minutes. Slowly add milk, stirring until thick and smooth. Simmer for 10 minutes. Remove from heat. Add cheeses, mustard, hot pepper sauce and artichoke pieces. Add ½ cup wine. Serve with chicken.

(An added bonus is that this can double as a wonderful vegetable dip—so you might want to make extra!)

VIENNESE PEAS

6 T. butter
4 T. flour
2 cups hot beef stock (or reduced canned broth)
4 T. sugar

½ tsp. salt (to taste)
¼ tsp. pepper
2½ lbs. frozen green peas
2 T. fresh parsley, chopped

Heat butter in medium saucepan. Add flour, making a roux. Add beef stock, stirring constantly until smooth. Simmer for 10 minutes. Add remaining ingredients and mix well until hot. Immediately remove from heat and serve. Can be made the day before serving and refrigerated. Serves 8.

For a terrific presentation . . .

4	2½-inch diameter zucchini, ends trimmed	3	T. butter, melted
			Salt

Peel strips lengthwise from zucchini, giving its exterior a striped appearance, then cut into 1½-inch lengths. Hollow out the zucchini pieces, forming cups by leaving ¼-inch sides and ½-inch base intact. In a large pot of salted boiling water, cook the zucchini until crisp-tender, about 4 minutes. Rinse with cold water and drain thoroughly. Brush inside and outside with melted butter and sprinkle inside with salt. Stand up in baking dish and set aside until ready to fill. (If you made these a day ahead, bring to room temperature before filling.) Fill zucchini cups with peas and bake in a preheated 375-degree oven until hot, about 10 minutes.

COEUR A LA CREME
with Peach Sauce

4	cups ice water		Pinch of baking soda
1	T. fresh lemon juice		Double thickness of cheesecloth

Combine water, lemon juice, and baking soda in medium mixing bowl. Cut 6 squares of cheesecloth large enough to line 6 oz. custard cups, leaving 2-inch overhang. Soak cheesecloth in water mixture while preparing creme.

Creme:

8	oz. cream cheese, room temperature	1½	tsp. vanilla
½	cup cottage cheese	½	vanilla bean, seeds only
½	cup powdered sugar, sifted	2	cups whipping cream

Beat cream cheese in large mixing bowl until soft and fluffy. Add cottage cheese and blend well. Add sugar, vanilla, and vanilla bean seeds and beat until smooth. In a separate bowl, whip cream until stiff and gently fold into cream cheese mixture.

Wring cheesecloths well and line each custard cup, leaving the 2-inch overhang. Spoon creme evenly into cups, smoothing gently. Fold cheesecloth over top and tap cups lightly to allow mixture to settle. Place on baking sheet and chill until firm, at least 2 hours. (Best if chilled overnight). To serve, carefully lift cloth from top of creme. Invert custard cups onto serving plates and unwrap carefully. Smooth with spatula if necessary. Serve with Peach Sauce (recipe follows). Can be prepared 3 days ahead and stored, in custard cups, in refrigerator. Serves 6.

Peach Sauce:

½	cup peach jam	1	cup frozen peaches
1	T. peach schnapps	2	T. sugar
	Dash of lemon juice		Pinch of cinnamon

Place all ingredients in food processor and process, until slightly chunky. Can be made ahead and refrigerated. Reheat slowly and serve warm.

A Texas Roll Call

Starter:
Texas Honey Salad

Entree:
Gulf Coast Sauté

Cilantro Pesto Rice

Avocado-Corn Salsa

Black Bean Rollups

Dessert:
Mexican Flan

TEXAS HONEY SALAD

Texas Honey Salad Dressing:

6   T. olive oil
3   T. balsamic vinegar
2   T. honey
1   tsp. ground cumin

1   tsp. chili powder
1   tsp. sugar
2   tsp. chopped green onions
Salt and pepper to taste
Hot pepper sauce to taste
    (optional)

Combine all ingredients in blender, until thick. Refrigerate. Can be made several hours ahead; however, bring dressing to room temperature before serving.

Salad:

2   medium heads butter lettuce
1   small head savoy
2   medium red onions, sliced in
    thin rounds
4   carrots, shredded

1   small jicama, cut in matchsticks
1   pkg. radishes, cut in rounds
1   pt. cherry tomatoes, quartered
1   bunch cilantro, for garnish

Prepare all ingredients in advance and refrigerate. When ready to serve, arrange on individual salad plates, in the order listed above. Serves 6.

GULF COAST SAUTÉ

Marinade and Sauce Base:

4 T. vegetable oil
2 T. sesame oil
4 tsp. grated orange peel
4 garlic cloves, minced
1 cup chopped green onions
1 cup low-sodium soy sauce
¼ to ½ tsp. chile oil, to taste
4 tsp. cilantro, chopped
4 tsp. ground cumin

2 T. brown sugar
2 T. fresh ginger, minced
1 16 oz. can chicken broth,
   reduced by ½
1 small jar chopped black olives
Splash of tequila (also a splash
   for the cook!)
Chile oil, to taste (or on the table
   for those seeking extra fire!)

Heat the two oils in large pan. Add orange peel, garlic, green onions; sauté. Add soy sauce, chile oil (if you dare!), cilantro, ground cumin, brown sugar, and ginger. Add reduced chicken broth and cook, very slowly, for 10 minutes. Taste to correct seasonings. Add black olives and tequila.

Seafood Sauté:

1½ lbs. large shrimp, peeled
    and butterflied
1   lb. large sea scallops, rinsed
    and dried

2 T. oil
2 whole lemons
Marinade (recipe above)

Divide marinade into two separate bowls. About 2 hours before serving, toss the shrimp in one bowl of marinade and the scallops in the other. Drain seafood (reserving marinade) and set aside. Pour marinade into small saucepan and bring to a boil. Reduce over low heat. Sauté shrimp in oil until cooked, and place in casserole dish. In the same pan, sauté scallops, being careful not to overcook. Add scallops to shrimp in casserole dish and pour reduced marinade over them. Garnish with halves of lemon.* Serves 4.

*For a nice touch, wrap the lemon halves in lemon netting.

CILANTRO PESTO RICE

Cilantro Pesto:

3 bunches fresh cilantro,
   stems removed,
   leaves coarsely chopped
   (about 2½ cups)
½ cup Parmesan cheese,
   freshly grated
½ cup pine nuts

¼ cup garlic, chopped
1 T. plus 1 tsp. chili powder
1 T. ground cumin
Dried, crushed red pepper to taste
Salt, to taste
¾ cup olive oil

Combine first 8 ingredients in food processor. With machine running, gradually add olive oil until incorporated. Season with more salt, pepper, etc., to taste. Make ahead.
   Pesto can be kept, refrigerated, for up to one week.

Rice:

⅓ cup canola oil

½ very large onion, chopped

1 cup rice

2 cups chicken broth

10 tomatillas (approximately), peeled and chopped

2 T. chopped green chiles

1 cup of cilantro pesto (recipe above)

Chopped parsley to garnish

Heat oil in large frying pan. Add chopped onion and cook until lightly browned. Lower heat and add rice. Sauté very slowly until the rice is browned and smells nice and toasty. Add chicken broth, tomatillas, and green chiles. Simmer, covered, for approximately 20 minutes, or until the liquid is absorbed. Take one cup of pesto, drained of the oil, and mix into rice. This can be made ahead and reheated.

AVOCADO-CORN SALSA

1 cup fresh or frozen corn kernels

¼ cup red pepper, chopped

¼ cup yellow pepper, chopped

¼ cup tomatoes, diced

½ fresh jalapeño pepper, minced

2 T. fresh cilantro, chopped

2 T. shallots, finely chopped

2 T. freshly squeezed lemon juice

1 tsp. hot pepper sauce

1 cup avocado, diced

Salt and pepper to taste

Cook corn in boiling water until just tender. Drain and cool completely. Transfer to a medium bowl. Add the remaining ingredients, except the avocado, and toss gently. Refrigerate, covered, up to 8 hours. When ready to serve, dice and mix in the avocado. Season with salt and pepper to taste. (This recipe was contributed by Vicki Rado.)

BLACK BEAN ROLLUPS

1 15-oz. can black beans, drained

2 T. granulated garlic

Sprinkle of dried, crushed red peppers

1 T. ground cumin

2 oz. goat cheese

½ cup mozzarella cheese

Black pepper to taste

8 large, homemade flour tortillas (can be purchased at a Mexican bakery or in the gourmet section of the grocery store)

Combine all ingredients, except the flour tortillas, in food processor and pulse until blended. Lay out flour tortillas, one at a time, keeping the others moist under a damp towel. Spread ¼ cup of the black bean mixture down the center of each tortilla and roll tightly, cigar style. Place in baking dish and cover with damp towel. This recipe makes approximately 12 rollups, which can be served whole or cut in half. The rollups can be made ahead, sealed tightly, and refrigerated. Heat in 350-degree oven for 10 to 12 minutes.

MEXICAN FLAN

8 T. dark brown sugar
1 tsp. ground cinnamon
3 whole eggs
2 egg yolks
8 oz. cream cheese

1 14-oz. can sweetened condensed milk
14 oz. whole milk
2 tsp. granulated sugar
1 tsp. vanilla
Pinch of salt

Mix brown sugar and cinnamon together and set aside. Combine 3 whole eggs and 2 egg yolks; beat with a whisk and set aside. Place cream cheese in a mixing bowl and beat until smooth. Add eggs, sweet milk, whole milk, granulated sugar, vanilla and salt, mixing until smooth. Divide and pack brown sugar and cinnamon mixture into the bottoms of 6-oz. custard cups. Place custard cups in a pan filled with 1 inch of water. Pour liquid into cups and set cups in water-filled pan. Bake at 350 degrees for 1 hour. When done, custard should spring back when touched or a silver knife inserted ½ inch into the center should come out clean.

Cool for 2 hours. Run a knife around edge of cups and turn onto serving plates. Chill before serving. Serves 8.

(This recipe was originally developed by a renowned Austin chef and our friend, the late Larry Adams. As chef at the Governor's Mansion, Larry's flan was served to many admirers. We have changed his caramelizing procedure. Instead of the traditional method, we like the quicker and easier approach of using packed brown sugar. The result is different, but delicious.)

Chapter 3

Austin's "White House"

ontinuing in the political vein, this chapter includes menus from parties held at the Texas Governor's Mansion, fondly referred to as "The Texas White House." Every state governor since Bill Clements' term has been served by Gourmet Gals & Guys, with parties ranging from the understated to the extravagant.

At a luncheon in honor of former First Lady Mrs. Rosalynn Carter, we created a special dessert known as the "Looner Schooner" — a delectable mousse that ended the meal in a flourish. Our formally clad waiters made a grand entrance as they presented trays of desserts. The raspberry mousse, served in formal shrimp-icers, was surrounded by pale green water into which we dropped dry ice, its smoke creating a startling, bold illusion of billowing clouds.

The weather intervened in one grand event at the Governor's Mansion in honor of England's Prince and Princess Michael of Kent. A glorious fall had settled in Austin, and with no talk of rain in the forecast for weeks, we prepared for an outdoor afternoon tea for 250-300 honored guests. The tables under a sizable tent were draped with delicate Battenburg lace tablecloths. The food preparation was being handled in the Mansion's Carriage House, a good street block away from the party. Just as all the food trays were arranged under the tent, except for the delicate tea sandwiches and scones, Mother Nature let her rip, rendering the prim green grounds an inundated sponge.

As the guests arrived, they were hurriedly escorted under the few umbrellas we were able to scavenge, to the receiving line where the attending nobles were slowly sinking into the dark Texas mud. Women's silk pumps pierced the ground and forever lost their colors, and the skirts of the pristine white tablecloths were splashed with mud. The delicate tea sandwiches were protected by plastic wrap, but the catering staff, clad in make-shift raincoats of huge plastic garbage bags, got soaked transporting them to the serving tables. The moral of the story, of course, is that the Scout maxim "Be Prepared" also applies to caterers. The rains eventually let up and the royal affair received rave reviews, so yet again we survived the fickle Texas weather and established a new cardinal catering rule in doing so. From that day forward, umbrellas are packed for every party!

The five menus that follow include several special recipes, among them one provided by Texas Governor's Mansion administrator Anne DeBois. The Mansion chef's recipe for Burnt Sugar Ice Cream Pie wowed a Spanish prince at a dinner hosted by former Governor and Mrs. Bill Clements. There is also an unbeatable Chicken Flauta recipe from the wife of former Governor Mark White, and an array of enticing cocktail party recipes created for political fundraisers for former Governor Ann Richards in addition to present Governor George W. Bush.

39

A Seated Dinner Honoring
His Royal Highness,
The Prince of Spain
hosted by Governor & Mrs. Bill Clements

Passed Hors d'oeuvres:
Dorothy Territo's Beignets

Starter:
Basil Lime Lobster Salad
Carrington Toast

Entree:
Harvest Veal
with Glazed Pears
Champagne Risotto
Acorn Squash Cups
*Dinner Rolls and Butter

Dessert:
Burnt Sugar Ice Cream Pie

*Recipe not included

DOROTHY TERRITO'S BEIGNETS

3 oz. Roquefort cheese, crumbled	8 sheets fillo pastry
3 oz. cream cheese, softened	¼ cup butter, melted
2 egg yolks	Fritter Batter (recipe follows)
Salt (optional)	Oil for deep frying

Combine first 4 ingredients and stir until mixed.

Fritter Batter:

1 cup all-purpose flour	1 cup milk
1 tsp. baking powder	¼ cup vegetable oil
½ tsp. salt	
1 egg	

Whisk together all ingredients until well mixed.

Assembly:

1 egg yolk, slightly beaten, for sealing fillo triangles

Follow fillo instructions for making triangle hors d'oeuvres, brushing pastry with butter. Place 2 tsp. cheese mixture on fillo strips and fold the strips into triangles. Seal the last fold with egg yolk. (Can be frozen at this point.) Heat oil in a deep fryer to 375 degrees. Dip triangles into prepared batter, shaking off the excess, and place in fryer, a few at a time. Do not crowd the beignets. Remove from oil when beignets are a light, golden brown; drain on paper towels. Can be served warm or at room temperature. Yields 40 beignets.

An alternate cooking method: Place beignets on baking sheet, without dipping in batter, and spray with cooking spray. Bake in 350-degree oven, middle rack, for approximately 10 to 12 minutes.

BASIL LIME LOBSTER SALAD

3	garlic cloves		Salt and pepper to taste
2	T. olive oil	4	cups romaine lettuce, sliced and tightly packed
1	T. balsamic vinegar		
2	T. fresh lime juice	1	cup watercress, trimmed and tightly packed
1	cup tomato, seeded and chopped		
1	cucumber, seeded and diced	1	lb. lobster meat, cooked and cut into bite-sized pieces
½	cup chopped green onions		
3	to 4 T. fresh basil, chopped		

Process the garlic, olive oil, vinegar, lime juice, tomato, cucumber, green onions, basil, salt and pepper in food processor until smooth, using the knife blade. Do this several days before serving and refrigerate, allowing the flavors to intensify.

When ready to serve, prepare the romaine lettuce, watercress, and lobster. Gently toss and coat the lettuce and watercress with the chilled dressing. Divide and mound on four individual serving plates; top with lobster claws. Serves 4.

CARRINGTON TOAST

¾	cup mayonnaise	½	cup Parmesan cheese
5	T. onion, finely chopped		Very thin sliced white bread
2	garlic cloves, minced	¼	cup parsley, chopped

Combine mayonnaise, onions, garlic, and cheese and mix thoroughly. Remove the crusts of the bread and cut into quarters. Generously spread cheese mixture on bread. Sprinkle with chopped parsley. Bake in 375-degree oven for 15 minutes. Yields approximately 24 toasts.

HARVEST VEAL WITH GLAZED PEARS

½ cup flour
½ tsp. salt
1 tsp. white pepper
1½ lbs. veal scallops, thinly sliced
1 T. clarified butter
1 T. olive oil
1 T. chopped shallots

2 T. + 2 T. pear schnapps (more if needed)
1 cup dry white wine
2 cups demi-glaze (or double strength beef broth)
Salt and pepper to taste

Combine the flour, salt, and white pepper. Lightly coat each slice of veal in flour mixture and set aside. (Reserve seasoned flour for Pear Sauce.) Heat butter and oil in a medium skillet. Add shallots; sauté over medium heat until soft. Sauté veal, a few pieces at a time, careful not to overcrowd, approximately 3 minutes per side. To each batch, add 1 T. pear schnapps and flambé. Place cooked veal on an oven-proof platter. Continue until all veal is cooked, adding more butter and oil as needed. Keep veal warm. Deglaze the skillet with white wine, scraping the sides and bottom with a wooden spoon. Reduce the wine by ½ and add the demi-glaze. Cook until liquid thickens. Add 2 T. pear schnapps. Adjust seasonings if needed and pour over veal. Serve with Pear Sauce and Glazed Pears (recipes follow). Serves 6.

Pear Sauce:

2 T. butter
2 T. seasoned flour from veal
¼ cup demi-glaze
¼ cup pear schnapps

1 cup half and half
2 T. sugar
Salt and pepper to taste

Melt butter in saucepan; add seasoned flour and cook for 2 minutes. Slowly add demi-glaze and pear schnapps. Cook until thickened. Add half and half, sugar, salt and pepper. Taste for seasonings. Serve warm over veal.

GLAZED PEARS

3 pears
1½ T. sugar

4 T. water
Cinnamon to garnish

Peel the pears, quarter, core and finely slice, not quite cutting through the stem end. Fan out. Brush the bottom of an unheated skillet with butter and sprinkle with the sugar. Add the water. Set the skillet over moderate heat and cook until the water and the sugar begins to thicken. Add pears round side down and cook until tender and glazed. Sprinkle with cinnamon. Place 2 fanned quarters on each serving of veal.

CHAMPAGNE RISOTTO

Warning: This is a time-consuming rice recipe, but well worth your efforts. Try it and see for yourself!

4½	cups fresh or canned chicken broth	1½	cups Arborio rice
3	T. unsalted butter	1	cup champagne plus ¼ cup
¼	cup onions, finely minced	¼	cup light cream
2	garlic cloves, minced	2	T. fresh parsley, chopped

In a large saucepan, simmer the broth. In a separate, heavy 4-quart saucepan, heat butter over medium heat. Sauté onions and garlic in the butter for 1 to 2 minutes, until softened, but not brown. Add rice to butter mixture and stir for 1 minute, making sure all grains are well coated. Add 1 cup of champagne, stirring until completely absorbed. Add the simmering broth ½ cup at a time, stirring frequently. Be sure that each addition is completely absorbed before adding the next ½ cup. Frequent stirring will prevent sticking. After approximately 18 minutes, the rice will be tender but firm. Add the remaining ¼ cup of champagne, cream, and parsley. Stir briskly to combine with rice. Serve immediately. Serves 4.

ACORN SQUASH CUPS

3	medium acorn squash	6	T. brown sugar
6	T. butter		Salt and pepper to taste

Cut squash in half, lengthwise. Remove seeds and place cut side down in oven-proof casserole dish, with 1 inch of water. Bake in 375-degree oven for ½ hour, or until tender. Remove from oven; pour off water. Turn squash upright and fill the cavity with butter and brown sugar. Return to oven for 10 minutes, or until sugar is melted and butter is bubbly. Sprinkle with salt and pepper. Serves 6.

BURNT SUGAR ICE CREAM PIE

This fabulous dessert was developed by Sarah Bishop, chef at the Texas Governor's Mansion.

¾	cup sugar	1	8-inch Gingersnap Pie Crust
1½	cups milk		(follows)
3	egg yolks		Whipped cream for garnish
	Pinch of salt		(optional)
3	T. cornstarch		Candied orange peel for garnish
1½	tsp. vanilla		(optional)
1½	cups heavy cream		

In a large heavy skillet, cook sugar over medium high heat, stirring constantly with a fork, until melted completely and a deep golden caramel. Remove from heat; stir caramel to prevent further darkening. Into the side of skillet, add milk carefully. (The caramel will harden when milk is added.) Cook caramel mixture over moderate heat, stirring, until the caramel is dissolved. Remove skillet from heat. In a bowl, whisk together egg yolks, salt, and cornstarch. Add caramel mixture in a slow stream, stirring. In a heavy saucepan, cook caramel mixture over moderate heat, stirring constantly with a wooden spoon until the mixture comes to a boil. Boil, stirring constantly, for 2 minutes. Strain the custard through a fine sieve into a metal bowl set in a larger bowl filled with ice and cold water. (This will cool the mixture down quickly.) Allow custard to cool, stirring; chill it, covered, until it is cold. Stir in vanilla and cream until mixture is combined well. Freeze mixture in ice-cream freezer, according to manufacturer's instructions.

Gingersnap Pie Crust:

1½ cups gingersnap cookies (approximately ½ box)

1/3 cup sugar

1 oz. unsalted butter, softened

¾ cup semisweet chocolate, melted

Whipped cream, sweetened

Candied orange peels

Preheat oven to 350 degrees. Break gingersnap cookies, and place in food processor; pulse until they are finely pulverized. Add sugar. Work in butter. Press into an 8-inch pie plate and bake for 8 to 10 minutes. Place in freezer to set up. When well chilled, remove from freezer and brush inside of pie crust with melted chocolate.

Assembly:

Spoon ice cream into pie shell; smooth with spatula. Store in freezer for 3 hours or until ready to serve. Garnish with sweetened whipped cream and candied orange peels. Yields 6 to 8 servings.

A Tea Honoring
Prince & Princess Michael of Kent
hosted by Governor & Mrs. Mark White

After meeting the Prince and Princess in a receiving line, the guests were served flutes of champagne with strawberries.

Passed Hors d'oeuvres:
Mock Cheese Blintzes
with Blueberry Sour Cream Sauce
Asparagus Rollups

Buffet:
Assorted Sandwiches:
Watercress Triangles

Open-faced Cucumber Rounds

Egg Salad Squares

Ham Salad Cornucopias

Caviar and Cream Cheese Flowers

Tuna Salad Fingers

Smoked Salmon Rollups

Sherried Mushrooms
served in a chafer, accompanied by miniature tart shells

Traditional Scones
with butter (or clotted cream) and Strawberry Jam

Pastries:
Raspberry Snails

Lemon Cassata Cups

Almond Butter Cups

Strawberry Cream Stars

*Traditional English Tea
with hot milk

Peach Tea Punch

*Recipe not included

MOCK CHEESE BLINTZES

This recipe is for a large quantity of wonderful Mock Cheese Blintzes, so make them, freeze them, and serve as needed. (It is always nice to have a special snack in the freezer, ready to serve.)

3	loaves white sandwich bread	½	tsp. vanilla
½	cup cinnamon	2/3	tsp. salt
2	cups sugar	¾	tsp. lemon peel
3	lbs. cream cheese	½	T. cinnamon
2	egg yolks	½	tsp. nutmeg
1	cup sugar	1	lb. butter, unsalted, melted

Prepare bread by removing crusts. Flatten, using a rolling pin or a pasta machine. Combine ½ cup cinnamon and 2 cups sugar and set aside. Beat cream cheese in a large mixing bowl. Add eggs and beat until creamy and smooth. Add 1 cup sugar and remaining ingredients (except melted butter). Spread on flattened bread, roll up (cigar style), and cut in half. Dip one side first in the melted butter, then in the cinnamon-sugar mixture. (The blintzes can be frozen at this point.) Bake in 350-degree oven for 12 to 15 minutes, on the upper rack of the oven. Serve with Blueberry Sour Cream for dipping. (Recipe follows.) The blintzes are best when served warm. Makes approximately 108 pieces.

Blueberry Sour Cream:

1	pt. fresh blueberries (if you have to use frozen berries, defrost them on paper towels to absorb most of the moisture)	1	pt. sour cream
		1	tsp. sugar
			Dash of nutmeg

Combine all ingredients. Chill before serving.

ASPARAGUS ROLLUPS

1	1 lb. loaf thin white sandwich bread	*Topping:*	
1	lb. cheddar cheese, shredded (4 cups)	1	cup Parmesan cheese
4	oz. cream cheese, softened	½	cup bread crumbs
Horseradish to taste		Dash of cayenne (for color)	
Cayenne pepper to taste		Dash of chili powder (for color)	
1	green pepper, chopped		
2	drops hot pepper sauce	8	oz. butter, melted
1	15-oz. can asparagus spears, drained		

Prepare bread by removing crusts and flattening, using a rolling pin or a pasta machine. Set aside, covered with plastic wrap or a damp towel. Combine cheeses, seasoning, green pepper, and hot pepper sauce; mix well. Spread cheese mixture evenly on slices of bread. Place an asparagus spear on one end of each slice and roll up, jellyroll style. Cut in half. Repeat until all bread and/or asparagus is used. Combine ingredients for the topping; melt butter. Dip one side of each rollup first in the butter, then in the topping. (Can be frozen at this point.) Preheat oven to 375 degrees. Bake for 10 to 12 minutes. Yields 4 dozen.

Basic Tea Sandwiches

Tea sandwiches are definitely "oldies but goodies." You never know when a king or queen will stop by! Most of the fillings can be made several days in advance; however, the sandwiches themselves should be made no more than one day ahead. When working with bread, always use damp towels and plastic wrap to cover and keep your finished product fresh and moist.

If refrigerator space is at a premium (and when is it not?) stack the sandwiches in a shirt box or shoe box until you are ready to make your trays. Naturally, this will not work with open-faced sandwiches, but it is a great space saver for the others. If possible, have some help for the last-minute open-faced sandwiches. Make your trays attractive by using several shapes on each tray. We like to use items that are easily accessible for tray garnishes, such as fresh pansies and other flowers and greens from the garden, sprigs of watercress, or lemon roses. Use your imagination to create a motif for each tray, giving special thought to eye appeal.

We have given you a specific menu for a Tea we served to English Royals at the Governor's Mansion. Because we served hundreds of guests, our menu is very involved, offering many choices. We suggest you serve three to four different sandwiches and as many sweets. We've found that if you plan on three "savories" and three to four "sweets" per person you will have the proper amounts.

With all this in mind, here are the recipes we served:

Basic Seasoned Cream Cheese for Tea Sandwiches:

8 oz. cream cheese, softened	1 T. chili sauce
1 small carrot, finely grated	Pinch of salt
¼ cup grated cheddar cheese	Dash of white pepper
2 T. green peppers, chopped and squeezed dry	Dash of Worcestershire
	Dash of hot pepper sauce
	Bread (1 loaf makes approximately 100 canapes)

Beat the cream cheese. Add remaining ingredients (except bread) and mix well. Chill. Can be made ahead. (We use this for Watercress and Cucumber Tea Sandwiches.)

WATERCRESS TRIANGLES

White bread   **Watercress**
Basic Seasoned Cream Cheese

Spread slices of bread with Basic Seasoned Cream Cheese mixture. Cut into triangles. Garnish with sprigs of watercress.

OPEN-FACED CUCUMBER ROUNDS

White bread   **Basic Seasoned Cream Cheese**
1 large cucumber (or more, if needed)   **½ cup nuts, finely chopped**

Score sides of cucumber lengthwise with tynes of fork. Cut in half, lengthwise; remove seeds and cut into ¼-inch slices. Spread bread with Basic Seasoned Cream Cheese mixture; cut into **circles** using a cookie cutter. Place a half-slice of cucumber on the cheese. Sprinkle the other half of the circle with chopped nuts.

EGG SALAD SQUARES

6 hard-cooked eggs, coarsely chopped
⅓ cup cream cheese, softened
½ tsp. salt
¼ tsp. white pepper
3 T. green peppers, chopped and squeezed dry
Thin sliced egg bread

Chop the eggs and set aside. Beat the cream cheese until smooth, adding the salt and pepper. Mix in the green peppers. Gently mix in the eggs. Spread egg mixture on bread; cut into squares.

HAM SALAD CORNUCOPIAS

32 thin slices of ham
32 thin slices of Swiss cheese
3 cups cooked ham, ground
2 T. Dijon mustard
2 T. light brown sugar
½ cup cream cheese, softened
Honey Dijon dressing

Trim sliced ham and Swiss cheese to the same size, approximately the size of a piece of white bread. Set aside. Combine ground ham, mustard, brown sugar and cream cheese. Lay out one slice of ham and spread with dressing. Place one slice of Swiss cheese on the ham. Cut in half, diagonally, forming triangles. Place 1 tsp. of ham mixture on each half and roll into cornucopias, securing with a frilled toothpick.

CAVIAR AND CREAM CHEESE FLOWERS

2 T. butter, softened
4 oz. cream cheese
2 T. white onion, finely chopped
White bread
Caviar (we like to use a variety — red, black, and yellow)
Capers

Mix butter, cream cheese, and onion together until smooth. Spread cheese mixture on bread; cut into flowers using a cookie cutter. Drain caviar and capers on paper towels. Decorate sandwiches with caviar and sprinkle a few capers on top.

TUNA SALAD FINGERS

2 6-oz. cans tuna, white meat packed in water, drained
1 T. lemon juice
2 T. black olives, chopped
¼ cup celery, finely chopped
⅓ cup mayonnaise
⅓ cup sweet pickle relish
Wheat bread

Combine all ingredients and spread bread with tuna mixture. Top with another slice of bread. Cut into **rectangular** "fingers."

SMOKED SALMON ROLLUPS

4   oz. unsalted butter, softened
3   oz. cream cheese, softened
¼   cup sour cream
5   oz. smoked salmon, chopped
3   T. fresh dill, minced
Dash of salt

Dash of pepper
1   tsp. lemon juice, or to taste

Rye bread
¼   cup melted butter
¼   cup parsley, chopped

Combine butter, cream cheese, and sour cream. Blend until smooth. Stir in the next five ingredients. Taste and correct seasonings, if necessary. Remove crusts and flatten the rye bread using a rolling pin or a pasta maker. Spread with cheese mixture and roll cigar style. Cut in half. Dip one end first in melted butter, then in chopped parsley.

SHERRIED MUSHROOMS

Sherry Sauce:
4   T. butter
1   T. garlic oil
4   T. onion, finely chopped
¼   cup flour
2   cups milk
¼   cup fresh parsley, finely chopped

¼   tsp. finely ground black pepper
½   tsp. chicken bouillon granules
1   T. Dijon mustard
Nutmeg to taste
½   cup sherry

In a medium saucepan, melt butter with oil. Add onions and sauté until golden brown. Add the flour and cook for 3 minutes. Add milk, 1 cup at a time, whisking until smooth. Add parsley, pepper, chicken bouillon granules, and mustard, stirring until smooth. Add a pinch of nutmeg and sherry, continuing to whisk. Cook on low heat for 10 minutes. If necessary, add more milk or sherry for proper consistency. Yields 2 cups.

2   T. onion, chopped
1   T. garlic, chopped
2   T. oil

1   qt. button mushrooms,
    brushed clean*
Chopped parsley for garnish
Toast triangles

Sauté onion and garlic in oil until golden brown. Add mushrooms and cook quickly over medium heat until browned. Add Sherry Sauce, gently tossing the mushrooms. Place in a water-lined chafing dish and sprinkle with chopped parsley (or finely chopped red peppers for additional color). Serve with toast triangles. Serves 12 to 15.

*If you are unable to find fresh button mushrooms, use small mushrooms, destemmed and sliced.

TRADITIONAL SCONES

½ cup white raisins, chopped and
   soaked in orange juice overnight
2 cups all-purpose flour
2 tsp. baking powder
½ tsp. baking soda
Pinch of salt
¼ lb. butter cut into pieces

5 tsp. sugar
2 eggs
1/3 cup light cream
1 tsp. vanilla
1 egg white, slightly beaten
Granulated sugar

The night before making scones, chop raisins and soak in orange juice. Sift the flour, baking powder, baking soda, and salt together. Using a pastry blender or 2 knives, cut in the butter until the mixture is coarse and crumbly. Add sugar and raisins. In a bowl, beat 2 eggs, then add the cream and vanilla. Slowly add the egg mixture to the dry ingredients, until the mixture just holds together. Wrap in plastic wrap and chill for 1 hour.

Preheat oven to 375 degrees. Spray a baking sheet with cooking spray. Turn out dough onto a floured board and knead gently for about 30 seconds. Roll ½-inch thick and cut into shapes using cookie or biscuit cutters. Brush tops lightly with beaten egg white. Sprinkle with sugar. Bake for 13 to 15 minutes or until lightly brown and puffed. Allow to cool on wire racks. Serve with clotted cream, fruit preserves, or flavored butters. Yields 18 scones.

RASPBERRY SNAILS

1 cup butter, unsalted
1 8-oz. pkg. cream cheese
2 T. sugar
½ tsp. vanilla
¼ tsp. salt
2 cups all-purpose flour

½ cup sugar
¾ cup walnuts, finely chopped
2 T. cinnamon
½ cup seedless raspberry
   preserves
2/3 cup mini-chocolate chips

Using a large mixing bowl, beat butter and cream cheese until light and fluffy. Beat in 2 T. sugar, vanilla, and salt. With the mixer on low, stir in flour until combined. Flour your hands and a work surface; knead the dough briefly, until just smooth — about 10 seconds. Divide dough into thirds. Shape each piece into a 5-inch circle, ¾-inch thick. Wrap well with plastic wrap and refrigerate for 1 hour or overnight.

Preheat oven to 325 degrees. Line 2 cookie sheets with parchment paper. Combine the remaining ½ cup sugar, walnuts, and cinnamon in a bowl.

On a floured surface with floured rolling pin, roll one piece of dough into a 14-inch circle. Spread top with 1/3 of the raspberry preserves, leaving a 1-inch border around the edge. Sprinkle with 1/3 of the cinnamon-sugar mixture; then sprinkle with 1/3 of the mini-chocolate chips. Gently press the chips into the dough. Cut the circle into 12 wedges with a sharp knife or pastry cutter. Starting at the wide edge, roll up each toward the point. Place rolls on cookie sheet, points tucked underneath, and shape into crescents. Repeat with remaining ingredients. Bake in lower third of oven 40 to 45 minutes, until lightly browned. Transfer to wire rack to cool. These cookies freeze well. Yields 3 dozen cookies.

LEMON CASSATA CUPS

Dough:
¾ cup butter
½ cup sugar
1 egg
2 cups flour
¼ tsp. salt
1 tsp. almond extract

Filling:
8 oz. cream cheese
2 eggs, beaten
½ cup sugar
¼ tsp. salt
3 T. lemon juice, freshly squeezed

Cream butter and sugar until light and fluffy. Add egg, blending well. Gradually add flour, salt, and almond extract. Press ½ tsp. of the dough into miniature muffin tins lined with miniature paper baking cups, forming the sides and bottom of the Cassata Cups. Refrigerate.

Preheat oven to 325 degrees. Combine cream cheese, eggs, sugar, salt, and lemon juice; mix well. Spoon enough cream cheese mixture into each cup to fill ¾ full. Bake for 20 minutes. Remove Cassata Cups from the muffin tins and cool on wire racks. May be frozen. Yields 5 dozen.

ALMOND BUTTER CUPS

Dough:
2 cups flour
1 cup butter
1 egg
¼ tsp. salt
½ cup granulated sugar
1 tsp. almond extract

Filling:
2 eggs
½ cup granulated sugar
½ tsp. almond extract
1 cup almonds, crushed

Combine all dough ingredients in food processor and mix well. Combine all filling ingredients and mix well. Line miniature muffin tins with paper cup liners and fill each cup with dough approximately the size of a walnut. Mold dough into the bottom and sides of the muffin cups to the rim. Pour the filling into each cup until approximately ¾ full. Preheat oven to 350 degrees. Bake 25 minutes, or until cups are puffy and lightly browned. Yields 3 dozen.

Alternative fillings:

Chocolate-Raspberry Filling:

6 oz. miniature, semisweet
   chocolate chips
1 12 oz. jar red raspberry jam
1 egg
¼ tsp. vanilla
1 T. Mexican coffee liqueur

Cheese Filling:

1 16-oz. carton cottage cheese,
   large curd
1 egg
½ cup sugar
½ tsp. vanilla
Lemon juice to taste

51

STRAWBERRY CREAM STARS

8 oz. cream cheese, softened   1 T. lemon juice
¼ cup confectioners sugar   1 qt. fresh strawberries
1/8 tsp. cinnamon

Combine cream cheese, sugar, cinnamon, and lemon juice in a mixing bowl and beat until smooth. Cover and refrigerate. (Can be made ahead.) Clean and hull strawberries. Place on paper towels, hulled side down. With a sharp knife, cut an "X" through the pointed end of each berry, being careful not to cut all the way through. Gently open the berry slightly. Using a pastry bag and a large star tip, pipe the filling into the center of the berries. Berries can be filled up to 2 hours in advance. Place filled berries in paper petit four cups for easy serving. Yields about 36 filled strawberries.

PEACH TEA PUNCH

This recipe was contributed by Anne DeBois, long-time administrator of the Texas Governor's Mansion, and developed by Mansion chef Sarah Bishop.

4 cups water
3 family size tea bags
4 cups mint, packed
1 12 oz. can frozen lemonade
2 bottles peach nectar (can be purchased at your local health food store)

2 1-liter bottles ginger ale
2 1-liter bottles soda
½ to 1 cup simple syrup (recipe follows — taste before adding)

Boil water; steep tea and mint for about 15 minutes. Remove tea bags. Leave mint in solution until cool. Strain into 2-gallon container. Add lemonade and peach nectar. Add ginger ale, soda, and simple syrup. Serve well chilled.

Simple Syrup:
1 cup sugar   ½ cup water

Bring to a slow boil until clear — about 4 minutes.

Mark White's Inauguration
A Reception at the Governor's Mansion

Luncheon Buffet:
Taco Sombreros

Miniature "Not Quite Barbecued" Brisket Sandwiches
with Wasabi Horseradish Spread

Marinated Shrimp

Linda Gale White's Chicken Flautas

Southwestern Pasta Salad

The Governor's Vegetable Platter
Pickled okra, baby carrots, mushrooms,
haricot verts, brussels sprouts, miniature corn,
colossal black olives, roma tomatoes

Fresh Strawberries
with Whoopie Sauce for dipping
(Always a favorite!)

The Sweets:
Cream Cheese Brownies

Praline Bars

TACO SOMBREROS

Filling:

1	cup tortilla chips, coarsely crushed	2	oz. ripe olives, diced
1	cup sour cream	2	T. taco sauce
1	egg, beaten		

Combine ingredients and refrigerate.

Sombreros:

1	lb. lean ground beef	1	T. cumin
1½	tsp. black pepper	½	tsp. salt
2	tsp. chili powder	2	T. ice water
2	tsp. granulated garlic	4	oz. cheddar cheese, shredded
1	tsp. onion powder		

Preheat oven to 375 degrees. Combine beef, seasonings, and ice water and mix. Using a heaping tablespoon of mixture, roll meat into balls. Press into small muffin tins – 1½-inch cups – forming a "tartlette" shell, covering the bottom and the sides of the cups. Into each sombrero shell, place a spoonful of the filling, mounding it slightly. Sprinkle the tops with shredded cheddar cheese. Bake at 375 degrees for 10 to 12 minutes. Remove immediately and serve. These can be cooled, frozen, and served later. In our years of catering, we have made literally thousands of these and they freeze very well. Reheat in 375-degree oven for 10 to 12 minutes or until hot. Yields about 30 Sombreros.

MINIATURE "NOT QUITE BARBECUED" BRISKET SANDWICHES

Marinade:

1 cup bourbon	¾ cup soy sauce
1 large onion, chopped	½ cup ketchup
3 T. Dijon style mustard	¼ cup brown sugar, packed
6 garlic cloves, crushed	1 cup strong coffee
¼ cup molasses	1/8 tsp. Worcestershire
4 slices of fresh ginger	Few dashes hot pepper sauce
Black pepper to taste	

1 beef brisket, 8 to 10 lbs., trimmed

Combine all ingredients for the marinade. Place brisket in an oven baking bag. Add marinade, closing tightly, and place in a large baking pan. Refrigerate for at least 24 hours.

Preheat oven to 250 degrees. Bake brisket, in the baking bag, for 5 hours or until a fork pulls out easily when pierced. Heat one-half of grill. Remove brisket from baking bag and place on grill, searing each side. Move brisket to "cold" side of grill and continue cooking for 10 to 15 minutes. Allow the brisket to cool to room temperature before slicing across the grain. Yields approximately 3 servings per pound.

Meanwhile, transfer the marinade to a saucepan, skim off all fat, and bring to a boil. Use this over the sliced brisket when reheating. Serve with your favorite barbecue sauce or Wasabi Horseradish Spread (recipe follows) and cocktail rolls.

WASABI HORSERADISH SPREAD

2 cups mayonnaise	Granulated garlic to taste
¾ cup Parmesan cheese, grated	Wasabi to taste (Attention:
¼ cup teriyaki sauce	it's HOT!)

Combine all ingredients and refrigerate. Yields 3 cups. Keeps well in the refrigerator.

MARINATED SHRIMP

This recipe was contributed by Linda Gale White and was developed by the late Larry Adams, chef to former Governor and Mrs. White.

4 lbs. large shrimp, cooked and peeled

Marinade:

1 cup fresh parsley, chopped	¼ cup Dijon mustard
1 cup tarragon vinegar	1 cup shallots, chopped
2 cups olive oil	1 cup white wine vinegar
8 T. crushed red pepper	2 tsp. salt, or to taste
4 serrano peppers, seeded and sliced	

Combine the marinade ingredients. Pour over the shrimp while still warm and stir occasionally. Allow to marinate for 24 hours, refrigerated. Drain the marinade and serve chilled.

LINDA GALE WHITE'S CHICKEN FLAUTAS

Marinade:

1 cup Italian salad dressing (fat-free is fine!)	½ tsp. granulated garlic
	½ tsp. onion powder
½ tsp. cumin	½ tsp. chili powder

Flautas:

1 5 to 6 oz. chicken breast	1 T. fresh parsley, chopped
3 T. butter	½ tsp. cumin
1 tsp. grated onion	½ tsp. chili powder
¼ tsp. minced garlic	White pepper to taste
¼ cup flour	4 cups oil for frying
¼ tsp. salt	8 corn tortillas
1 cup chicken stock or broth	

Early in the day combine all marinade ingredients. Add chicken breast and marinate for 6 hours.

Preheat grill. Remove chicken from marinade and grill for 3 minutes on each side. Dice into small pieces.

In a medium skillet, melt butter; add onions and garlic and sauté until just softened. Blend in flour and salt. Add chicken stock and cook until thickened. Add spices and herbs. Stir in chicken and cook slightly. Heat oil to 350 degrees. Soften tortillas in hot oil, one at a time, and place approximately 2 T. of chicken mixture in each tortilla. Roll into cigar-sized flautas. (Cut in half for hors d'oeuvre size flautas.) Secure with toothpicks. Fry at 350 degrees until crisp and lightly browned. Drain on paper towels. Serve with your favorite avocado sauce or guacamole. Yields 8 large or 16 small flautas.

SOUTHWESTERN PASTA SALAD

This recipe is another family favorite of former Governor Mark and Linda Gale White.

2 lbs. medium shrimp, cooked, shells removed	1 red pepper, julienne strips
1 green pepper, julienne strips	1 red onion, sliced
1 bunch cilantro, chopped	½ cup olive oil
4 ears fresh corn, cooked and shucked	½ cup balsamic vinegar
1 15-oz. can black beans, rinsed	4 tomatoes, chopped
	1 12-oz. bag spiral pasta, cooked
	Salt and pepper, to taste

Combine all ingredients. Serve on a bed of fried corn tortilla strips. Serves 8.

THE GOVERNOR'S VEGETABLE PLATTER

(So named because we developed this assortment of marinated vegetables specifically for this event, and it is still a favorite!)

Pickled okra	Brussels sprouts
Baby carrots	Miniature corn
Button mushrooms	Colossal black olives
Haricot verts	Roma tomatoes

Marinade #1:

1¼ cups vegetable oil	1½ tsp. salt
½ cup red wine vinegar	½ tsp. black pepper
3 T. tarragon vinegar	1 tsp. basil
3 T. onions, minced	1 tsp. dry mustard
1 tsp. granulated sugar	

Mix all ingredients in a blender. Refrigerate for 24 hours and use as a marinade for vegetables or as a salad dressing. Yields 1½ cups.

Marinade #2:

½ cup olive oil	⅛ tsp. crushed red pepper
¼ cup lemon juice, freshly squeezed	1 garlic clove, minced
1 tsp. salt	1 T. fresh basil, chopped
¼ tsp. green pepper, diced	

Combine all ingredients and whisk briskly. Refrigerate for 24 hours and use as a marinade for vegetables, or as a salad dressing. Yields 1 cup.

GOVERNOR'S PLATTER CARROTS

Marinated Carrots:

1	7-oz. jar sun-dried tomatoes
½	cup vegetable oil
1	cup granulated sug
1	T. Worcestershire s
1	T. salt
1	tsp. prepared must

¾ cup vinegar
5 cups baby carrots, blanched
er, chopped
pped

Combine tomatoes, oil, s   in food processor and mix until well ble   n a bowl. Pour
dressing over vegetables   e serving.

2	12-oz. pkgs. of s
	chocolate chips
1½	14-oz. cans swee
	condensed milk
1	13-oz. can evaporated milk
⅛	cup light corn syrup

liqueur

Melt chocolate chips in a double boiler over hot (not boiling) water. Add sweetened milk and blend well. Add evaporated milk, corn syrup, vanilla, almond extract, liqueur, brandy, and salt. Mix well. Remove from heat and cool completely. (Store in wide-mouthed jars, because the sauce thickens as it cools.) Serve warm with fruit as a dipping sauce or over ice cream or dessert of your choice. Can be refrigerated for up to one month. Yields 6 cups of heavenly chocolate!

CREAM CHEESE BROWNIES

Brownies:

2	pkgs. brownie mix (total of 43 oz.)
⅓	cup brandy
⅓	cup Mexican coffee liqueur
½	cup vegetable oil

1 tsp. vanilla
4 eggs
Pinch of salt

In a large mixing bowl, combine all ingredients and blend, at half speed, until just mixed. Set aside.

Filling:

2	8-oz. pkgs. cream cheese, softened
¼	cup butter, softened
½	cup sugar

1 tsp. vanilla
2 T. cornstarch
4 egg yolks

Cream together softened cream cheese and butter. Add sugar, vanilla, and cornstarch. (Scrape the bowl and beaters.) Add the egg yolks.

Frosting:

4 oz. unsweetened chocolate
6 T. butter
4 cups powdered sugar (sifted)

Pinch of salt
$\frac{1}{8}$ cup water
1 tsp. vanilla

Preheat oven to 350 degrees. Line a 12 x 18-inch or two 9 x 13-inch pans with foil and spray with baking spray. Spread bottom of pan with 1/3 of the brownie mixture. Add remaining brownie mix and cheese filling in alternating portions and swirl together with a knife. Bake for 35 to 40 minutes. Allow brownies to cool in pan. Freeze brownies when cool. For frosting, melt chocolate and butter over hot water in a double boiler. Add powdered sugar and salt, alternating with water. Add vanilla and mix well. While still frozen remove brownies from pan; remove foil. Frost and cut into desired size. Freezes well. Yields 36 two-inch brownies.

PRALINE BARS

12 graham crackers
1 cup butter or margarine
1½ cups light brown sugar

1½ cups chopped pecans
1 tsp. vanilla
1 tsp. imitation rum flavoring

Line a 15x10x1-inch jellyroll pan with whole graham crackers. Bring butter and sugar to a rolling boil and cook for 3 minutes, stirring with a whisk. Remove from heat. When the bubbling stops, add the nuts, vanilla, and rum flavoring. Spread mixture evenly over crackers. Bake at 350 degrees for 10 minutes. Cut each cracker into pieces, at the natural scored lines. Yields approximately 4 dozen cookies.

"Fun for Funds" Cocktail Party
A Political Fundraiser

"Pennies From Heaven"

Passed Hors d'oeuvres:
Shrimp Italiano

Buffet:
Braccioli
Beef roulade with savory Italian filling — Texas style

Antipasto
Zucchini Pizzas
Tortellini with Herbs
and White Wine Sauce

Dessert:
Tiramisu
Chocolate Mint Brownies

Accompanying beverages were Texas wines and Texas beers

SHRIMP ITALIANO

Marinade:

¼ cup olive oil
2 T. lemon juice
1 T. fresh parsley, chopped
1 tsp. sugar
1 garlic clove, finely chopped

¼ tsp. black pepper
1 T. fresh basil, chopped
¼ tsp. dried oregano
1/3 cup green onions, chopped

2 lbs. large cooked shrimp (15-16 per pound)

Combine marinade ingredients. Add shrimp and refrigerate up to 8 hours.

BRACCIOLI

This is a delicate version of the classic Italian rolled meat filled with a farce of vegetables and herbs. Our rendition lends itself to a broader venue than the traditional braised entree. It does well as a hot main course or sliced into ½-inch rounds served at room temperature for a cocktail party.

Filling:

3   10-oz. pkgs. frozen, chopped spinach, defrosted and squeezed dry
1   cup mayonnaise
⅓   cup onion, chopped

½   tsp. oregano
2   tsp. parsley, chopped
1   cup grated Parmesan cheese

1   flank steak, approximately 2 lbs.
1½ to 2 cups toasted breadcrumbs
Olive oil

Salt and pepper
Granulated garlic

Combine all the filling ingredients and set aside. Preheat oven to 325 degrees. Place the flank steak between sheets of plastic wrap on a heavy board. Using a tenderizing mallet, flatten the steak to ¼-inch thick. Remove the plastic wrap and spread the filling evenly over the meat, leaving a 3-inch border at the far end of the meat for sealing the rolled meat. Sprinkle breadcrumbs over the spinach mixture. Roll the beef, making sure its grain runs the length of the roll, so that slices will be across the grain. Tie the meat with butcher's twine. Brush with olive oil and season with salt, pepper, and garlic. Sear in a very hot skillet using ⅛ cup oil, then roast in a heavy baking pan in preheated oven for about 50 minutes, or until internal temperature is 160 degrees. Let meat "rest" before slicing. Serves 8.

ANTIPASTO

1   14-oz. can artichoke hearts, drained
½   lb. button mushrooms
½   lb. fresh green beans, blanched
1   large head curly leaf lettuce, separated and washed
1   8-oz. can pitted ripe olives, drained
1   10-oz. can colossal green olives, drained

1   red pepper, sliced in strips
1   green pepper, sliced in strips
½   lb. mozzarella cheese, sliced
4   oz. salami, thinly sliced
2   2-oz. cans anchovy fillets, drained
Pepperoncinis
Cherry tomatoes

Marinade for vegetables:

½   cup olive oil
½   tsp. sugar
Salt and pepper

¼   cup lemon juice
1   garlic clove
Dash of red pepper

Combine marinade ingredients in blender and mix thoroughly. Pour marinade over artichokes, hearts, mushrooms, and blanched green beans. Allow to marinate overnight. Drain before serving. (You could also use your favorite Italian salad dressing as a marinade.)

Arrange the lettuce leaves on a large platter and place all the remaining Antipasto ingredients, alternating the colors for eye appeal. Serves 10.

ZUCCHINI PIZZAS

1   15-oz. container of ricotta cheese
1   tsp. fresh parsley, chopped
1   tsp. fresh garlic, chopped
10 leaves fresh basil, minced
Dash of black pepper
Dash of red pepper flakes
¼   tsp. salt

1   T. Parmesan cheese
2   medium zucchini,
    2½ inches in diameter
10 dinner-sized hard rolls
1   cup of your favorite pizza sauce
2   cups mozzarella cheese, grated
Parmesan cheese

Preheat oven to 350 degrees. Combine the ricotta, parsley, garlic, basil, peppers, salt and Parmesan cheese in food processor and blend well. Refrigerate.

Trim ends of zucchini and slice diagonally into 3/8-inch ovals. Cut hard rolls in half and scoop out center, leaving 1/4-inch crust. Generously spread cheese mixture inside rolls; add a slice of zucchini. Top zucchini with 1 T. pizza sauce and follow with a generous sprinkling of grated mozzarella. Top with Parmesan cheese. Bake for 10 minutes or until cheese is melted. Serve immediately. Yields 20 pizzas.

TORTELLINI WITH HERBS AND WHITE WINE SAUCE

½   cup butter
1   T. olive oil
2   T. finely chopped garlic
2   T. shallots, chopped
¾   cup dry white wine
3   T. fresh parsley, chopped plus
    2 T. for garnish
2   tsp. fresh basil, chopped
½   tsp. oregano

Dash of nutmeg
1   cup heavy cream
½   tsp. salt
Pepper to taste
3   dashes hot pepper sauce
½   cup sour cream
18 oz. cooked tortellini pasta
1   cup Parmesan cheese

Melt the butter and oil in a large skillet. Sauté garlic and shallots for 3 to 4 minutes over low heat. Add wine, 3 T. chopped parsley, basil, oregano, nutmeg, heavy cream, salt, pepper and hot pepper sauce and blend. Remove from heat and add sour cream. Whisk until smooth.

Toss the wine sauce with the tortellini. Add Parmesan cheese and toss again. Top with 2 T. chopped parsley for garnish.

This dish holds well in a warm oven or can be reheated in the microwave.

TIRAMISU

"Tiramisu" is Italian for "pick me up," and is the perfect name for this wonderful dessert. It tantalizes your taste buds, even after a full dinner. Our version of this classic uses cream cheese, instead of the mascarpone, but in no way compromises the rich flavor. It is a "hurry up and wait" dessert, as we think it is best when served after being refrigerated for at least 24 hours, allowing the flavors to blend completely.

1	8-oz. pkg. cream cheese	1	cup strong coffee or espresso, chilled
1/3	cup sugar		
1	oz. Marsala wine	2	T. brandy
1	tsp. white vanilla	2	3-oz. pkgs. ladyfingers (24)
1	cup whipping cream, whipped	1	cup semisweet chocolate, shaved

In a mixing bowl, beat cream cheese and sugar until light and creamy. Blend in wine and vanilla. Fold in whipped cream. In a separate small bowl, combine coffee and brandy and set aside.

Assembly:

Split each ladyfinger in half. Dip the ladyfinger halves, cut side down, in the coffee-brandy mixture. Line the sides and bottom of a 9-inch square baking dish with the cookies, dipped side down. Evenly spread 2 cups of the cheese mixture over the ladyfingers and sprinkle with ½ cup shaved chocolate. Repeat procedure using the remaining ladyfinger halves dipped in coffee-brandy. Top with cheese mixture and shaved chocolate. For storage, place toothpicks in the corners and center of Tiramisu and cover with plastic wrap. Refrigerate for 24 hours. Remove toothpicks and cut into 3 x 3-inch squares. Yields 9 servings.

CHOCOLATE MINT BROWNIES

This recipe was contributed by former Governor Ann Richards.

Brownie:

½	cup butter	1	cup sugar
2	squares unsweetened chocolate	½	cup flour
2	eggs	1	tsp. vanilla
½	tsp. salt	½	cup nuts, chopped

Melt butter and chocolate. Let cool. Beat eggs, salt, and sugar. Add chocolate. Mix in flour and add remaining ingredients. Bake at 325 degrees in an 8 x 8-inch pan, coated with cooking spray, for 25-30 minutes. Cool.

Filling:

2	T. butter	1	tsp. peppermint flavoring
1	cup powdered sugar	1	drop green food coloring

Mix all ingredients and spread on top of cooled brownies. Refrigerate until cold.

Glaze:

1	1-oz. square unsweetened chocolate	1	T. butter

Melt chocolate with butter and spread over cold brownies. Refrigerate. Cut into squares and serve. Yields 16 brownies.

Chapter 4

Ladies Who Lunch

unching is an art whose true patrons are unfortunately diminishing in number daily. This chapter is a tribute to the women who carry on the tradition of leisurely lunching, some of Texas' most gracious hostesses who have not forgotten the beauty of an extended midday meal, be it among friends, colleagues, or clients.

The menus in this chapter include lunches and brunches served to honor the ladies of the Texas House and the Senate, former First Lady Mrs. Lady Bird Johnson and members of her renowned National Wildflower Research Center, and others.

Many of our lunches were the centerpiece of another Texas tradition—the afternoon Ladies' Sewing Club. Part of the social fabric for decades, the object of today's Sewing Club, as any good member knows, is not to create quilts or clothes but to spend time catching up with dear friends, possibly to play bridge, but certainly to eat, drink, and be merry. Some of the Sewing Club lunches we serve are extremely formal affairs, with gleaming table settings and multiple courses. Others are more casual, featuring one-plate luncheons.

Mrs. Allan Shivers, late wife of the late Texas Governor Allan Shivers, and a Sewing Club hostess with whom we worked for years, can be credited with teaching us much of what we know about serving formal occasions. Mrs. Shivers was a sophisticated hostess who became one of our early mentors. Her knowledge of quality service became our guideline.

Another client also stands out in our memory. As the former director for Special Services of the University of Texas System, Mrs. Nancy Payne was the coordinator for all official functions of the University of Texas System, a hefty title which included events at The University of Texas in Austin and fifteen component institutions—nine academic and six medical. Nancy's job was one that carried awesome event planning responsibilities, but she possessed amazing finesse and always radiated an unrivaled pre-party calm. A special mention goes to Nancy's husband Joe, who acted as an unofficial taster for Gourmet Gals & Guys.

Take time in this crazy, hurried world for resurrecting the art of lunching. The following midday menus will provide you with inspiration.

Seated Luncheon
for Lady Bird Johnson
in Celebration of
the National Wildflower Association

Grilled Swordfish Salad
with Roasted Garlic Dressing

Fresh Fruit Salad
with Yogurt Sauce

Molded Gazpacho

*Assorted Miniature Muffins, Rolls
with whipped butter

Dessert:
Ice Cream Cones
Filled with Angel Chocolate Mousse,
garnished with whipped cream flowers
and punctuated with berries or candied flowers

* Recipe not included

GRILLED SWORDFISH SALAD

Marinade:

¼	cup balsamic vinegar	¼	cup fresh basil
¼	cup concentrated grapefruit juice	2	tsp. cilantro
¼	tsp. sesame oil	1	tsp. cumin
2	T. olive oil	¼	tsp. black pepper
2	T. water	2	garlic cloves

Combine all ingredients in blender or food processor until smooth. Can be made several days ahead. Yields ¾ cup.

Grilled Swordfish:

1½ lbs. fresh swordfish fillets (approximately 4 oz. per person)

Marinate swordfish for 4 hours. Grill fish over a medium-hot grill for approximately 4 minutes per side. Baste with marinade while grilling. Set aside.

Roasted Garlic:

4   large heads garlic (do not use
     elephant garlic)
½   cup olive oil
½   cup dry vermouth

½   cup red wine
Dash of coarsely ground
    black pepper

Preheat oven to 350 degrees. Remove the outer skins of garlic heads. Place the garlic heads and the remaining ingredients in a small casserole lined with foil. Seal the foil tightly and bake until garlic is soft—approximately 1 hour. Remove garlic and cool. Lightly squeeze each garlic clove from its skin. You should have 1 cup.

Grilled Swordfish Roasted Garlic Salad Dressing:

1   cup roasted garlic (above)
2   T. fresh lemon juice
1   T. Dijon mustard
1½ tsp. anchovy paste (optional)*
1½ tsp. Worcestershire

Dash of hot pepper sauce
½   tsp. salt
1   tsp. ground black pepper
2/3 cup olive oil

Place garlic, lemon juice, Dijon mustard, anchovy paste, Worcestershire sauce and pepper sauce in a blender and mix until smooth. Add salt and pepper. With blender turned on, slowly add olive oil. This dressing may be made ahead; however, bring to room temperature before serving. If the dressing is too thick, add 1 or 2 T. water. Yields 2½ cups.

* Olives may be substituted for anchovy paste.

Salad and Assembly of Ingredients:

3   heads romaine lettuce
1   head leaf lettuce to line plates
    (8 nice leaves)
6   4-oz servings grilled swordfish,
    sliced

Croutons of your choice
1   pt. cherry tomatoes
Anchovies, small shrimp or
    crab meat (optional)

Wash, dry, and tear romaine lettuce into bite-sized pieces. Toss well with Roasted Garlic Salad Dressing. Line each serving plate with a large piece of leaf lettuce. Mound dressed romaine on lettuce cup; add sliced swordfish, croutons, cherry tomatoes, and anchovies. Serve remaining dressing separately. Yields 6 servings.

YOGURT SAUCE FOR FRUIT SALAD

2   8-oz. fruit flavored yogurts
    (we use strawberry-banana
    non-fat yogurt)
1   T. rum, optional (or any liqueur
    of your choice)
1   T. sugar

1/8 tsp. nutmeg
¼   tsp. cinnamon
1   tsp. orange juice concentrate
1   tsp. honey
1   tsp. white vanilla

Combine ingredients and refrigerate. When ready to serve, place fruit of your choice in a lettuce or soufflé cup. Top with Yogurt Sauce. Yields 2 cups.

MOLDED GAZPACHO

2	pkgs. unflavored gelatin	1	cucumber, pared and diced
18	oz. tomato juice	1	red onion, finely chopped
Splash of olive oil		1	green pepper, diced
⅓	cup red wine vinegar	1½	tsp. salt
¼	tsp. hot pepper sauce	⅛	tsp. coarsely ground pepper
1	14.5-oz. can tomatoes, peeled and diced	2	garlic cloves, minced

Dissolve unflavored gelatin in ¾ cup tomato juice over low heat. Remove from heat and add remaining tomato juice, olive oil, vinegar and hot pepper sauce. Transfer to a bowl and set in ice until it starts to gel. Fold in the remaining ingredients. Spray mold or custard cups with cooking spray and pour in gazpacho. Refrigerate for 24 hours. Serve with your favorite avocado sauce. Yields about 6½ cups.

ICE CREAM CONES
WITH ANGEL CHOCOLATE MOUSSE

This dessert was presented to Mrs. Lyndon Johnson as part of the "Keep Texas Beautiful" campaign. The mousse-filled cones, decorated to look like wildflowers, were secured with floral pins in country-style baskets. Each guest was presented with a packet of bluebonnet seeds along with the dessert "flowers."

1	12-oz. bag chocolate chips	¼	cup sugar
½	cup evaporated milk	1	cup frozen whipped topping
2	T. brandy	1	cup whipping cream, whipped
1	tsp. almond extract	1	angel food cake, torn into small pieces
2	tsp. vanilla		
2	T. Mexican coffee liqueur	24	cake-style ice cream cones
3	eggs, separated		

Melt chocolate chips over low heat or in a microwave. Stir in evaporated milk until mixture is no longer stiff. Add brandy, almond extract, vanilla, and liqueur and allow to cool slightly. In a separate bowl, beat egg yolks. Beat small amount of chocolate mixture into yolks; then add remaining chocolate and mix well. Beat egg whites until foamy; add sugar and beat until stiff peaks form. Fold egg whites into chocolate mixture. Add whipped topping and whipped cream. Add angel food cake pieces and toss together. Fill ice cream cones with chocolate mousse; refrigerate until set, at least 4 hours. Decorate with Stabilized Whipped Cream (recipe follows) and just before serving, garnish with colorful candied flowers. Yields 24 servings.

STABILIZED WHIPPED CREAM

This whipped cream can be used to outline and decorate with a star or shell tip, or served as a frosting.

1	tsp. unflavored gelatin		¼	cup powdered sugar
4	tsp. cold water		½	tsp. white vanilla
1	cup heavy whipping cream		½	tsp. brandy

Combine gelatin and cold water in small saucepan. Let stand until thick. Warm over low heat, stirring constantly, until gelatin dissolves (about 3 minutes.) Remove from heat and cool slightly. Whip cream, sugar, vanilla, and brandy until slightly thickened. With the mixer set on low speed, gradually add the gelatin to whipped cream mixture. When the gelatin is completely absorbed, whip at high speed until stiff.

Brunch Buffet for the Senate Ladies Club

at Bauer House, The University of Texas

Banana Rumaki

*Orange and Tomato Juices

Nancy's Brunch Casserole

Reba's Orange Rolls, *Cinnamon Rolls and *Croissants

with assorted flavored butters and spreads

Breakfast Torte

Cheese Blintzes

Served with Red Hot Apple Glaze

*Recipe not included

BANANA RUMAKI

1 lb. bacon	½ cup brown sugar
½ cup orange juice concentrate	½ tsp. cinnamon
1 cup water	3 large bananas, not quite ripe
1 tsp. white vanilla	55 toothpicks
1 T. rum (optional)	

Preheat oven to 350 degrees. Slice bacon strips in half. In a large skillet, partially cook bacon until soft and slightly browned. Do not allow to overcook as crisp bacon will not wrap. Drain on paper towel.

Combine orange juice concentrate, water, vanilla, and rum in a medium bowl and set aside. In a separate small bowl, combine brown sugar and cinnamon.

Cut bananas into 1-inch slices; cut each slice in half. Soak banana pieces in orange juice mixture, drain, and toss with sugar/cinnamon mixture. Wrap each banana section with a strip of bacon and secure with a toothpick.

Bake on a nonstick baking sheet for 8 minutes. Serve immediately. Yields approximately 54 pieces.

NANCY'S BRUNCH CASSEROLE

This recipe was contributed by Nancy Payne.

4	15-oz. cans yellow or white hominy		Salt and pepper, to taste
2	4-oz. cans green chiles, chopped	2	cups Monterey jack/colby
½	cup sour cream		cheese, combined, shredded

Preheat oven to 325 degrees. Spread 2 cans of hominy in a greased 9 x 13-inch casserole dish. Top with all of the green chiles. Spread sour cream over the green chiles and sprinkle with salt and pepper. Spread remaining 2 cans of hominy and top with the cheese. Bake for 20-25 minutes, or until cheese is bubbly. Can be prepared a day ahead and baked just before serving. Serves 12.

REBA'S ORANGE ROLLS

1	pkg. active dry yeast	½	cup sour cream
¼	cup warm water	6	T. + 2 T. melted butter
¼	cup sugar	2¾	to 3 cups all-purpose flour
1	tsp. salt	¼	cup toasted coconut for
2	eggs		garnish*

Coconut-Sugar Mixture:

¾	cup coconut	2	T. grated orange rind
¾	cup sugar		

Glaze:

¾	cup sugar	2	T. orange juice
½	cup sour cream	¼	cup butter

Preheat oven to 350 degrees. Dissolve yeast in warm water. Add sugar, salt, eggs, sour cream, and 6 T. butter. Gradually add flour to form stiff dough. Cover and let rise in a warm place until doubled, about 45 to 60 minutes. While dough is rising, combine coconut, sugar, and grated orange rind. Knead dough on well floured surface about 15 times, then divide in half. Roll half of dough into a 12-inch circle. Brush with 1 T. melted butter. Sprinkle with half of coconut-sugar mixture. Cut into 12 wedges and roll each wedge, crescent style, starting at the wide end and rolling toward the point. Place rolls point-side down in a well greased 9 x 13-inch pan, forming three rows. Repeat with second half of dough. Allow rolls to rise in a warm place until doubled in size, about 45 to 60 minutes. Bake for 25 to 30 minutes. Leave in pan for glaze and garnish.

While rolls are baking, combine ingredients for glaze in a small saucepan. Gently boil for 3 minutes, stirring occasionally. Pour glaze over warm rolls and sprinkle with toasted coconut. Yields 24 rolls.

* To toast coconut, bake in a shallow pan for 5-10 minutes or until golden brown, stirring occasionally.

HONEY BUTTER

1	cup butter, softened	7	T. honey

Place butter in a small mixing bowl and beat until smooth. Add honey until light and fluffy. Yields 1¼ cups.

LEMON BUTTER

1	cup butter or margarine	1/3	cup fresh lemon juice
½	cup sugar	1/8	tsp. salt
1	T. grated lemon peel		

Melt butter in the top of a double boiler. Stir in sugar, lemon peel, lemon juice, and salt. Heat until sugar is dissolved. Remove from heat. Beat until the mixture is thick and smooth. Refrigerate. Yields 1½ cups.

BREAKFAST TORTE

1	lb. puff pastry	*Omelets:*	
		6	eggs
1	T. oil	2	tsp. fresh chives, chopped
1	T. butter	2	tsp. fresh parsley, chopped
1	lb. fresh spinach, blanched and drained	½	tsp. dried tarragon
		1	T. butter
2	garlic cloves, minced	Salt and freshly ground pepper	
¼	to ½ tsp. nutmeg		
Salt and freshly ground black pepper		8	oz. ham, grated
		8	oz. Swiss cheese, grated
		1	egg, beaten

Lightly grease an 8-inch springform pan. Roll ¾ lb. of the puff pastry to ¼-inch thickness and line the bottom and sides of pan. Keep remaining pastry covered and refrigerated.

Heat oil and butter in a large skillet. Add spinach and garlic; sauté for 2 to 3 minutes. Season to taste with nutmeg, salt, and pepper. Remove from heat and set aside.

For omelets: Lightly beat the eggs, herbs, salt and pepper to taste. In an 8-inch skillet over medium heat, add 1 T. butter and fully coat the bottom of the pan. Pour in ½ of the egg mixture and stir briefly. As eggs begin setting, lift the omelet's edges, allowing liquid to run underneath. When eggs are completely set and the top of omelet is no longer moist, slide the omelet onto a warm plate. Repeat with remaining butter, and egg mixture.

Assembly:

Preheat oven to 350 degrees. Layer ingredients in prepared springform pan in this order: 1 omelet, ½ spinach mixture, ½ cheese, ½ ham. Repeat layering in reverse order, using remaining ingredients.

Roll remaining pastry to ¼-inch thick. Cut out an 8-inch circle and place over omelet. Seal well to pastry liner by pinching the edges together with your fingers or the tynes of a fork. Draw the wedged servings desired directly on the pastry with the tip of a knife and decorate with leftover pastry cut into flower shapes. Brush with beaten egg. Place the springform pan on a baking sheet and bake until golden brown, about 70 to 75 minutes. Cool for 20 minutes. Remove from pan and serve warm. Yields 12 servings.

CHEESE BLINTZES

Crepe Batter:

½ cup water
½ cup milk
½ tsp. salt
4 eggs, beaten
1 cup flour
1½ T. butter, melted and cooled

Combine water, milk, salt, and eggs in a blender until ingredients are combined. Slowly add flour and blend until smooth. Add the cooled, melted butter, in a slow, steady stream. Refrigerate at least 1 hour.

Heat a lightly greased 6-inch omelet pan. Using a ¼ cup measure with a spout, pour batter in the middle of the pan and swirl rapidly to cover the sides and base. Cook only until the crepe begins to pull away from the sides of pan and the top is dry. Do not allow the crepe to brown. Turn out on a towel cooked side up. Re-butter the pan and repeat until batter is used. Do not stack crepes until they have cooled, then stack browned side up. Refrigerate.

Cheese Blintz Filling:

1 8-oz. pkg. cream cheese, room temperature
2 egg yolks
4 T. sugar
½ tsp. salt
1 tsp. white vanilla
1 tsp. cinnamon
Pinch of nutmeg
1 tsp. lemon juice
15 oz. small curd cottage cheese, drained of all liquid

Beat the cream cheese until smooth. Add egg yolks, sugar, salt, white vanilla, cinnamon, nutmeg, and lemon juice and blend well. Add cottage cheese and mix. (Mixture will be lumpy.) Refrigerate.

Assembly and Cooking:

Spread 1 T. of blintz filling in the center of the cooked side of crepe. Fold, envelope-style. Chill or freeze until ready to cook.

Butter a skillet with unsalted butter and cook blintzes, seam-side down, over medium heat for 3 minutes on each side, or until golden brown. (Blintzes may also be baked for 20 minutes at 350 degrees on a lightly-oiled cookie sheet.)

Serve with Red Hot Apple Glaze (recipe follows), sour cream and cinnamon-sugar mixture, fruit preserves, or blueberries. Yields 8 to 10 blintzes.

RED HOT APPLE GLAZE

4 apples, peeled, cored and sliced
1 T. lemon juice
3 T. butter
1 T. cornstarch
1 6-oz. can concentrated frozen apple juice
1 cup water
Dash of nutmeg
4 -oz. pkg. hot cinnamon candy
Pinch of salt
2 T. brandy

Toss apples in the lemon juice immediately after slicing. Melt butter over medium heat; add cornstarch and stir until smooth. Add apples, apple juice, water, nutmeg, candies and salt. Cook over medium high heat until the apples soften. Add brandy. Cook for 10 more minutes. Cool. Process mixture in a blender or food processor until slightly chunky. Serve warm over heated Cheese Blintzes. Yields 4 cups.

Texas Legislative Ladies Club
at Bauer House, The University of Texas

A One-Plate Seated Luncheon

Greek Chicken Salad
with Tarragon Vinaigrette Dressing
*Sliced Kiwi Garnish
Sun-dried Tomato Monkey Bread and Butter

Dessert:
Lemon Tart
garnished with mint leaves

*Recipe not included

GREEK CHICKEN SALAD

3 cups Tarragon Vinaigrette marinade and dressing (recipe follows)
8 6-oz. marinated, broiled, sliced chicken breasts
2 heads romaine lettuce, or 16 nice leaves to line the plates
3 bunches fresh spinach, washed, dried and torn, to equal 8 cups

8 hard-cooked eggs, sliced
½ lb. mushrooms, sliced
8 tsp. pine nuts
½ lb. feta cheese, crumbled
16 Greek olives
8 lemon slices
8 cherry tomatoes, halved
2 14-oz. cans artichoke hearts, drained and quartered

Tarragon Vinaigrette:
¾ cup dry white wine
¼ cup dried tarragon
½ cup white onions, chopped
1 cup white wine vinegar
½ tsp. Dijon mustard
1½ cups olive oil

1½ cups vegetable oil
2 tsp. granulated garlic
⅛ tsp. white pepper
1 tsp. sugar
1 tsp. salt

Combine wine and dried tarragon in a small saucepan. Over medium heat, reduce to 3 T. Set aside. Purée onions, wine vinegar, and Dijon mustard in a food processor or blender. With the machine running, add the oils in a steady stream. Add the Tarragon Vinaigrette, garlic, pepper, sugar and salt and blend. Rrefrigerate. Allow to come to room temperature and shake well before serving. Yields 3 cups.

Broiled Chicken:

Marinate chicken breasts in 1 cup of Tarragon Vinaigrette for 3 hours. Remove chicken from marinade and broil 3 minutes per side, basting regularly with the marinade while cooking. Cool and cut into serving slices. This can be made a day ahead.

Assembly:

On a large dinner plate, layer the salad in the order of ingredients listed above, placing the chicken slices after the sliced mushrooms. Use the lemon slices, cherry tomatoes, and artichoke hearts as garnish. Sprinkle each salad with Tarragon Vinaigrette and season with freshly ground black pepper to taste. Pour remaining Tarragon Vinaigrette in serving boats and place on the table. Yields 8 servings.

SUN-DRIED TOMATO MONKEY BREAD

2   loaves uncooked frozen bread, slightly defrosted

¾   cup butter, melted (1½ sticks)

1   cup Parmesan cheese

½   cup marinated sun-dried tomatoes, drained and chopped

½   cup fresh chives, finely chopped

½   cup mozzarella cheese, cut into small chunks

Place the slightly defrosted bread on a lightly floured surface. Cut the loaves in half length-wise; cut each half into 6 pieces. (Each loaf will yield 12 pieces.) Grease a large bundt pan. Dip each piece of bread first in melted butter, then in Parmesan cheese. Layer the pieces of bread in the bundt pan. Sprinkle bread with sun-dried tomatoes, chives and cheese, making sure that none of the additional ingredients are exposed to the surface of the pan, as they will burn. Continue alternating the bread pieces sprinkling each layer with sun-dried tomatoes, chives and mozzarella cheese, ending with a final layer of bread pieces. Cover with a clean, dry towel and allow to rise in a warm, draft-free area, for 1 hour, or until double in size.

Preheat oven to 375 degrees. Bake for 25 to 30 minutes, or until golden brown. Remove bread from pan immediately. Makes 1 loaf.

LEMON TART

1   cup all-purpose flour

⅛   tsp. salt

½   cup unsalted butter

2   T. confectioner's sugar

¼   tsp. grated lemon peel

Yolk of 1 large egg

1   tsp. water

Combine flour and salt and set aside. Beat butter in mixer until light; add sugar and lemon peel. Beat in egg yolk and water. Reduce speed to low and add flour and salt, until just combined (mixture will be crumbly). Wrap and refrigerate for 2 hours.

Preheat oven to 400 degrees. Roll pastry between 2 sheets of floured wax paper into a 12-inch circle, ⅛ inch thick. Fit into 10-inch tart pan with removable bottom. Line pan with foil and fill with dried beans, to prevent pastry from puffing. Bake for 10 minutes. Remove from oven and remove beans and foil. Bake for an additional 12 to 15 minutes, until golden brown. Cool completely in pan on wire rack.

Filling:

1	tsp. unflavored gelatin		Yolks of 4 large eggs
½	cup fresh lemon juice (divided in half)	1	T. grated lemon peel
		¼	cup unsalted butter, cut in pieces
1	cup granulated sugar	¾	cup whipped cream, beaten stiff

Sprinkle gelatin over ¼ cup lemon juice and set aside until softened, about 5 minutes. Combine remaining ¼ cup lemon juice, sugar, egg yolks, and lemon peel in a double boiler. Cook over simmering water, stirring constantly, until mixture is thick, about 10 minutes. Add gelatin mixture and cook, stirring, until completely dissolved, about 2 minutes more. Remove from heat and stir in butter until melted. Transfer to a bowl and cool completely. Fold in whipped cream and pour into prepared crust. Refrigerate 2 hours or overnight. Garnish with curly lemon peel and mint. Yields 10 servings.

Austin-Tatious
A Texas Ladies' Sewing Club

Hors d'oeuvres:
Clam Supreme

Seated Luncheon:
Fresh Asparagus
with Lime Hollandaise Sauce
Lobster Salad
Nonnie's Popovers and Sweet Butter

Dessert:
Mexican Coffee Parfait

CLAM SUPREME

This recipe was contributed by friend and mentor the late Marialice Shivers.

8 oz. cream cheese
1 T. cream
1 T. clam juice (reserved from clams)
2 6 ½-oz. cans minced clams, drained well
2 tsp. onion, finely minced
1 tsp. fresh garlic, minced
1 heaping tsp. fresh parsley, chopped
Dash of hot pepper sauce
10 brown and serve cloverleaf dinner rolls
3 T. butter
Chopped parsley
Parmesan cheese

Mix the cream cheese until light, adding the cream and clam juice slowly. Add minced clams, onion, garlic, parsley, and hot sauce and mix until smooth.

Cut the rolls into three sections. Scoop out the center of each section leaving about 1/8-inch crust on the sides and bottom. Lightly butter and fill with the clam mixture. (Can be made a day ahead up to this point and refrigerated.) When ready to serve, sprinkle with chopped parsley and Parmesan cheese. Bake on a cookie sheet in 350-degree oven for 10 minutes.

FRESH ASPARAGUS WITH LIME HOLLANDAISE SAUCE

42 asparagus spears, pencil thin
Lime Hollandaise Sauce (recipe follows)

6 yellow teardrop tomatoes
12 red onion rings

Lime Hollandaise Sauce:

5 T. white wine vinegar
¼ cup chopped green onions
2 T. lime juice
1 cup butter (2 sticks)

4 T. heavy cream
4 T. sour cream
1 tsp. granulated garlic

Combine vinegar, chopped green onions, and lime juice in a small saucepan. Reduce to 2 T. Cut butter into 16 pieces. Reduce heat to low and add butter, 3 pieces at a time, whisking constantly, until mixture is smooth and thick. Remove from heat and add heavy cream, sour cream, and granulated garlic. If made ahead, reheat over very low heat, whisking constantly. Yields 1¼ cups.

Steam fresh asparagus until tender but crisp. Remove from heat immediately and immerse in cold water to stop cooking.

Arrange cooled asparagus on individual salad plates, 7 per serving. Top with warm or room temperature Lime Hollandaise Sauce. Garnish with yellow teardrop tomatoes and red onion rings. Yields 6 servings.

LOBSTER SALAD

4 whole lobsters, 1 to 1¼ lbs. each

Dressing:

¾ cup mayonnaise
¾ cup sour cream
4 tsp. brandy
2 T. white wine
2 tsp. horseradish
½ tsp. fresh squeezed lemon juice
1 tsp. fresh parsley, chopped
1 tsp. minced garlic
¼ cup olive oil
½ cup sherry wine vinegar
2 tsp. sugar
½ cup red bell pepper, chopped
Salt and pepper to taste

Plate garnish:

6 cups lettuce, washed and torn
1 lemon, cut into 8 slices
1 cucumber, sliced
8 fresh mushrooms, cleaned and
    sliced

Steam the lobsters the day before serving and refrigerate.

To prepare lobsters for the salad, carefully remove the claws and tails, reserving for garnish. Remove the meat; cut meat into bite-sized pieces.

Combine all the dressing ingredients in the food processor and mix until smooth. Toss the lobster meat in a small amount of the dressing. Refrigerate.

To serve: Place approximately 1½ cups lettuce on each serving plate. (We prefer large buffet plates.) Drizzle dressing over the lettuce. Divide the lobster meat into 4 equal servings, mounding on each plate, as if the salad were the "body" of the lobster. Position the reserved claws and tails on the salad plate, recreating the lobster shape. Garnish with lemon, mushrooms, and cucumbers. Serves 4.

NONNIE'S POPOVERS

3 eggs
1 cup milk
3 T. oil

1 cup all-purpose flour, sifted
½ tsp. salt

Preheat oven to 400 degrees. Grease 8 5-oz. popover pans, muffin tins or custard cups and place them on a baking sheet. In a large mixing bowl, beat eggs, milk, and oil until combined. Slowly sift flour and salt into egg mixture; beat just until smooth. Pour batter into prepared pans, filling half full. Bake for 45 to 50 minutes, or until golden brown. Serve warm or at room temperature. Yields 8 popovers.

MEXICAN COFFEE PARFAITS

This is a simple, do ahead dessert that is easy to serve.

In 6-oz. wine or small parfait glasses, layer first 6 ingredients in the following order:

1 cup chocolate wafers, finely ground
Brownie Chunk ice cream
Cappuccino ice cream
Dash of Mexican coffee liqueur

Whoopie Sauce (see p. 57)
Sprinkle of chocolate wafer crumbs
Whipped cream, for garnish
Candy coffee beans, for garnish

Freeze, covered, for at least 8 hours. 10 minutes before serving remove from freezer. Garnish with whipped cream and candy coffee beans. Yields 4 oz. per guest.

Cocktail Buffet for Liz Carpenter

Lieutenant Governor's Suite in the Capitol

Cocktail Buffet:
Craig's Bourbon Salmon

Mix & Match Stuffed Mushrooms

Eggplant and Goat Cheese Spread

Artichoke and Lemon Ring
with Mock Hollandaise Sauce

Fruited Brie

Dessert:
Political Pie

CRAIG'S BOURBON SALMON

3	cups soy sauce	2	oz. sesame oil
1	cup bourbon	1	tsp. chili powder
½	cup fresh garlic, minced	3	lbs. fresh salmon filets,
½	cup fresh ginger, minced		skinned and boned
⅓	cup black pepper		

Combine the soy sauce, bourbon, garlic, ginger, pepper, sesame oil, and chili powder and blend well. Pour mixture over the salmon and marinate for 2-3 hours, refrigerated.

Remove from marinade and "cold smoke" for 4 hours, following the manufacturer's instructions on smoker. Preheat oven to 350 degrees, and finish the salmon, baking until flaky. Serve at room temperature. Salmon can be smoked the day before serving and refrigerated. Serve with Cucumber Dill Sauce (see p. 18). Serves 16 for hors d'oeuvres.

Cold smoke method:
The theory of cold smoking is to use a heavy smoke, without allowing the smoking area temperature to reach over 180 degrees. Follow the directions on your smoker. After smoking the salmon for 4 hours, finish cooking in a 350-degree oven until the salmon is flaky. Serve at room temperature. (Salmon can be smoked the day before serving and refrigerated.)

Method for grilling on a double burner gas grill:
Heat one side of the gas grill to 180 degrees. Soak wood chips in water and sprinkle on the coals. Position the salmon over the "cold" side of the grill and let cook for 2½ to 3 hours, adding wet wood chips as needed for continual heavy smoke. Finish cooking in the oven as described above.

CHEESE STUFFED MUSHROOMS

36 large mushrooms, brushed,
    stems removed

½ tsp. fresh garlic, chopped
½ tsp Worcestershire
1/8 tsp. white pepper

¼ tsp. dry mustard
1 cup mayonnaise
1 cup Parmesan cheese
2 T. scallions, chopped
3 dashes hot pepper sauce
¼ cup breadcrumbs

Preheat oven to 375 degrees. Combine all filling ingredients. Stuff mushrooms and bake for 12 to 15 minutes, until slightly browned on top. Filling can be made 2 days in advance. Serves 8.

CRAB STUFFED MUSHROOMS

12 large mushrooms, brushed,
    stems removed

½ cup fresh or canned crabmeat,
    picked clean (imitation Krab is a
    budget-minded substitution)

2 large cloves garlic, minced
1 T. fresh parsley, chopped
1 T. sherry
2 T. cream cheese, softened
Dash of hot pepper sauce
Salt and pepper to taste

Preheat oven to 350 degrees. Mix crabmeat, garlic, parsley, sherry, cream cheese, and hot pepper sauce. Stuff mushrooms, place on baking sheet, and bake 12 to 15 minutes. Serves 4.

ISLAND MUSHROOMS

1 lb. large mushrooms, brushed,
    stems removed

1/3 cup green onions, whites only
2 garlic cloves, minced
1 slice fresh ginger, chopped
2 T. vegetable oil
1 T. sesame oil

½ lb. ground pork
½ lb. ground chicken
½ cup cracker crumbs
2 T. soy sauce
2 tsp. sugar
1 tsp. spicy Thai sauce
1 T. sherry

Preheat oven to 375 degrees. In a medium skillet, sauté scallions, garlic, and ginger in vegetable and sesame oil until slightly soft. Add ground pork and chicken and sauté until well browned. Remove mixture from heat and add remaining ingredients. Generously fill the mushrooms. Heat on a baking sheet for approximately 10 to 12 minutes or until hot. Mixture can be made early in the day. Serves 6 to 8.

SPINACH FILLED MUSHROOMS

28 large mushrooms, brushed,
    stems removed

1 cup fresh spinach, washed,
    stems removed
2 dashes hot pepper sauce
    (or to taste)
1 T. Worcestershire

1 tsp. fresh garlic, chopped
¼ cup mayonnaise
½ cup Swiss cheese, grated
½ cup fresh Parmesan, grated
1/8 tsp. white pepper
1/8 cup sherry
¼ cup breadcrumbs
Dash of nutmeg

Preheat oven to 375 degrees. Mix all filling ingredients in a food processor. Fill mushrooms and bake on a baking sheet for 12 to 15 minutes. Serves 8.

EGGPLANT AND GOAT CHEESE SPREAD

4 T. olive oil
1 small onion, chopped
1 shallot, minced
1 T. fresh chives, minced
1 T. fresh garlic, crushed
1 medium eggplant, peeled and diced
1 medium red bell pepper, diced
1 medium green bell pepper, diced

1 medium zucchini, diced
2 small tomatoes, diced
1 carrot, finely chopped
¼ cup red wine vinegar
½ tsp. black pepper
½ tsp. salt
8 large fresh basil leaves, minced
Dash of hot pepper sauce
2 oz. Texas goat cheese

Heat olive oil in heavy large saucepan over high heat. Add onion, shallot, chives, and garlic; cook for 1 minute, stirring. Add eggplant, red and green bell peppers, zucchini, tomatoes, carrots, vinegar, pepper, salt, basil, and hot pepper sauce. Reduce heat and cook until vegetables are very tender, stirring occasionally, about 35 minutes. Remove from heat and allow to cool. Cover and refrigerate. Can be prepared 1 day ahead. When ready to serve, reheat slowly. Place in chafing dish and sprinkle with goat cheese. Serve with pita bread or pita chips. Serves 8 to 10.

ARTICHOKE AND LEMON RING

8 artichokes, cooked, cooled, cut in
    half, lengthwise, with choke removed
10 large lemons, halved, with scalloped
    edges
3 heads leaf lettuce, separated,
    washed and dried

1 12-inch styrofoam ring
Floral greening pins
Floral picks
1 14-inch platter
2 bunches parsley, washed
Paprika for garnish

Attach leaf lettuce to styrofoam ring with greening pins. Evenly space artichoke halves, cut side down, around the ring, securing the top and bottom of each artichoke with floral picks. Alternate the scalloped lemons with the artichoke halves by inserting more floral picks through the back side of the ring. (Cut floral picks to size.) Fill in blank areas with parsley. Sprinkle paprika lightly on the lemon edges. Add cherry tomatoes and olive for garnish. Cover with plastic wrap; refrigerate. (Artichokes can be cooked and refrigerated the day before, and the ring can be assembled 6 to 8 hours ahead.) Place the Artichoke Ring on a platter lined with leaf lettuce. Serve with Mock Hollandaise Sauce in an artichoke which has been cooked and scooped-out.

MOCK HOLLANDAISE SAUCE

½ cup butter (1 stick)
¾ cup mayonnaise
1 cup sour cream
1 T. granulated garlic

2 T. Parmesan cheese
1 T. fresh lemon juice
1 T. fresh parsley, chopped
Dash white pepper
Dash of hot pepper sauce, to taste

Melt butter in medium saucepan over low heat. Remove from heat and add mayonnaise and sour cream, whisking briskly until smooth. (It is important to remove from the heat to insure the proper consistency.) Return pan to heat on the lowest setting. Whisk in remaining ingredients. Serve at room temperature. Yields 2½ cups.

FRUITED BRIE

This recipe is dedicated to our good friend, Jean Graeber. It's her all-time favorite, and probably will become a favorite of yours, too.

2 sheets puff pastry
1 1-kilo Brie (9-inches round)
½ to 2/3 cup brown sugar
1½ to 2 cups walnut pieces, chopped

2 fresh pears, peeled, cored and thinly sliced
Cinnamon and sugar mixture

1 egg, beaten with 2 T. water

On a floured surface, roll out one sheet of puff pastry to half its original thickness. Cut out an 11-inch circle and set aside. Roll out second sheet of puff pastry to half its original thickness and cut a 10-inch circle. Set aside, reserving scraps for garnish.

Center the 11-inch puff pastry circle on the bottom of a 9-inch springform pan. Place the Brie on the puff pastry and press a thin layer of brown sugar on top. Sprinkle walnuts over the sugar, again pressing down. Toss the pear slices in sugar/cinnamon mixture, and arrange the fruit in a circular pattern on the Brie. Fold up the sides of the puff pastry, surrounding the Brie and fruit. Brush the pastry edges with water. Place the 9-inch circle of puff pastry on top of Brie, folding and pinching pastry crusts together, sealing well. Cut out decorative designs from the reserved pastry scraps, such as flowers, stems and leaves, and garnish the top of pastry.

Preheat oven to 350 degrees. Line a cookie sheet first with a layer of heavy foil, then parchment paper. (This will aid in cleanup!) Brush the top of the pastry with egg/water mixture and bake on the cookie sheet for 15-20 minutes or until golden brown. Serves 20 as an hors d'oeuvres.

POLITICAL PIE

Crust:

3   cups cream-filled chocolate
     sandwich cookies, finely chopped

½ cup roasted, salted cocktail peanuts

½ cup granulated sugar

5   T. butter

Preheat oven to 350 degrees. Spray a 9-inch springform pan with cooking spray. Combine all the ingredients in a food processor and mix well. Press the mixture to ¼-inch thickness on the bottom and sides of the springform pan. Bake for 12 minutes. Let cool.

Filling:

2   T. butter

3   T. sugar

½ cup peanut butter

20 oz. vanilla caramels

1½ cups cocktail peanuts,
     finely chopped

1   cup whipping cream

Melt butter in a saucepan over medium heat. Add sugar, stirring to dissolve, until mixture is golden brown. Remove from heat and add peanut butter, caramels, peanuts, and whipping cream. Return to medium heat and cook for 2 minutes. Pour mixture into crust and cool.

Topping:

½ lb. bittersweet chocolate

2   cups whipping cream

2   T. butter

4   egg yolks

6   egg whites

3   T. sugar

In a double boiler, melt chocolate with whipping cream. Remove from heat and let cool. Cream the butter in a medium mixing bowl, and add egg yolks, one at a time. Beat in chocolate/cream until mixture is stiff. In a separate bowl, beat egg whites until soft peaks form; beat in sugar, a little at a time, until stiff peaks form. Stir ¼ of the egg whites into chocolate mixture; then fold in remaining egg whites. Pour over pie and refrigerate for 2 hours or overnight. Slice 1 hour prior to serving and return to refrigerator. Garnish with whipped cream. Serves 12.

Chapter 5

For Women Only . . .

his chapter is for women only: those of you who told us you don't cook anymore. How long do you want to be a slave to the kitchen? Are you willing to be doomed to the purgatory of preparing three meals a day, forever? If not, this chapter is about making foods easier, quicker, and more fun. Some of you are busy with your jobs in the work force. Others are limited by time constraints dictated by busy families, and still others just hate to cook. You have been there, done that, and no longer want to wear that apron. You have retired your pots and pans, used your ovens for storage, decked your stovetops to suit the season, and carpeted your kitchen in white. You have taken a serious stand against the five-course meal!

However, considering that you are reading this cookbook, it's obvious that you still have interest in food. We think there are different kinds of women in the culinary craft of cooking. First, the "couldn't-care-less" gals who have never been interested in the preparation of food; maybe they lack the cooking gene, for whatever reason. They have nothing against food, as long as they don't have to prepare it. Their credo is, "That's why God made take-out!"

Next, are those of you who admire the culinary arts and talent of others, but can't quite master the cooking confidence you desire, no matter how many cookbooks you own, how devoted you are to Emeril 101, or how many cooking schools you've attended. The ability alludes you—it's always just beyond your reach. But you persist, trying to get your kitchen act together, in spite of your shortcomings.

Then there are those of you who always did, still do, and always will find food fascinating and wonderful. The thought of entertaining, and trying new recipes, sends shivers of pleasure down your spine. Using your "Martha" skills, you are either the envy of your friends, or they think you're absolutely crazy. You're the one who takes a cookbook to read in bed. Yes, we know who you are!

Cooking and entertaining, as we have known it, has evolved. It's no longer your mother's kitchen! Today's woman is a combination of all of that we've described, plus those who feel the need to cook, but really don't want to anymore. Our lives now include so many diverse opportunities, that standing in the kitchen making meals, is not a top priority. In fact, for many of us, it's extinct. Today's gourmet kitchens, with high-tech, "Jetson" appliances are often only places to be admired, not utilized. But, the truth is, you still have to eat; you still want to entertain.

Entertaining can still be in your blood. Let's probe the possibilities.

Women, arise from where you are and think of this as our personal intervention to help you plan for minimal time in the kitchen and maximum time with your guests and family. Believe it or not, the rest of this chapter details foods readily available, and already prepared, requiring little or no work. We're going to mention the obvious; almost every restaurant, deli or grocery store will make a huge variety of trays, not the mention pizza, chicken wings, and sub sandwiches. The trick is to make it your own. One idea is to take your own ovenproof casserole dish to your favorite restaurant and ask them to provide you with the entree of your choice. Warm it up at home and serve with salad and bread. Voila! Dinner is served. (Choose foods that will reheat well, such as entrees with sauces and the obvious, casseroles, being sure to get specific heating instructions.)

We hate to burst your bubble, but many of today's restaurants use prepared foods to save on labor costs. There are wholesale businesses that cater specifically to restaurants, with a huge variety of pre-prepared menu items. Warehouse stores have now given us the same opportunities. These stores are certainly not a secret, but knowing how to use their prepared items is. Hours saved in the kitchen translate to extra time with your guests, and these stores can be the salvation for those of us without time or without that cooking confidence. Warehouse stores, as well as specialty grocery stores, are plethoras of treasures! We've scoured the aisles and found several prepared, quality foods, which, with imagination, can be made to taste like homemade. Some of these foods can even be served as suggested on the packaging, without additional seasonings or sauces. (Be sure to throw the box away before the guests arrive!)

Before we begin talking about foods from warehouse stores, keep in mind that unfortunately, the same foods are not always available and often, some of our favorites are considered seasonal. So, when you're warehouse shopping, be flexible, and if it's a food you really like, stock up on it. Always read the instructions for preparation and decide if the food item fits your party plan. Consider the size and number of your ovens when making your choices.

LET'S TALK APPETIZERS

- Various brands and flavors of eggrolls that we've tried and found delicious, providing they are served hot and crisp. Accompany them with sauces from Chapter 11, the Las Vegas Luau, page 189.
- Quiches (sprinkle with additional Feta or Parmesan Cheese before baking)
- Scallops with Bacon (brush with Teriyaki Sauce before baking)
- Coconut Shrimp (serve with eggroll sauces)
- Jamin Shrimp (serve with a Jerk Sauce)
- Cooked, Peeled and Deveined Frozen Shrimp (defrost, season to taste with salt, pepper, and granulated garlic, toss in marinade of your choice, or Italian salad dressing. Accompany the shrimp with the sauces from Chapter 7, page 126.
- New York style Roasted Garlic Bagel Crisps, instead of French Bread Rounds, are great with Bruschetta Spread, Olive Tapenade, or Pesto.
- Marinated Fresh Mozzarella Balls, served on Baquette slices brushed with seasoned olive oil, and baked in a 350 degree oven until melted are always popular. (You will be oven-bound for this delicious treat. You can never serve enough!)
- Garlic Artichoke Dip (add granulated garlic, a dash of hot pepper sauce, 5 oz. defrosted chopped spinach, squeezed dry, and Parmesan Cheese to taste. Top with additional Parmesan Cheese and heat in microwave oven until cheese is melted. Serve with tortilla chips or Pita Bread, or stuff in mushroom caps.

SOUPS AND SANDWICHES

- Harry's Brand Soups are all wonderful and convenient. Our favorite one is the Tortilla Soup, to which we add chicken broth (instead of water), black beans (drained and rinsed), corn and leftover cubed chicken. Heat and serve with crushed tortilla chips, sour cream, shredded cheese, cubed avocados, and sprigs of cilantro.
- Wraps (sandwiches rolled with various ingredients) come in different flavors. Serve them with gourmet mustard and/or mayonnaise.

QUICK & EASY MEALS

- Thai Kitchen makes noodles in three flavors. Follow the instructions on the box, and add your own cooked chicken, beef, pork, seafood, and/or stir-fried vegetables.
- Penguin Natural Foods makes gourmet pasta salads in three flavors. Again, add tuna, meats or vegetables, if desired.

FROZEN ENTREES

- Mandarin Orange Chicken
- Don Miquel Chicken and Beef Fajitas (fully cooked, can be used in salads, for filling enchiladas, or the good old fashioned way, with flour tortillas and condiments)
- Ravioli (there is a large variety of flavors to choose from. They can be served cold in salads—very trendy—or as appetizers, accompanied by your favorite marinara sauce.)

DESSERTS

- We found a large assortment of imported cookies, our favorites being Almond Thin Biscuits and Just Desserts Petite Palmiers. Both of these cookies are light, airy and not too sweet—perfect with coffee or tea.
- Ghiriadelli Triple Brownie Mix is to die for (and tastes homemade!) when you add 2 Tbls. vanilla, and 2 Tbls. brandy to each recipe. Do not overbake!
- Sometimes you'll find frozen Cream Puffs, Cheesecakes, Eclairs, Tiramisu, and Assorted Petite Fours. Dress up any of these desserts by placing them on a pool of raspberry sauce (page 18) or chocolate sauce (Whoopie Sauce, page 57.)
- Some of the Warehouse Stores' bakeries have wonderful desserts, including an All American Chocolate Cake (see above for sauces), Caramel Apple Pie, and fabulous seasonal Pumpkin Pie. Use your own fresh, whipped cream on top and you'll think you're eating Mom's!

Part of the fun of warehouse shopping is munching on the samples—a veritable shopping smorgasbord! You can also pick up inexpensive serving pieces such as water-based chafers for buffet service. While you're at it, select beautiful fresh flowers for your centerpiece.

We would be remiss if we didn't mention that prepared foods have additives and preservatives. Manufacturers understand that people are much more conscious about what they eat. They now list the nutritional information as well as the ingredients. If you chose to eat more natural foods, they are available, already prepared, at specialty grocery stores. These stores are usually more than willing to let you taste-test before you buy. The quality of these foods is generally excellent, and the foods are freshly prepared.

Remember, like fashion, foods change. The crostini, popular today, may not be the hors d'oeurves of tomorrow. We are not saying that a lamb chop's hemlines will go up and down, knowing that a lamb chop is just a lamb chop. In the last few years we have watched dinner plates go from miniscule amounts of food, to stacked, layered towers, to Mom's home cooking, with low-carb foods being one of the trendy diets. We've become a society of food conscience consumers, and yet, no one passes up garlic mashed potatoes! Vegetables might be roasted in healthy exotic oil, but who among us won't indulge in chocolates and champagne? Enough said!!!

Chapter 6

For Men Only ...

ow that you've read this far into the book, this chapter is for all of you who have said to us, "But I don't cook anymore!" Actually, neither do we. Hooray for all of us. Since publishing *Texas Tuxedos to Tacos* we have both retired, and cooking has taken a back seat in our lives, much to the chagrin of our husbands. Ironically, Mike and Robert have both become excellent cooks. Robert makes an exquisite turkey breast and Mike has become so accomplished, everything he prepares is welcomed and wonderful. Pardon us while we brag, but they are both charming, wonderful hosts, as well. We include their favorite recipes later in this chapter.

The status of men in the kitchen has changed. Want to know why? WOMEN—all of us—that's why! We, as a group, have created our own chefs extraordinaire, who are learning to fend for themselves, because we, too, are prominent in the work force, while at the same time diapering the babies, raising our children, and trying to keep our houses beautiful. Yes, we are WOMAN. This has created great challenges for the men of the world. Gone are the days when the man of the house arrived home to a piping hot dinner on the table, with the children scrubbed, tubbed and ready for bed. In his work world he might be the CEO of a company, but in his home world, he's a Renaissance Man, because here, there's no "glass ceiling." He gardens, drives carpools, coaches the kids' athletic teams, and is a scout leader. He's also comfortable in the aisles of the grocery store and is more than intimate with his own kitchen. This dad who makes serious business decisions daily, now gets home to a quick hug and a kiss from his wife, who has had an equally busy day, three hungry kids, and a soccer game in twenty minutes. Sitcom this isn't; this is Reality! In years gone by, his choices for dinner would have been the three "P's"—pizza, popcorn, or pancakes. Today's man however, can prepare a three-course dinner, without breaking a sweat, thanks to the ingenuity of the prepared food industry. The choices are endless.

This man of the house, master of his own fate, goes back to his roots. A caveman existence turned modern. The caveman had to learn to hunt his own food. But instead of hunting in the woods with a weapon, the modern Survivor has neon lights guiding his way through the grocery store. As his ancestors, today's man also needs fire. On his own, as if by magic, he learns that there is a stove and an oven. He realizes that there are spices, marinades and rubs to season the food. But best of all, to his delight, he finds that there are grills, smokers, and spits, either gas or charcoal. These devices have become his favorite fire source.

Do you see yourself in this picture, or do you have a different lifestyle? If so, just delete the wife and kids from above, and you're there. So, whether you are self-taught, or had a coach at your side, either way, someone has to cook dinner!

Men, we don't want to have too much fun at your expense, because we know that you are becoming exceptional cooks. More of you enjoy perfecting this craft and recognize that cooking is a delicious labor of love.

Both of our fathers loved to prepare Sunday breakfast for our families. It has become a tradition passed down to the next two generations. No matter how you celebrate Sundays, whether with your immediate family or the extended variety, there is something special about the luxury of being together, without the day-to-day pressures of the work week. That's what makes weekends! Eggs are the staple of breakfast. Keep in mind, you have it on good authority, that cholesterol isn't a problem when eggs, of any description, are served with Mimosas or Bloody Marys! Here's a Sunday Starter followed by some of our families' favorite brunch foods.

A BULLISTIC BRUNCH COCKTAIL

The following recipe is the way we like this cocktail, but naturally, you can use less alcohol, if desired. As is, they go down smoothly and can sneak up on you!

½ to 1 cup orange juice
¼ cup Vodka
¼ cup white wine

1 T. strawberry preserves
¼ cup Strawberry Schnapps
1 cup Champagne

Pour orange juice into a blender and blend until frothy. Add the Vodka, white wine, strawberry preserves, and Strawberry Schnapps; blend until well mixed. Pour ½ cup of Champagne into each of two of your best champagne glasses. Fill each glass with the blended mixture, and garnish each glass with a fresh strawberry. Serves 2. Skol!

MIKE'S SWEET POTATO EGGS BENEDICT

This is one of my favorite breakfasts, but is a welcome meal anytime of the day. Also, any leftover biscuits are wonderful just as biscuits!

6 Sweet Potato Biscuits (recipe follows)
12 eggs
12 slices Canadian bacon, sizzled

1 cup Mock Hollandaise sauce
(see Chapter 5, page 81)
Chopped fresh parsley for garnish,
optional

Poach the eggs. Sizzle the Canadian bacon. Warm Sweet Potato Biscuits in the oven, and while you're at it, warm the individual plates, too. Split the biscuits in half, placing two halves on each plate. Place one slice of sizzled Canadian bacon on each biscuit half; put one poached egg on the Canadian bacon, top with Hollandaise sauce and sprinkle with parsley. Serves 6.

SWEET POTATO BISCUITS

1½ cups flour
1 T. baking powder
½ tsp. salt
⅛ cup sugar

½ cup shortening
¼ cup milk
1½ cup sweet potato, cooked,
mashed and cooled

Preheat oven to 375 degrees. Sift dry ingredients together in a bowl. Cut in shortening, using a pastry blender or knives. Mix milk and sweet potato until smooth. Blend potato mixture into the dry ingredients. Drop by large spoonfuls onto baking sheet and bake for about 20 to 25 minutes, or until done, and lightly browned on edges. Makes 6 large, moist biscuits.

RESTAURANT FRENCH TOAST

2 cups canola oil
3 eggs (Egg Beaters can be substituted)
1 cup fat-free Half-and-Half
1 cup complete pancake mix

1 tsp. vanilla extract
1 tsp. rum, optional
6 slices white bread, cut in half
  (don't use thick Texas toast)

Heat oil in a medium fry pan until a cube of bread fries quickly. In a medium bowl, combine and beat the eggs, Half-and-Half, pancake mix, and vanilla. Dip each piece of bread in the batter, turning to coat. Using tongs, transfer to fry pan. Do not crowd. Fry both sides until golden brown. Cover finished French Toast with paper towel until ready to serve. Serve with hot syrup, powdered sugar, or cinnamon/sugar mixture. Serves 4. Freezes and reheats well.

SIMPLY FRUIT

Any variety of the freshest fruits in season can be used for this recipe, but nothing compares to fresh berries! The flavor enhancers are the sugar/cinnamon mixture and the vanilla, but you could also add melted and cooled marmalade, or any fruit-flavored schnapps, to taste.

2 cups blueberries
1 cup blackberries
2 cups strawberries, sliced
1 T. white vanilla
1 to 2 T. sugar/cinnamon mixture
  (recipe follows)

½ cup orange marmalade,
  melted and cooled, optional
Fruit-flavored schnapps, optional
Fresh mint, for garnish

Wash the berries and dry them on paper towels. In a medium bowl, combine the berries with the vanilla and sugar/cinnamon mixture; toss gently. (Mix in marmalade and/or schnapps, if desired.) Garnish with sprigs of fresh mint, if available. Serves 6 to 8.

SUGAR/CINNAMON

1 cup granulated sugar
2 T. cinnamon (or, to taste)

Pinch of nutmeg
1 cinnamon stick

Mix ingredients together and store in a sugar-shaker jar with the cinnamon stick. Keeps indefinitely.

We asked men from various backgrounds to share their cooking stories and some of their favorite recipes. We learned that their stories are similar to one another, and maybe, to yours. Here are a few favorite recipes from our "Grill Professors." These men love to cook, not because it's their profession, but because it's their passion. A common thread through their stories and recipes is their families' and friends' influence. Besides our husbands, Mike and Robert, we present the rest of the willing participants with their most-loved or secret recipes.

MIKE'S LENTIL SOUP

My mother was a wonderful Swedish cook. One of my fondest memories is walking home from school on a cold, wintery, Chicago day and knowing by the aromas drifting from the kitchen window that she was preparing my favorite soup.

1 lb. dry lentils	1 potato, diced
2½ quarts water	1 cup celery, chopped
1 large ham bone or pork hock	1 bay leaf
1 large onion, chopped	¼ tsp. dry mustard
2 cloves garlic, minced	salt and pepper, to taste
1 large carrot, diced	

Follow the package directions for sorting and washing the lentils. Combine all ingredients and bring to a boil. Simmer for 1½ to 2 hours until very tender, stirring occasionally. (Additional simmering time enhances the flavors.) Remove ham or pork hock and set aside. Remove bay leaf. Process remaining ingredients in the food processor or blender for a smooth and creamy soup. Chop meat and add back to soup. If additional liquid is needed, use chicken broth or vegetable broth.

ROBERT'S BREAST OF TURKEY

Being the husband of a caterer, it's not easy to try my hand at cooking. In my mind, however, this is my famous turkey breast.

1 Breast of Turkey	Granulated garlic
⅓ cup of your favorite mustard (I like smoky mustard)	Paprika
	Olive Oil spray
⅓ cup Mayonnaise	

Preheat oven to 300 degrees. Combine the mustard and mayonnaise. Starting at the small end of the turkey breast, work your fingers under the skin, separating it and removing it from the meat, all the way to the neck cavity. Under the skin, spread a thick layer of the mustard/mayonnaise mixture over the breast meat, and sprinkle with granulated garlic. Carefully replace the skin. Spray entire breast with olive oil spray, sprinkle with granulated garlic and paprika. Place turkey breast on a baking pan and roast slowly, for approximately 2–3 hours, until the juices run clear when pierced with a fork (Time will depend on size of breast.) Instant-read thermometer should read 160 degrees. Leftover meat can be used for salads and sandwiches.

Gregg Krumme, ATTORNEY-AT-LAW

To earn money during high school, I worked on the cook line; first at Cocos and later at Chi Chi's Mexican restaurant. This was my first taste of cooking and real work. My mom could smell me coming home. My "cooking boots" stayed in the garage. Later, during college, while waiting tables at places like the Skirvin Plaza in Oklahoma City, I was exposed to some of the finer points of food preparation from schooled chefs. Among other things, I picked up the skill of speed-chopping a plethora of items with a chef's knife (no food processor needed).

Now as a practicing lawyer, cooking is a great way to unwind. A home project of "building some shade" for an outdoor patio morphed into a full-fledged outdoor kitchen. This is my favorite place to have a healthy pour of wine and prepare some good food. This leg of lamb recipe is wonderful for special occasions. Enjoy with a nice Pinot Noir.

EAST MEETS WEST LEG OF LAMB

1	6-8 pound bone-in leg of lamb	8	thin slices of fresh ginger,
8	cloves garlic, cut into thin strips		cut into slivers

Marinade and Sauce

¼	cup Worcestershire sauce	2	T. olive oil
½	cup soy sauce	2	T. butter
½	cup brown sugar, packed	2	T. sesame oil
4	T. Dijon mustard	2	T. garlic, minced
	(or 3 T. Chinese mustard)	1½	T. fresh ginger, minced
2	T. fresh lemon juice		Salt and pepper to taste

In a heavy saucepan, combine marinade ingredients. Cook over medium heat for approximately 3 minutes or until thick. Stir frequently to prevent the sugar from sticking or burning. Remove from heat and allow to cool. Using a sharp paring knife, make slits in the leg of lamb 1 inch deep and 1 inch apart. Alternately, insert garlic and ginger into the slits. Place ½ of the marinade and the lamb in a large plastic bag. Refrigerate for 24 hours (or at least overnight), turning the bag frequently. Remaining sauce will be used for basting during cooking and as an accompaniment for the lamb when served.

This lamb is perfect cooked on a spit on your grill. Or set your grill for indirect cooking and place a drip pan in the center. Preheat to medium. Remove the lamb from the marinade and place on the grill over the drip pan. Brush with more sauce. (Discard the used marinade.) Cover the grill and cook for approximately 2 to 2½ hours, basting frequently with the sauce. Whether cooking on a spit or by indirect heat, use an instant-read meat thermometer to determine the doneness you prefer, 140 degrees for medium-rare and 160 degrees for medium. Remove to a cutting board, brush again with the sauce, and allow to "rest" for 10 minutes before carving. Meanwhile, reheat the remaining sauce and serve with lamb. Serves 10. (This is a variation of a recipe from The Barbecue Bible, by Steven Raichlen.)

John Langston, ASSISTANT MANAGER, THE DRISKILL HOTEL, AUSTIN, TEXAS

As a small child, my grandmother, "Ma." was my best friend. Ma was a charming southern lady and helped my mother with the kids and the cooking. We were what you would refer to as a "meat and potatoes" family. Every night a proper dinner was served. Proper, in my family, was a good southern meal. Country-fried anything and everything. I still remember the day that Ma caught the can of Crisco on fire! The Crisco can, filled with bacon drippings, was a permanent fixture on the stovetop. It seemed like the preparation for everything from green beans to fried eggs began with a scoop out of the Crisco can. That is how Ma seasoned food.

My career in the Luxury Hotel industry has provided incredible opportunities to travel the world and enjoy outstanding food and although I really appreciate good food, I am not a chef. However, on occasion and in the company of very trusted friends, I will prepare a meal. Comfort food. Nothing fancy. When I cook, I cook like my grandmother did, minus the Crisco. Years later, and more fine dining experiences than I can recall, I still love fried okra.

MA'S SOUTHERN FRIED OKRA

4 cups okra, sliced $\frac{1}{2}$ inch thick	$\frac{1}{2}$ tsp. pepper
$\frac{1}{2}$ cup yellow cornmeal	2 eggs, beaten
$\frac{1}{2}$ cup flour	cooking oil
1 tsp. salt	

Heat $\frac{1}{4}$ inch cooking oil in frying pan. Combine cornmeal, flour, salt and pepper in a large bowl. Dredge okra in beaten eggs, then dredge in flour-cornmeal mixture. Place okra in heated frying pan and cook on medium heat until golden brown. Stir occasionally so that all sides get brown. Drain on paper towel.

Recipe options:
- 2 16-oz. bags of frozen sliced okra (thawed) may be used in place of fresh okra.
- For extra spice, substitute garlic salt and cayenne pepper in place of salt and black pepper.
- Bacon drippings can be substituted for cooking oil.
- Hum 5 choruses of "The Yellow Rose of Texas" during cooking.

Jeff Schafer, SALES AND EVENTS COORDINATOR, BALCONES SPRINGS CONFERENCE AND RETREAT CENTER, MARBLE FALLS, TEXAS

As sales and event coordinator for a retreat and conference center, I assist clients in finalizing their meeting plans, as diverse as choosing their menus to a myriad of other fun and educational events, including horseback rides through the beautiful Texas Hill Country. Prior to this, however, my friend, Ernie and I were youth workers. I rented an old ranch house—so old, in fact, that the oil lamp in the kitchen was electrified and the fireplace still had an arm to swing a pot over the fire for cooking. In addition to these quaint touches, it had four essential elements to living as a Texan who longs for the Caribbean: a huge limestone barbeque, two palm trees, a great patio and THE perfect front porch. Ernie and I had a standing Friday/Saturday and sometimes, Sunday, BBQ party with whomever was free to come. Ernie was raised in Puerto Rico, so he made the Pina Coladas and dessert, and I cooked the food. Combine Ernie's Pina Coladas, Jeff's BBQ in a Bag, and Ernie's Puerto Rico Plantains with guitars, Caribbean music, friends, and laughter for a great, casual BBQ!!

My friend, Ernie, joined the army and was promoted to captain. On December 28, 2003 he became a casualty of war in Iraq. He is my hero, and I submit these recipes in his memory.

JEFF'S BBQ-IN-A-BAG

For every two people: You can modify the ingredients to your liking; almost any combination of veggies, meat and fruit come out delicious.

1	green/red/yellow pepper, core removed	1	1015 Texas Sweet Onion
2	whole corn on the cob; remove "silk" but leave corn in the husk	4	carrots
½	fresh pineapple; peel and remove core, cut into rings or half-rings. Reserve juice for marinade. Reserve the remaining pineapple half for Pina Coladas	1	lb. chicken/beef/pork/venison —any one, or a variety!

Marinade: Combine the reserved pineapple juice, ½ bottle Teriyaki sauce, 1 bottle Worcestershire sauce, and any spices or herbs that you prefer. I like fresh garlic, fresh parsley, sliced fresh jalapeno peppers, and LOTS of course-ground black pepper.

Cut meat and vegetables into "can't fall through the grill"-size pieces and place in a Ziploc bag. Add marinade, and refrigerate overnight, turning it over every once in awhile. When you are ready to BBQ, pour the marinade into a saucepan and bring it to a boil. Since I'm a sauceboy, I always cook the marinade and use it as a basting and dipping sauce. Remove the meat and vegetables from the bag and put them on the grill to cook, turning occasionally, until done. Serve immediately and pass the warm sauce.

ERNIE'S PINA COLADAS

Essential to the success of the BBQ event is the pre-testing and perfecting of the Pina Coladas before your guests arrive. This usually happens on the night before the BBQ, or the morning/afternoon/evening of the event.

Step 1: **In a blender, combine**
½ **cup Coco Lopez Cream of Coconut**
1 **cup fresh pineapple juice**
  (canned juice can be substituted)

A few chunks of fresh pineapple
A few glugs of Puerto Rican Rum.
  (I am a 4-glug guy)

Step 2: **Fill the blender with ice and blend to a smooth, frosty slush that will make you hear the ocean's waves lapping on a golden strip of sand! If you want to impress the chicks, serve in a fresh coconut shell with a paper umbrella and a straw, but if it's just the guys, keep it simple and just pass the blender around.**
Step 3: **Drink. Beware of brain freeze.**
Step 4: **If you don't hear waves, repeat Steps 1, 2, and 3, as necessary.**

ERNIE'S PUERTO RICO PLANTAINS

For every two people:
1 **large plantain, peeled and sliced into ½-inch pieces.**
½ **cup flour**

1 **T. brown sugar**
1 **tsp. cinnamon**
½ **tsp. ginger**
¼ **tsp. cayenne pepper**

Combine the ingredients in a plastic bag and shake until all plantain pieces are well coated. Remove fruit from bag and sauté in butter until golden brown and tender, about 2-3 minutes. Serve with honey.

Jack Holmes, Chiropractor and Child Advocate Volunteer

I began cooking under the direction of my mother as a child. My father was so helpless in the kitchen he couldn't even boil water. Mom was bound and determined not to turn her three sons out onto some unsuspecting bride the way her mother-in-law did to her. Mom was a great cook and exposed us to a wide variety of food. She insisted we eat what was placed before us and as a result, I learned to like just about everything but sauerkraut.

I love to eat good food. I tell people I live to eat rather than eat to live. I also love to cook for company or special events. My work as a chiropractor and my volunteer activities as an advocate for children who are victims of abuse or neglect, or children in crisis, does not leave the time or desire to come home and fix dinner every night. As a result, I have learned to cook BIG once or twice a week, which provides me with delicious leftovers.

When I entertain, I want to spend time with my friends, not doing a messy, last-minute sauté, so I look for simplicity in menu planning. I have actually had guests who see a spotless kitchen ask if I was still planning to serve dinner! The recipes I have included here can be prepared ahead and be pulled from the refrigerator or the oven and placed on the buffet.

OVEN ROASTED VEGETABLES

This is a technique, not a specific recipe. Use a combination of your favorite vegetables or just a single vegetable, such as asparagus.

Olive Oil
1   **small eggplant with skin**
2   **large yellow onions**
2   **green peppers**
2   **red peppers**

3   **yellow squash with skin**
1   **lb. package baby carrots**
Kosher salt and fresh cracked
     pepper to taste

Cut all above vegetables into 1-inch chunks. Toss with enough olive oil just to coat. Lay out onto jellyroll pan or pans. Do not exceed one layer thick. Cover with fresh cracked pepper and kosher salt, to taste. Bake at 350 degrees for 30 minutes or until the edges begin to caramelize. Serve immediately or transfer to an ovenproof dish to be re-heated later.

GARLIC BRISKET

1   10-13 lbs. Cry-o-vac Brisket
1   head fresh garlic, separated into
     unpeeled, individual cloves
13 oz. BBQ cooking sauce
     (I use the whole 13 oz. jar of
     Woody's brand sauce)

Worcestershire Sauce
Liquid Smoke

Trim most of the fat off brisket and place fat side up, onto heavy aluminum foil that is large enough so ends and sides can be brought up and over the top and sealed shut. Cut pockets in checkerboard pattern over the top of brisket. Stuff with unpeeled garlic cloves. Pour and spread cooking sauce over the top of brisket. Sprinkle with 2 – 3 T. Worcestershire sauce and 3 – 4 drops of liquid smoke. Seal brisket tightly in foil, making sure no leaks develop. Place wrapped brisket in a large pan. Bake at 250 degrees for 10 hours. Slice and serve with sides of your choice, or shred with a fork and wrap in flour tortilla with salsa, cheese, sour cream, and onions.

PESTO PASTA SALAD

To make Pesto:
4-6 large garlic cloves, peeled
3   cups firmly packed fresh
     basil leaves

¾   cup pine nuts
1   cup grated Reggiano-
     Parmesan cheese
¾   cup good cold-pressed olive oil

In food processor, chop garlic. Add basil, pine nuts and cheese. While chopping, drizzle in the olive oil. Continue to blend until completely mixed. Use pesto immediately (approximately 1 heaping T. per person) or put pesto into plastic ice cube trays and freeze for 24 hours. Transfer pesto cubes to Ziplok bag for future use.

For the Pesto Pasta Salad:
Cook the pasta of your choice as per directions. Drain and return to cooking pan. Add just enough good olive oil to coat pasta when tossed. Add pesto (approximately 1 heaping T. or one defrosted cube per serving) and toss thoroughly. Place pasta in a serving bowl and sprinkle with additional Parmesan cheese. For pasta salad, chill before serving. Can be served immediately, hot, as a wonderful entrée.

Variation:
Add vegetables and/or leftover cooked chicken, cut into chunks.

JACK-O-MOLE

This is my version of the South-of-the-Border favorite. NOTE: The number of avocados and tomatoes used will depend on their size. I generally use 1 medium avocado and 1 medium Roma tomato per serving.

Avocados
Roma tomatoes
1 small red onion
Olive oil

Balsamic vinegar
Kosher salt
Fresh cracked black pepper

After halving the avocados, remove seed. Use a knife to cut through the "meat" of the avocado, but not the skin, going down lengthwise, then twice across. Use a small spoon to scoop chunks out of the skin. Chop the tomatoes. Cut the red onions into small slivers, lengthwise. The ending ratio should be 75-80% avocado/tomato, to 20-25% red onion. Drizzle with olive oil and balsamic vinegar. Add salt and pepper to taste. The guacamole can be made two hours ahead. Place the avocado pit in the bowl and cover with plastic wrap.

Todd Schroeder, MANAGER, CHRISTIAN DIOR, NEIMAN MARCUS

I was never an imaginative cook, although I love and appreciate gourmet foods and flavors. I was raised in the 1950s and 1960s, when the emphasis seemed to be on efficiency rather that fancy, and anything frozen and pre-prepared was considered a marvel (forgive me, Mom.) In the late 1990s I stumbled, by pure chance, into the position of Assistant Epicure Buyer at Neiman Marcus. At first I was shocked when my boss would try one bite of a product sample and toss the rest into the wastebasket, but I gradually learned to distinguish between the mediocre, the good, the great, and the fabulous. I still do not cook a great deal; after all, Texas is the land of the grill, and mine gets fired up about four nights a week. I have one easy method of seasoning—I sprinkle some Jane's Crazy Mixed Up Salt on whatever I'm cooking and throw it on the grill!

However, I have a few favorite family recipes that I hope you'll try and enjoy.

CHICKEN DIVAN

This is how I make use of my leftover grilled chicken. It's simple and satisfying.

2	large, cooked boneless skinless chicken breast halves	1	can cream of mushroom soup
1	bunch of broccoli crowns	5	slices of your favorite cheese

Preheat oven to 350 degrees. Steam broccoli crowns until almost done. Cube chicken breasts; heat in microwave until hot, about 2 minutes. Place the chicken, broccoli crowns, and cream of mushroom soup in a 8 x 8-inch baking pan. Mix thoroughly. Layer the cheese slices on top of mixture to cover, and bake at 350 degrees for 20 minutes or until the cheese starts to brown. Serves 2–3 VERY generously as a single dish meal. (And if there's more, it makes great leftovers!)

LINDA'S MARINATED SHRIMP AND MUSHROOMS

My brother, Bryant, and his wife Linda are two of my favorite people. They live in Glenview, Illinois, where they enjoy entertaining their neighbors and friends. When I visit them, I ask them to spoil me with either one of these two recipes.

1	package Good Seasons Italian dressing mix	1	lb. fresh mushrooms, washed and stemmed
1	cup cider vinegar	1	large onion, sliced and separated into rings
½	cup vegetable oil		
2	T. water		
2	lbs. shrimp, cooked, peeled, and deveined		

Combine dressing mix, vinegar, oil and water. Add shrimp, mushrooms and onion. Cover and marinate in the refrigerator for 4 hours. Drain and serve cold. Serves 8.

BRY'S MOOSE, VENISON, OR ANTELOPE STROGANOFF

There aren't too many moose, venison, or antelope in the Chicago suburbs, so if Bryant doesn't have the opportunity to go game hunting with his buddies, these meats are often available in specialty meat markets.

¾ to 1 lb. round, sirloin or tenderloin
    steak, cut into strips ½ inch thick
    by 2-3 inches long
2 T. butter
1 medium/large onion, coarsely chopped
1 clove garlic, chopped
8 oz. sour cream
2 tsp. Worcestershire sauce

2 T. catsup
1 4-oz. can sliced mushrooms,
    drained
1 can cream of mushroom soup
1 tsp. salt (or garlic salt)
1 tsp. finely ground black pepper
Splash of red wine or dry sherry,
    if desired

In a large frying pan, melt the butter. Saute the onions and garlic until soft but not browned. Add meat and brown on all sides. Add remaining ingredients and slowly heat to barely bubbling, stirring frequently. Reduce heat and simmer for a minimum or 20 minutes, stirring regularly. Additional time and stirring improves the blending of flavors. Serve over lightly buttered wide or goulash noodles.

    Serves 4.

Roland Geretti, MD, Retired

Being born into an Italian family means having delicious food available at all times. Mom has a love for the art of cooking and in her younger years she prepared food for a parish rectory in Italy. I thought most people ate tasty meals and I never questioned its source. College and medical school allowed me little time to learn Mom's secrets. Naturally, when I married a non-Italian wife, along with love, food was on top of my list for having a happy and satisfying marriage. Diligently, my loving wife learned the family secret recipes. Being busy with my medical practice and helping to raise our three children left me little time for anything else. Now, forty-two years later, I am finding time to cook some of the delicious family recipes. Italians have a love for fresh vegetables. Here are some recipes that are easy and delicious.

ITALIAN GREEN BEANS

1 lb. fresh green beans	¾ tsp. granulated garlic
3 T. balsamic vinegar	salt and pepper to taste
3 T. extra Virgin olive oil	

Put green beans in enough water just to cover; then add about 1 T. salt to the water. Bring to a boil and then lower heat to medium; cook for about 8 minutes. The beans should be soft but still firm. Drain in a colander, pouring cold sink water over the beans to stop the cooking process. Gently drain beans on a towel for a few minutes to get out the excess water. Put the green beans into a flat dish and toss with the remaining ingredients.

CAULIFLOWER DELIGHT

1 medium head of cauliflower	2 T. butter
¼ cup olive oil	¾ tsp. granulated garlic
½ cup bread crumbs	salt and pepper to taste
¼ cup grated Parmesan cheese	

Cut the cauliflower into small, bite size pieces. Put into a pan and just cover with water; then add about 1 T. salt to water. Boil for about 5 minutes; do not overcook. Drain in a colander. Meanwhile, add half of the oil to a frying pan. When oil is hot, add the cauliflower and cook on medium heat for a minute or two. Add remaining ingredients. Gently turn. Everything will start to brown. When it reaches the desired crispness, remove from heat and serve. Adjust seasonings according to your own tastes.

Ciao!!

Chapter 7

Putting On The Glitz

s we mentioned in our introduction, catering has often been compared to a theatrical production. Many travelers come to Texas anticipating a scene out of the Wild West. We like to respond with a little drama, altering their perception of our state by treating them to the unexpected. Menus included in this chapter were served in unique atmospheres, each presenting its own challenges.

Being a caterer in Texas means having to overcome some of the pre-conceived notions many visitors, "foreigners" to the Lone Star State, have about Texas. We often work with large national corporations, who come to the heart of Texas expecting cactus and cowboys but are transported beyond the state's proverbial boundaries by our cosmopolitan and sophisticated foods.

One such elegant affair was hosted by Mrs. Margaret McDermott, who was traveling to cities all over the United States hosting benefits for the prestigious New York Metropolitan Museum. The arrangements for Mrs. McDermott's party in Texas' capitol were unforgettable. Under the soaring, rose-granite rotunda on the second floor of the State Capitol building, tables to serve the 75

to 100 guests were formally set. It was the first time a party had been hosted outside the governor's office. What proved most challenging for us wasn't dazzling the guests with our food, but tending to the formal table settings in a record thirty minutes. Congress was in session until 6:00 P.M. that day, and though the party started at 7:00 P.M., we weren't allowed entrance to the second floor staging area until 6:30. As Mrs. McDermott's guests finished their tour of the Capitol and arrived outside the governor's office, we greeted them, the sweat wiped from our brows, with hot hors d'oeuvres passed on lavishly garnished silver trays. The chaos had turned to calm and the pink granite halls had been transformed into a soothing garden setting with music from twin harpists, soft lighting, and twinkling trees which surrounded the elegantly set tables.

Another noteworthy event began one otherwise normal morning. At 11:00 A.M., the phone rang. It was a favorite client who needed a cocktail party catered. Nothing unusual about that. A major business coup for Austin had been accomplished and a celebration was in order. The glitch was that the party for the out-of-town VIPs would be that afternoon. We had five hours to develop a menu, prepare the food, and hire the staff for 100 guests. The foods had to be elegant, but easy to prepare in the given time. We chose to pass all the hors d'oeuvres, as time didn't permit a buffet. This story, too, ends happily, as everything came together, our client was thrilled, and Austin had another addition to its high-tech family. We have included this menu as it offers an impressive yet practical option for those who choose to prepare their party in advance.

Time and weather aren't the only complications we've experienced. Occasionally, we are faced with something totally beyond our control, like the time we were serving a formal garden dinner party for 100 guests at the elegant, hilltop home of one of Austin's prominent citizens. Hors d'oeuvres and drinks were being passed, and we were at work in the kitchen when the Austin skyline went black. The electricity all over Austin had failed, and house and gardens were plunged into darkness. It promised to be a long evening! Fortunately, the phones still worked, so we sent an S.O.S to our warehouse staff, requesting our entire supply of portable cooking equipment. While we waited, we lit the night with votive candles, ever present in our party equipment box. Within twenty minutes we were cooking on gas and instead of courting disaster, we had truly memorable fun. Dinner was delayed for only a short time, and the guests were in awe of the magic we worked without the benefit of electricity. Our clients loved responding to the often asked question: *"And where were you when the lights went out in Austin?"*

All the menus in this chapter should help you in turning an otherwise ordinary affair into an evening to remember.

Monsanto
A formal seated dinner
Black Tie

Hors d'oeuvres in the Great Hall:
Artichoke Bites
Shrimp Los Trios
Mexican Shrimp

Texas Shrimp

Classic Marinated Shrimp
Jeweled Crab Claws

Entree:
Chicken Royale
*Sautéed Snow Peas and Baby Carrots
Wild Rice Pilaf
*Dinner rolls and butter

*Salad:
Limestone lettuce, clear vinaigrette dressing,
Saga cheese, grapes and French bread

Dessert:
Strawberries with Chocolate Cream

*Recipe not included

ARTICHOKE BITES

1 cup unsalted butter
2 tsp. fresh parsley, chopped
1/8 tsp. basil
1/8 tsp. oregano
½ tsp. fresh garlic, chopped

¼ lb. Gruyere cheese, grated
Salt and pepper to taste
Melba toast or toast points
1 can artichoke hearts, drained
  and chopped

Combine butter, parsley, basil, oregano, garlic, and cheese. Blend until smooth. Salt and pepper to taste. (Can be made ahead and refrigerated, but bring to room temperature before using.)

Spread butter/cheese mixture on Melba toast and top with chopped artichokes. Bake at 350 degrees until hot. Serve immediately. Yields 3 cups.

SHRIMP LOS TRIOS

The following shrimp sauces, served with traditional boiled, peeled shrimp, give this all-time favorite new marks of distinction.

Classic Seafood Sauce:

2 cups ketchup
2¾ cups chili sauce
¾ cup horseradish (start with ½ cup
  and increase to your personal taste)

1 tsp. granulated garlic
1 tsp. Worcestershire
1 tsp. lemon juice
2 dashes hot pepper sauce

Combine all ingredients and mix well. Stores well in refrigerator. Yields 5 cups.

Sombrero Sauce:

2 cups Classic Seafood Sauce
  (see previous recipe)
1/8 bunch cilantro, washed and
  chopped (or to taste)
¼ cup picante sauce

1 tsp. cumin
1 tsp. oregano
1½ T. chili powder
1 tsp. sugar
2 tsp. freshly squeezed lime
  juice

Combine all ingredients and mix well. Yields 2 cups.

Texas Seafood Sauce:

4 oz. cream cheese
4 oz. sour cream
¼ cup fresh parsley, chopped
3 T. shallots, chopped
1 T. red bell pepper, chopped

¼ cup tequila
½ cup green chiles, chopped
1½ T. taco seasoning
Salt and pepper, to taste
Hot pepper sauce, to taste

Mix all ingredients together. Taste for seasonings. Yields 2½ cups.

JEWELED CRAB CLAWS

12 Snow crab claws

Filling:

½ lb. scallops, drained and finely
   chopped
½ lb. uncooked shrimp, shelled,
   deveined, dried and finely chopped
1 tsp. Chinese rice wine

1 T. cornstarch
1 egg white
½ tsp. salt
¼ tsp. white pepper

Remove crabmeat from claws. Add remaining ingredients and mix well. Chill filling until firm.

Coating:

½ cup all-purpose flour
2 eggs, slightly beaten
2 cups panko (Japanese dried breadcrumbs available at Oriental market)

Vegetable oil for deep frying

Assembly:

Divide filling into 12 equal portions. With moistened fingers, mound one portion on end of each claw. Refrigerate 30 minutes.

Dredge filling end of claw in flour, and dip into beaten eggs. Coat completely in panko. Arrange claws on baking sheet and chill for 30 minutes.

Heat oil to 350 degrees. Fry crab claws in batches, careful not to crowd, until golden brown. Yields 12 hors d'oeuvres.

CHICKEN ROYALE

6 6-oz. boneless, skinless chicken
   breasts, halved

Granulated garlic
White pepper

12 thinly sliced pieces of ham

½ cup Gruyere cheese

Season chicken breasts with granulated garlic and white pepper. Cover and refrigerate. When ready to prepare, pound breast halves until thin, using the smooth side of mallet. Place 1 slice of ham lengthwise on each chicken breast.

Filling:

3 T. olive oil
½ lb. fresh mushrooms, sliced
1 T. garlic, minced
2 T. dry sherry

1 tsp. freshly squeezed lemon juice
2 cups Swiss cheese, grated
Salt and pepper, to taste

In a large skillet over medium heat, sauté the garlic and mushroom in olive oil for 3 minutes. Stir in sherry and lemon juice and cook for 2 to 3 minutes. Add grated cheese; remove immediately from heat. Salt and pepper to taste.

Assembly:

Preheat oven to 350 degrees. Place a heaping tablespoon of filling at one end of each ham-lined chicken breast half. Roll tightly and place seam side down in a large, heavy baking dish. Pour sauce over chicken (recipe follows). Bake for 25 minutes. Remove from oven and sprinkle with Gruyere cheese. Return to oven for 4 to 5 minutes, or until cheese is melted. Serves 6.

Sauce:

4	oz butter	2	T. dry white wine
2	T. flour	1	T. sherry
1	T. tomato paste	4	T. brandy
1	tsp. Dijon mustard	½	tsp. pepper
1¼	cups chicken broth	½	tsp. salt
1	cup whipping cream		

Melt butter in a medium saucepan. Add flour and whisk. Add tomato paste, mustard, and chicken broth. Cook until smooth and slightly thickened. Gradually add whipping cream; add wine, sherry, brandy, and stir to blend. Add salt and pepper.

WILD RICE PILAF

1	large onion, finely diced	3	T. fresh carrot, grated
2	T. olive oil	¼	cup chopped parsley
1	cup precooked wild rice	1	T. granulated garlic
1	cup uncooked white basmati rice	½	T. salt
4	cups chicken broth		Dash white pepper
1	cup champagne		

In a large skillet, sauté onion in oil until transparent. Add rices and chicken broth. Add champagne, carrots, parsley, and seasonings and bring to a boil. Reduce heat, cover and cook over medium-low heat for approximately 35 minutes, or until the rice is cooked. Serves 6 to 8.

STRAWBERRIES WITH CHOCOLATE CREAM

8	oz. cream cheese, softened	½	tsp. vanilla extract
½	cup powdered sugar		(or almond, if you prefer)
3	T. cocoa	1	pt. of very large strawberries
⅛	tsp. salt		(or 3 strawberries per serving)

Beat the cream cheese in a small mixing bowl. Sift together the sugar, cocoa, and salt. Add to cream cheese and beat well. Add vanilla.

Remove the hull of each strawberry and drain on paper towel. Carefully cut an "X" in the pointed end of each strawberry, taking care not to cut all the way through the berry. Gently pull the sections apart.

Using a pastry bag fitted with a star tip, pipe chocolate cream cheese into each strawberry. Refrigerate for up to 4 hours before serving. To serve, sprinkle sifted powdered sugar on each dessert plate; place 3 filled strawberries on the sugar. Garnish with a whole strawberry, cut and fanned.

The University of Texas Board of Regents

Formal Seated Dinner

Hors d'oeuvres:
Cheese and Papaya Quesadillas

Starter:
Painted Plate Salad
with Creamy French Dressing

Entree:
Trio of Tenderloins
Beef Tenderloin with Red Wine Sauce
Pork Tenderloin with Mustard Sauce
Loin Lamb Chop with Mint Sauce

Almond Potatoes
*Bread of choice and butter

Dessert:
Texas Snowballs with Chocolate Sauce

Assorted Liqueurs

*Recipe not included

CHEESE AND PAPAYA QUESADILLAS

4 oz. Mexican cheese, softened
2 oz. goat cheese
1 tsp. garlic, chopped
¼ cup onions, chopped
¼ cup green onions, chopped
1 small red bell pepper, finely chopped

1 tsp. cilantro, chopped (optional)
Salt and pepper to taste
Chopped jalapeños (optional)
2 cups papaya, mashed
16 flour tortillas (6½ inches)
2 T. vegetable oil

Mix the Mexican cheese and goat cheese in a food processor. Sauté the garlic, onions, and red pepper until soft; add this mixture with the cilantro, salt, pepper, and jalapeños. Add to the cheeses. Gently stir in the mashed papaya. Spread approximately 2 T. on a flour tortilla; cover with another tortilla and press together lightly. Add small amount of oil to hot skillet and sauté each side of the quesadilla until lightly browned and the cheeses are melted. Drain on paper towels and cut into quarters. Serve immediately. Yields 64 hors d'oeuvres.

108

PAINTED PLATE SALAD
with Creamy French Dressing

This salad requires a large plate to allow room for the arrangement of all the ingredients. It has great eye appeal and makes a wonderful impression, especially when placed on the table prior to your guests being seated.

Creamy French Dressing:

1	cup olive oil	6	T. wine vinegar
3	garlic cloves, crushed		Salt and ground black pepper
¾	cup mayonnaise		to taste
½	cup sour cream		Anchovy paste to taste (optional)
¾	tsp. dry mustard		

In food processor, blend all ingredients together. For a thinner dressing, add milk. (Can be prepared several days in advance.) Yields approximately 2½ cups of dressing.

16 leaves of assorted greens (radicchio, Belgium endive, purple kale, etc.)
8 cups fresh spinach, washed, dried, destemmed, and chilled
Salt and pepper
6 oz. Enoki mushrooms, washed and destemmed (optional)
Creamy French Dressing (recipe above)
8 radishes, thinly sliced
32 artichoke hearts
24 cucumber slices
16 cherry tomatoes
24 thinly sliced red onion rings
2 medium carrots cut into 2½-inch slivers
Toasted pine nuts
Edible flower, for garnish

Line each serving plate with 2 lettuce leaves. Toss the spinach in a small amount of Creamy French Dressing, lightly coating the leaves; sprinkle with salt and pepper. Mound 1 cup spinach to one side of each plate and arrange the remaining ingredients around the plate. Pass chilled salad forks. (When selecting ingredients, choose the finest and most unusual vegetables.) Serves 8.

TRIO OF MEATS MARINADE

Marinade:

1½ cups vegetable oil
1 T. sesame oil
½ cup light soy sauce
¼ cup Worcestershire sauce
1 T. dry mustard
1/8 cup Umbushi vinegar
1 T. garlic, chopped
1 T. Hoisin sauce
½ cup honey
Salt and pepper to taste

Meats:

1 lb. beef tenderloin
1 lb. pork tenderloin
4 rib lamb chops

For garnish:

Parsley
Enoki mushrooms
Orange slices
Mint leaves

Combine all ingredients in a blender and mix until marinade is thick and smooth. Divide equally into three bowls, one for each meat. Remove fat from meats. Cut the beef tenderloin and pork tenderloin into four 3-oz. portions. Marinate meats, covered and refrigerated, for up to 8 hours, turning twice.

When ready to cook, remove all three meats from marinade. Sprinkle beef, pork, and lamb chops with pepper and granulated garlic. Broil (or grill) 3-5 minutes per side, or until done. Serve on warmed dinner plates, placing each meat on the appropriate Trio Sauce (recipes follow). Garnish with parsley, Enoki mushrooms on the beef, an orange slice on the pork, and mint leaves on the lamb. Serves 4.

TRIO OF TENDERLOIN SAUCES

Nothing is as special as a Trio of Tenderloins – beef, pork, and lamb – combined artfully with a trio of delectable sauces.

BASIC SAUCE (Base for Trio of Sauces)

¼ cup butter	4 sprigs of parsley
¼ cup flour	7 whole peppercorns
6 cups beef stock or broth	3 T. ketchup
2 small onions, quartered	Dash of hot pepper sauce
2 celery ribs, cut in half	Dash of Worcestershire sauce
2 small carrots, peeled and quartered	Salt and pepper to taste
2 bay leaves	

Melt butter over low heat; add flour and cook slowly until roux is medium brown. Gradually add the beef broth, blending thoroughly. Add all remaining ingredients and simmer, covered, for approximately 1 hour. Strain sauce through a sieve. Transfer cooked vegetables and ½ cup of sauce to blender and mix until smooth. Transfer puréed vegetables back to sauce and stir. Check seasonings. Yields 3 cups.

Evenly divide sauce into 3 bowls for preparation of trio sauces to accompany the Trio of Tenderloins.

Beef Tenderloin Wine Sauce:

1 cup Basic Sauce (see previous recipe)	1/8 tsp. salt
½ tsp. fresh parsley, chopped	½ cup red wine

Add parsley and salt to the Basic Sauce and reheat. Add wine and stir. To serve, ladle 1/8 cup Wine Sauce on each dinner plate and place beef tenderloin on top of sauce. Serves 4.

Pork Tenderloin Mustard Sauce:

1 cup Basic Sauce (see previous recipe)	¼ tsp. dry mustard
1 T. Dijon mustard	¼ cup dry white wine

Add Dijon mustard and dry mustard to the Basic Sauce and reheat. Stir in white wine. To serve, ladle 1/8 cup Mustard Sauce on each dinner plate and place pork medallions on top of sauce. Yields 4 servings.

Loin Lamb Chop Mint Sauce:

1 cup Basic Sauce (see previous recipe)	1 T. fresh mint, chopped
¼ cup mint jelly	

Add mint jelly and chopped mint to the Basic Sauce and reheat, blending well. To serve, ladle 1/8 cup Mint Sauce on each dinner plate and place lamb chop on top of sauce. Yields 4 servings.

ALMOND POTATOES

¼	cup vegetable oil	2	eggs
2	large onions, chopped	3	cups cooked or riced potatoes
2	garlic cloves, minced	1	tsp. salt
¼	cup butter	½	tsp. white pepper
½	cup water	1	cup toasted, sliced almonds, finely chopped in food processor
6	T. flour	¼	cup dried parsley

Sauté onions in oil in a medium skillet over medium-low heat until tobacco brown. This process takes approximately 30 minutes. Add minced garlic and cook for 2 more minutes. Drain onions on paper towels and set aside.

Combine butter and water in a small saucepan over low heat until butter is melted and water boils. Increase heat to medium and add flour. Remove from heat and whisk until smooth. Add eggs, one at a time, beating after each addition. Cover and cool, but do not refrigerate.

Combine prepared potatoes, onions, and cooked egg mixture and blend thoroughly. Add salt and pepper. Preheat oven to 375 degrees. Combine almonds and parsley. Spray your hands with cooking spray and roll potato mixture into walnut-sized balls. Coat completely with the almond/parsley mixture and place on greased baking sheet. Bake for 12 minutes, turning once, or until cooked through. Yields 24 potato balls.

TEXAS SNOWBALLS

This dessert is exceptionally rich, but well worth the additional calories!

10	oz. semisweet chocolate, chopped	5	eggs
¾	cup strong coffee or espresso	1	T. dark rum or coffee liqueur
1¼	cups sugar	2	pt. whipping cream
12	T. unsalted butter, room temperature		Whoopie Sauce (see p. 57)

Preheat oven to 350 degrees. Grease a 5½ by 9-inch loaf pan. In a double boiler, melt the chocolate, brewed coffee, and sugar over low heat. Set aside to cool for 10 minutes. Transfer the mixture to a medium mixing bowl, and add the butter, mixing on low until incorporated. Add the eggs, one at a time, mixing thoroughly after each addition. Stir in the dark rum. Pour the mixture into the prepared loaf pan and bake for 1 hour. Mixture will be puffed and cracked. Cool to room temperature on a rack. Cover and refrigerate at least 8 hours or overnight.

To serve:

In a chilled bowl, whip the cream until it forms stiff peaks. Using an ice cream scoop or two spoons, shape the chocolate into 2-inch balls. Using a pastry bag fitted with a decorative star tip and filled with whipped cream, pipe each chocolate Snowball with whipped cream. Cover each serving plate with ¼ cup warmed Whoopie Sauce and top with Texas Snowball. Yields 12 balls.

Sematech

Cocktail Party at Bauer House, The University of Texas

(This party was unique because the initial phone call was at 11:00 A.M., party and food choices confirmed at 1:00 P.M., and all was ready to be served as the guests arrived at 6:00 P.M..)

Hors d'oeuvres passed: Beef Tenderloin

sliced and served on miniature rolls spread with mustard and horseradish sauces

New Orleans Chicken

with Cajun Marinara Sauce

Grilled Andouille Sausage

brushed with jalapeño jelly

Baked Oysters

Queso Tejano Triangles

Mexican Coffee Truffles and Fresh Strawberries

BEEF TENDERLOIN FOR SANDWICHES

1 cup butter, softened	Herbed Mayonnaise
3 garlic cloves, minced	(see p. 212)
¼ cup parsley, chopped	Honey Mustard
1 beef tenderloin, approximately	(see p. 212)
3½ lbs. trimmed	Horseradish Sauce
3 dozen small rolls	(see p. 212)

Preheat oven to 400 degrees. Combine butter, garlic, and parsley. Spread mixture over meat. On a rack in a shallow baking pan, roast meat for 10 minutes. Lower oven temperature to 325 degrees and continue to roast for 25 more minutes for medium rare. (Add 10 additional minutes for medium.) Allow the meat to rest for 20 minutes before slicing thin for sandwiches.

Cut rolls in half, spread with your choice of sauces, and add 1½-oz. sliced beef tenderloin. Serve at room temperature. Yields 3 dozen hors d'oeuvres sandwiches.

NEW ORLEANS CHICKEN

2 whole boneless, skinless chicken breasts	1 tsp. oregano
Salt, pepper and granulated garlic	1 tsp. salt
½ cup flour	½ tsp. black pepper
½ cup pecans, finely chopped	Cayenne pepper (if you want a
3 tsp. chili powder	spicier flavor)
1 tsp. cumin	Vegetable oil for frying

Cut chicken into approximately 48 bite-sized pieces. Sprinkle with salt, pepper, and granulated garlic. Combine flour, pecans, chili powder, cumin, oregano, salt and pepper, and cayenne. Toss chicken pieces in flour mixture, coating evenly. Refrigerate for 4 hours. Sauté chicken pieces, a few at a time, in a small amount of oil. Drain on paper towels. Cooked chicken can be held in an oven on low temperature for 30 minutes. (It can also be flash frozen and reheated in a 375-degree oven for 12 to 15 minutes.) Serve accompanied by Cajun Marinara Sauce (recipe follows) for dipping.

Cajun Marinara Sauce:

1 cup onion, chopped	4 T. olive oil
1 green pepper, diced	2 T. oregano
6 garlic cloves, chopped	2 T. basil
8 oz. marinara sauce (your favorite)	1 T. Italian seasonings
1 6-oz. can tomato paste	3 T. Pickapeppa brand sauce
1 15-oz. can tomato sauce	½ tsp. sugar
1 14½-oz. can diced tomatoes	Red pepper flakes, to taste
½ cup Romano cheese, grated	

Sauté onions, green pepper, and garlic in oil until soft. Add remaining ingredients and simmer, uncovered, for 30 minutes. Serve with New Orleans Chicken.

GRILLED ANDOUILLE SAUSAGE

For a full-fledged New Orleans cocktail party, include this easily prepared version of Andouille Sausage.

1 lb. Andouille Sausage (allow 2 oz. per person, for hors d'oeuvres)	1 jar jalapeño jelly, melted

Grill the sausage over medium heat for approximately 20 minutes. Remove from grill and glaze with melted jelly. Cut into bite-sized pieces. This is very spicy. If your palate tends toward a milder taste, substitute a less spicy sausage.

BAKED OYSTERS

Oysters (20 oz. or approximately 20 oysters)
1 bottle Worcestershire sauce
½ cup fresh cracker crumbs
½ cup fresh breadcrumbs
½ tsp. Fines Herbes

1 tsp. onion powder
½ tsp. black pepper
½ tsp. paprika
¼ tsp. salt
1 tsp. granulated garlic

Drain and rinse oysters. Place in a bowl and cover with Worcestershire sauce. Refrigerate 4 hours. Combine the remaining ingredients, blending the spices well. Dip each oyster in the mixture. Refrigerate for an additional hour. Spray a baking sheet well with cooking spray and bake oysters for 15 minutes or until they have curled. Serve immediately with toothpicks or on top of your favorite cracker.

Alternative cooking method:
The coated oysters can also be sautéed in oil, until curled.

QUESO TEJANO TRIANGLES

½ cup Monterey cheese, grated
½ cup cheddar cheese, grated
½ cup mayonnaise
½ cup red onion, finely chopped
Dash of hot pepper sauce

1 T. salsa
2 T. fresh parsley, chopped
¼ cup Parmesan cheese

24 flour tortillas (6½ inches)

Mix all the ingredients, except tortillas. (Cumin or chopped fresh basil can be added for variation.) Spread 2 tablespoons of the mixture on half of each flour tortilla, fold in half, and sauté on both sides in a lightly oiled skillet, until golden brown. Remove from pan and cool for 5 minutes. Slice into triangles. These can be passed with your favorite spicy dip, or served alone.

MEXICAN COFFEE TRUFFLES

These delicacies must be prepared well in advance of serving and should definitely be stored out of sight, as temptation will certainly prevail for any chocoholic!

6 1-oz. squares semisweet chocolate
¼ cup butter
2 T. sweetened condensed milk
3 T. Mexican coffee liqueur
½ tsp. almond extract

¾ cup powdered sugar
Pinch of salt

2 T. powdered sugar
2 T. unsweetened cocoa powder
Mexican coffee liqueur

Melt chocolate squares and butter in a 1-quart saucepan over very low heat or in a microwave on low, stirring frequently until blended and smooth. Remove from heat, stir in sweetened milk, liqueur, and almond extract. Using a wooden spoon, beat in the powdered sugar and salt until thoroughly blended. Cool to room temperature; refrigerate 1 hour, until firm. Shape mixture into 1-inch balls and refrigerate.

In a small bowl stir 2 T. each of powdered sugar and unsweetened cocoa and mix well. Roll each truffle in Mexican coffee liqueur and sugar/cocoa mixture, coating completely. Store Truffles in a tightly covered container in the refrigerator for 48 hours. Roll again in Mexican coffee liqueur, then in the sugar/cocoa mixture. Return to airtight container and refrigerate for 2 weeks. Allow to stand at room temperature for 15 minutes before serving. Stores well in refrigerator. Serve mingled with fresh strawberries. Yields 24 Truffles.

Dinner Honoring
Former First Lady Betty Ford

Salad:
Warm Brie Salad

Entree:
Orange-glazed Cornish Hens
with Sweet Potato Salsa
Stuffed with rice and dried Bing cherries

Vegetable Flan

*Dinner rolls and butter

Dessert:
Une Bombe de Glace

* Recipe not included

WARM BRIE SALAD

Warm Brie Dressing:
¼ cup olive oil
½ cup fresh mushrooms, diced
4 tsp. fresh garlic, minced
4 tsp. green onion, chopped
4 tsp. Dijon mustard
½ cup balsamic vinegar
10 oz. double cream Brie cheese, rind removed
Salt and pepper to taste

Salad:
6 cups mixed greens
2 cups fresh mushrooms, sliced
1 pg. Enoki mushrooms for garnish
Croutons, fresh or packaged

Dressing:
Warm olive oil in a large skillet; add diced mushrooms, garlic, and green onions. Cook until soft. Remove from heat and add the remaining ingredients, mixing well. Return to heat; stir over low heat until the sauce is smooth. Add salt and pepper to taste.

To serve:
Divide salad evenly among serving plates; add the sliced mushrooms. Ladle 1/3 cup of Hot Brie Dressing over greens. Add Enoki mushrooms and croutons for garnish. Serve immediately. Yields 6 servings.

ORANGE-GLAZED CORNISH HENS

4 cornish hens
Granulated garlic
White pepper

Glaze:
4 T. orange marmalade
4 T. brandy
4 T. Orange Sauce (recipe follows)

3 cups chicken broth
1 cup orange juice
2 cups rice
1 pkg. dried Bing cherries
Paprika

Clean and dry the cornish hens. Sprinkle body and cavity with granulated garlic and white pepper. Refrigerate.

In a medium saucepan, combine the chicken broth and orange juice. Bring to a boil. Add rice and dried Bing cherries. Reduce heat; cover and simmer until cooked. Allow to cool. Preheat oven to 325 degrees. Stuff each hen with 1 cup rice. Truss legs; sprinkle with paprika. Place hens in roasting pan and bake for 30 minutes. Meanwhile, make the Glaze by combining the orange marmalade, brandy, and Orange Sauce. Baste hens with Glaze, tent with aluminum foil and bake for another 30 minutes. Turn oven to 400 degrees, baste again, and bake until browned. Serve with remaining Orange Sauce.

Sauce:
3 T. butter
1 T. garlic, minced
2 T. green onion, chopped
3 T. flour
1 14 ½-oz. can beef broth
½ cup fresh orange juice
1 T. orange peel
¾ cup orange marmalade

1/8 tsp. white pepper
2 T. ketchup
2 tsp. English tea broth
5 dashes hot pepper sauce,
   or to taste
¼ tsp. ginger
Pinch of salt
½ cup brandy (or white wine)

Melt butter in a heavy saucepan and sauté the garlic and green onions until soft. Add flour and cook until light brown. Add the broth, orange juice, orange peel, marmalade, white pepper, ketchup, English tea broth, and remaining seasonings. Simmer slowly for 20 minutes. Add brandy. This is a hearty sauce, but can be strained before serving if you want a lighter version. Serve with Orange-Glazed Cornish Hens. Yields 2 cups.

SWEET POTATO SALSA

1½ lbs. sweet potatoes, peeled and
    diced (approximately 3 cups)
2   large carrots, peeled and diced
1   large red bell pepper, chopped
2   apples, peeled, cored and diced
½ cup onions, chopped
1   T. oil
½ cup white grape juice concentrate

4   T. orange juice concentrate
½ tsp. sugar
1   tsp. salt
4   tsp. red chili powder
¼ tsp. cinnamon
¼ tsp. ground ginger
¼ tsp. white pepper
1   tsp. fresh parsley, chopped

Parboil the sweet potatoes and carrots for 3 minutes. Drain and plunge into cold water, to stop cooking. In a large skillet, sauté the bell pepper, apples, and onions in oil. Add the remaining ingredients; simmer for 5 minutes. Combine all ingredients, including the potatoes and carrots; taste for seasonings. Can be served warm or at room temperature. Salsa is best when made several days in advance. Yields 4 cups.

VEGETABLE FLAN

Don't let the length of this vegetable recipe scare you off! It is well worth the extra effort. You will get rave reviews from family and friends.

1   lb. fresh green beans, trimmed
    and cut in half
24 small whole fresh green beans
    for garnish
1   T. + 3 T. olive oil
½ cup onions, finely chopped
1/3 cup shallots, finely chopped
2   garlic cloves, minced

½ cup carrots, finely chopped
¼ cup turnip, finely chopped
2   cups sour cream
6   eggs
1   tsp. salt
1   tsp. white pepper

Wash and prepare green beans, reserving 24 small whole beans for garnish. Steam, uncovered, until just tender; rinse with cold water. Finely chop (but do not purée) the beans in a food processor.

Heat 1 T. oil and sauté onions, shallots, and garlic until soft; remove from skillet and reserve. Add 3 T. oil to skillet and sauté carrots and turnips over medium heat until cooked, but firm. Set aside.

Beat sour cream, eggs, salt and pepper until well mixed. Pour ½ of sour cream mixture into the onions and ½ into the carrots-turnip mixture.

Assembly:

Preheat oven to 325 degrees. Lightly grease 12 5-oz. custard cups. Arrange custard cups in a roasting pan, and fill the pan with hot water until the water reaches halfway up the sides of cups. Divide the beans and pack down evenly in the 12 custard cups. Then pour ¼ cup of the onion mixture into each cup, followed by ¼ cup of carrot mixture. Bake for 55 minutes or until a knife comes out clean. To serve, run a knife around the edge of the cups and invert onto plates. Garnish with whole beans. Yields 12 flans.

UNE BOMBE DE GLACE

1 packaged brownie mix
½ gallon vanilla ice cream
1 cup miniature chocolate chips
½ gallon French Silk ice cream

Chocolate Glaze (see
   Chocolate Cherry Surprise
   cookies, p. 205)
Whipped cream

Prepare and bake the brownies in a 9 x 13-inch pan according to package directions. Set aside and allow to cool completely.

Line a 1-gallon bowl with plastic wrap, allowing the wrap to hang over the edges of the bowl. Allow the ice cream to soften slightly. Using a spatula, coat the sides and bottom of the bowl with the vanilla ice cream, distributing evenly. Sprinkle the ice cream with miniature chocolate chips. Fill the remaining space with French Silk ice cream. Cover and return to freezer until the ice cream is frozen.

Cut a circle of brownie the same diameter as the bowl of ice cream to form the base of the Bombe. Make the chocolate glaze. Remove from the heat and allow to cool.

Place the round brownie on a serving platter. Turn out the frozen ice cream onto the brownie. Remove the plastic wrap and slowly pour the cooled chocolate glaze over the Bombe, allowing it to harden. Return to freezer. (Can be "frosted" with whipped cream at this point.)

Remove from the freezer 10 minutes before serving. Using a heavy serrated knife, slice the Bombe into individual servings and top with whipped cream. Yields 15 servings.

Celebration Honoring
the Metropolitan Museum of Art

Hosted by Margaret McDermott
at the
State Capitol of Texas

Black-tie seated dinner party

Hors d'oeuvres:
Sun-dried Tomato and Olive Tartlettes
Sausage en Croute

Starter:
Green Salad with Vintner Salad Dressing
Wine — Fall Creek Vineyard Delache Chardonnay 1987

Entree:
Beef Tenderloin with Mushroom Duxelle
with Merlot Wine Sauce
Wines — Clos du Bois Chardonnay and Rutherfod Hill Merlot
Baked Sweet Onions
*Glazed Baby Carrots
*Dinner rolls and butters

Dessert:
Tulle Cookie Baskets
with Raspberry Cloud Mousse
on Vanilla Sauce and Raspberry Sauce

*Recipe not included

SUN-DRIED TOMATO TARTLETTES

Dough:

8 oz. cream cheese
½ cup butter, softened

1 cup flour
1/8 tsp. granulated garlic
Dash of salt

Filling:

1 cup onions, chopped
2 T. vegetable oil
1 large tomato, finely chopped
10 sun-dried tomatoes, finely chopped
¼ cup black olives, chopped
1 T. basil

1½ tsp. oregano
¾ tsp. black pepper
½ cup Parmesan cheese
¼ cup pine nuts, toasted
½ cup mozzarella cheese, shredded
¼ cup goat cheese
1 tsp. red pepper flakes

Combine dough ingredients in a food processor and process until soft. Using a teaspoon, form the dough into balls and press into ungreased miniature muffin tins, covering the bottom and sides.

Sauté onions in oil on medium heat until browned. Add remaining ingredients, except cheeses and red pepper flakes and cook for 5 minutes. Remove from heat; stir in cheeses and red pepper flakes.

Preheat oven to 350 degrees. Fill the tart shells with sun-dried tomato filling mixture and bake for 25 minutes. Let cool on wire racks. The baked tartlettes freeze well. (See p. 108 for flash freezing method.) When reheating frozen tartlettes, cook in a 325- degree oven for 25 minutes. Yields 4 dozen tartlettes.

SAUSAGE EN CROUTE

1 pkg. phyllo pastry, cut in half, vertically
1 cup butter, melted

6 dozen whole sausage links
½ lb. Swiss cheese, shredded

Preheat oven to 375 degrees. Brush 1½ sheets of phyllo dough with butter. Fold in half. Place one sausage and some of the shredded cheese at one end and roll, cigar style. Cut ends evenly and then cut each roll in half. Bake for 10 to 12 minutes on an ungreased cookie sheet, until lightly browned. Yields 144 hors d'oeuvres.

These freeze well. Before serving, defrost and reheat in a 350-degree oven.

VINTNER SALAD DRESSING

½ cup vegetable oil
½ cup olive oil
2 T. balsamic vinegar
1 T. sugar
2 garlic cloves, minced

½ cup white wine
½ tsp. dry mustard
¼ tsp. paprika
1/3 cup shallots, chopped
Salt and pepper to taste

Combine all ingredients in a food processor and blend well. Yields 1¼ cups.

BEEF TENDERLOIN WITH MUSHROOM DUXELLE
with Merlot Sauce

4 oz. beef tenderloin per person	Black pepper, to taste

Marinade:

¼	cup olive oil	3	garlic cloves, chopped
¾	cup soy sauce	½	bunch green onions, chopped
1	T. Worcestershire sauce		

Duxelle Filling:

4½	cups fresh mushrooms, finely chopped	2	T. butter
3	shallots, finely chopped	½	cup white wine
1½	cups green onions, chopped	1	T. brandy
			Salt and pepper to taste

The day before serving, combine marinade ingredients. Marinate tenderloin overnight in the refrigerator, rotating the meat several times.

Sauté mushrooms, shallots, and onions in butter for approximately 3 minutes. Reduce heat and add wine and brandy. Simmer for approximately 10 minutes. Remove meat from marinade. Pat dry and season lightly with salt and pepper. Preheat oven to 400 degrees. Using a sharp knife, make a lengthwise pocket in the tenderloin, leaving the ends closed. Fill slit with Mushroom Duxelle and tie with butcher's twine. Place meat on a rack in a roasting pan and cook for 10 minutes. Reduce heat to 325 degrees; continue to cook for approximately 20 minutes, or until meat reaches desired temperature.* (Remember, always use a meat thermometer.) Remove from oven immediately, place on platter, and allow to "rest" for 10 minutes before slicing. Serve with Merlot Sauce (recipe follows).

* We prefer beef "medium rare." Cooking beef beyond the "medium" point diminishes its flavor.

Merlot Sauce:

2	T. butter	1	T. tomato paste
2	T. shallots, chopped	½	tsp. black pepper
2	cloves garlic, chopped	¼	tsp. dry mustard
2	T. flour	½	tsp. sugar
½	cup Merlot wine		Pinch of ground ginger
1	cup beef broth		Salt and pepper to taste

In a medium saucepan, melt butter and sauté the shallots and garlic for approximately 4 minutes. Add flour and whisk until smooth. Slowly add wine and beef broth, whisking until well blended. Add remaining ingredients; taste for salt and pepper.

BAKED SWEET ONIONS

6	medium sweet onions, peeled and cored (we use Texas 1015)	6	T. honey
			Salt, pepper, and paprika
6	T. butter		Breadcrumbs
6	T. soy sauce		

Preheat oven to 350 degrees. Spray baking pan with cooking spray and put onions in pan. In the middle of each onion, place 1 T. of butter, soy sauce, and honey. Sprinkle with salt, pepper, and paprika. Cover and bake for 60 minutes, basting with juices at least twice. Uncover; sprinkle with breadcrumbs and return to oven for 15 minutes, basting once. Yields 6 servings.

TULLE COOKIE BASKETS WITH RASPBERRY CLOUD MOUSSE

Several cookie sheets for baking
6 T. butter
1/3 cup packed brown sugar
3 T. light corn syrup
1/3 cup flour
½ cup ground blanched almonds

1 tsp. vanilla
Raspberry Cloud Mousse (recipe
   follows)
Vanilla Sauce (recipe follows)
Powdered sugar
Assorted fresh berries for garnish
Mint leaves, for garnish

Preheat oven to 350 degrees. Grease and flour a cookie sheet. Combine butter, brown sugar, and corn syrup in a saucepan and cook, stirring constantly, over medium heat until butter melts and mixture boils. Remove from heat. Stir in flour and almonds and blend thoroughly. Stir in vanilla.

For each large cookie, drop 2 tsp. of batter onto a heavy baking sheet. Though this looks like very little dough, the cookies need plenty of room for spreading, so place only 2 cookies on a sheet at a time. Bake 6 to 8 minutes or until a rich golden color. Cool 1 to 2 minutes on the baking sheet. While the cookie is still warm, remove from the cookie sheet with a spatula and place it on the outside of an inverted large custard cup, forming a lace cookie cup. Cool completely on the cup, then remove and store in an airtight container. The cookies should be stacked with wax paper inside each cookie cup. When ready to serve, fill with Raspberry Cloud Mousse (recipe follows). Prepare serving plates with Vanilla Sauce (recipe follows) and Raspberry Sauce (p. 18), swirled with the tip of a knife, forming a design. Place mousse-filled Cookie Basket on sauces and garnish with mint leaves and berries. Sprinkle with sifted powdered sugar.

Raspberry Cloud Mousse:

1 3-oz. pkg. raspberry gelatin
1 cup boiling water
1 10½-oz. pkg. frozen
   raspberries, defrosted and
   drained, reserving juice
1 cup vanilla ice cream, softened

1 cup whipping cream
2 T. powdered sugar
2 T. raspberry liqueur
2 tsp. vanilla
Reserved juice from raspberries

Dissolve gelatin in boiling water. Fold in raspberries and ice cream, combining well, and refrigerate for 20 minutes. Whip the cream on low until slightly thickened, while adding powdered sugar a little at a time. Continue beating on high until soft peaks form. Add liqueur, vanilla, and enough of the reserved raspberry juice for a rich pink color. Fold in the gelatin mixture, combining well. Refrigerate for 12 hours. Serve in Tulle Cookie Baskets.

Vanilla Sauce:

½ cup sugar
¼ lb. unsalted butter, cut into pieces

½ cup light cream
2 tsp. vanilla extract
1 oz. white rum

Combine sugar, butter, cream, vanilla, and white rum and bring to a boil. Lower temperature to simmer and continue to cook until slightly thickened. Serve with Tulle Cookie Baskets filled with Raspberry Cloud Mousse.

Cocktail Buffet
for
Caroline Hunt

Austin Celebration of
the Anniversary of the Mansion at Turtle Creek

Passed Hors d'oeuvres:
Escargot in Mushroom Caps
Momma Roz's New York Pate

Cocktail Buffet:
Caviar with Buckwheat Blinis and condiments
Crab Claws
With Cocktail and Remoulade Sauce
Shrimp Rumaki
Diana's West Coast Salmon Tartare
Chicken Hawaiian
With Gingered Apricot Sauce
Crudites

Dessert:
*Miniature Chocolate Cups
Served with assorted liqueurs

*Recipe not included

ESCARGOT IN MUSHROOM CAPS

8   oz. escargot, drained and rinsed
4   T. butter
1   T. olive oil
¼   loaf French bread, cubed
5   cloves garlic, finely chopped
1   shallot, finely chopped

2   T. cognac
¼   cup Madeira
Salt and pepper, to taste
36 large mushroom caps,
    destemmed and cleaned
2   T. chopped parsley

Melt the butter and olive oil over medium heat in a heavy pan. Add the cubed bread, garlic, and shallots and sauté until the bread cubes have browned. Add the cognac and Madeira (cooking until absorbed). Salt and pepper to taste.

Place an escargot on each mushroom cap and pack down the filling on and around the middle of each cap. Bake in a 350-degree oven until hot (12-15 minutes). Serves 8-10 escargot lovers.

MOMMA ROZ' S NEW YORK PATÉ

7   T. oil
1   T. chicken base seasoning
2   medium onions, sliced
1   lb. chicken livers, washed,
    drained and patted dry

6   hard-cooked eggs
Salt and pepper to taste
⅛   cup brandy

In a medium skillet, heat oil and chicken base. Add onions and cook over medium-low heat until tobacco-brown. (This process cannot be hurried, as it brings out the sweetness of the onions and creates the main flavor of the pate.) Once browned, remove the onions from pan using a slotted spoon, and place in food processor bowl. In the same skillet, sauté the chicken livers in the remaining oil until well cooked. (The inside should be browned.) Add the eggs to the onions and chop. Add the chicken livers and remaining juices from the pan to the egg-onion mixture, and blend thoroughly. (If the mixture is too dry, add 1 T. melted butter.) Place mixture in a bowl. Add salt and pepper to taste; stir in the brandy. The paté will be slightly loose — the consistency of jello. It will become firm when chilled. Serve with cocktail rye bread or crackers. Serves 12 to 15.

BUCKWHEAT BLINIS

1⅓ cups milk
1   egg
1   T. oil
¾   cup buckwheat pancake mix
1   T. dried parsley

1   T. Parmesan
1   T. mozzarella cheese, shredded
1   tsp. garlic powder
2   drops hot pepper sauce

In a medium bowl, beat egg and milk together. Stir in oil. Add pancake mix and remaining ingredients; mix lightly. Pour 1 T. of batter on a medium-hot griddle. Flip when the batter bubbles. Remove from heat and cool. Repeat. Serve blinis with caviar and condiments. (See p. 132 for the complete description of setting up a caviar bar.) Yields 1¼ cups batter, or approximately 20 blinis.

Condiments for Caviar Bar:
Chopped red onions
Chopped egg whites
Chopped egg yolks

Capers
Sour cream
Herbed Cream Cheese (see recipe this chapter)

COCKTAIL SAUCE
FOR CRAB CLAWS OR SHRIMP

1 cup ketchup
1 cup chili sauce
2 T. white, cream-style, prepared horseradish
2 drops hot pepper sauce

1 T. lemon juice
½ tsp. white pepper
1 T. granulated garlic
1 tsp. Dijon mustard

Combine all ingredients in a large bowl and mix well. Refrigerate for 24 hours before serving. Yields 2 cups.

REMOULADE SAUCE

2 cups mayonnaise
2 tsp. dry mustard
2 to 3 garlic cloves, finely minced
1 T. gherkin pickles, minced

1 T. capers, drained and chopped
1½ T. fresh parsley, minced
1 T. fresh tarragon, minced
1 tsp. anchovy paste (optional)

Combine all ingredients and mix thoroughly. Cover and refrigerate for at least 2 hours prior to serving. Yields 2½ cups.

SHRIMP RUMAKI

¼ cup scallions, chopped
1 4-oz. can green chiles, drained and chopped
1 4-oz. can water chestnuts, drained and chopped
⅓ cup breadcrumbs
1 clove garlic, crushed

1 tsp. teriyaki sauce
1½ cup cheddar cheese, grated
1½ cup Monterey jack cheese, grated
8 slices bacon, slightly cooked
24 large raw shrimp, peeled, deveined and butterflied, tail on
24 toothpicks

Preheat oven to 350 degrees. Combine scallions, green chiles, water chestnuts, breadcrumbs, garlic, teriyaki sauce, and cheeses in small mixing bowl. Cut partially cooked bacon strips into thirds. Place 1 tsp. filling into each butterflied shrimp; wrap with bacon and secure with a toothpick. Place shrimp on a slightly oiled baking sheet and bake for 8 to 9 minutes, or until opaque. Remove toothpicks before serving. Yields 24 hors d'oeuvres.

DIANA'S WEST COAST SALMON TARTARE

1 lb. fresh salmon fillet, skin removed	1 T. fresh lemon juice
½ cup onions	1 tsp. fresh dill
¾ tsp. capers, or to taste	1 tsp. horseradish
	Black pepper to taste

Place salmon in the food processor and chop, leaving the salmon chunky. Remove, and refrigerate. (This yields approximately 1 cup of packed salmon.) Chop onions in food processor. Remove and place in medium bowl.

Chop capers, lightly, in food processor and add to onions. Combine salmon, capers, and onions and mix by hand. Add lemon juice, dill, and horseradish, tasting after each addition, so as not to overpower salmon. This hors d'oeuvre should be made close to party time and refrigerated until served.

Serve surrounded by thin rye squares, extra chopped onion, capers, and very thin slices of lemon.

CHICKEN HAWAIIAN

This has always been a buffet favorite.

1 10-12 oz. whole chicken breast, boneless and skinless	Granulated garlic
	White pepper

One day prior to serving, season chicken breast with garlic and pepper. Cover and refrigerate overnight. When ready to prepare, cut into approximately 24 to 30 bite-sized pieces.

1 cup complete pancake mix	1 cup club soda
1½ tsp. ground ginger	Vegetable oil for frying — at least
1½ tsp. granulated garlic	½ inch in pan
¼ tsp. white pepper	2 cups flaked coconut
1/8 tsp. salt	

In a large bowl, combine pancake mix, ginger, garlic, pepper and salt. Add club soda and stir until well mixed. Heat oil to 350 degrees. Dip chicken pieces in pancake batter; roll in coconut and shape into balls by rolling chicken in your hands. Fry a few pieces at a time, until light golden brown. Do not crowd. Drain on paper towel. (As you fry, remove excess coconut from the oil with a slotted spoon, and add more oil, if necessary.) Can be done ahead to this point. Preheat oven to 350 degrees. Reheat for 10 to 12 minutes or until heated through. Serve with Gingered Apricot Sauce. Serves 6.

To Flash Freeze: Put individual chicken pieces (or any individual food item to be frozen) on a cookie sheet, uncovered, in the freezer until frozen solid. Remove from cookie sheets, package in plastic freezer bags, and return to freezer. Follow directions for reheating.

GINGERED APRICOT SAUCE

1 cup apricot preserves	½ tsp. teriyaki sauce
½ tsp. ground ginger	¼ cup club soda
½ tsp. granulated garlic	Dash of hot pepper sauce

Melt the preserves in a small saucepan. Add remaining ingredients and cook for 5 minutes over medium-low heat. Cool. Serve with Chicken Hawaiian. Yields 1¼ cups sauce.

CRUDITES

SMOKED OYSTER PATÉ

1 medium garlic clove, crushed	⅛ tsp. white pepper
1 medium shallot, chopped (or 1 T. onion)	Dash of hot pepper sauce
2 8-oz. pkg. cream cheese	1 3¾-oz. can smoked oysters, drained and chopped
2 tsp. Worcestershire	
¼ tsp. salt	½ cup pecans, finely chopped (use only if making a log)

In a mixing bowl, mix garlic, onion, cream cheese, Worcestershire, salt, pepper, and hot pepper sauce until well blended. Gently fold in chopped smoked oysters. To serve, pipe paté into prepared cherry tomatoes (see instructions below) using a large pastry tip.

Another way to serve this wonderful paté is as a spread. Before adding the oysters, spread cream cheese mixture on a rectangular piece of foil, approximately 8x10 inches. Spread the mashed smoked oysters over the cheese. Cover loosely with plastic wrap and refrigerate for several hours until firm, or overnight. Roll like a log, using a long narrow spatula to help release the cream cheese from the foil. Roll log in chopped nuts, covering completely. Garnish with parsley and serve with crackers. Yields approximately 2½ cups.

Preparation of cherry tomatoes: Cut off tops of tomatoes and remove pulp. Drain upside-down on paper towel for at least one hour before filling.

HERBED CREAM CHEESE

1 8-oz. pkg. cream cheese	½ tsp. Worcestershire
1 tsp. basil	1 garlic clove, minced
1 tsp. dill weed	1 tsp. chives

Combine all ingredients in a mixing bowl. Refrigerate for 4 hours, allowing flavors to blend. Bring to room temperature before serving. One of our favorite ways to serve this is piped into snow peas using a medium star tip.

WHITE BEAN TEQUILA DIP

1   15-oz. can butter beans
1   red pepper, diced
3   green onions, chopped (using the
      white and the green)
¼   bunch fresh cilantro, minced
Dash of hot pepper sauce, to taste

1   tsp. lime juice
1   tsp. garlic powder
1   T. teriyaki sauce
1   T. tequila
1   cup sour cream

Combine all ingredients except the sour cream in a food processor and mix well. Fold in sour cream. Refrigerate for 6 hours, or overnight. Serve spread on prepared Belgium Endive leaves or alone with chips. Yields 3½ cups.

SCALLOPS ON CUCUMBERS

½   lb. sea scallops
3   T. lime juice
3   English cucumbers

Dash of salt
Pinch of ground cloves
Pinch of cayenne pepper
2 to 3 T. creme fraiche

Cut scallops in half; toss with 2 T. lime juice and refrigerate no more than 2 hours. Peel and cut cucumbers into 24 1-inch thick slices. Using a melon baller, make a shallow well in the center of each piece. Drain the scallops; combine with remaining 1 T. lime juice, seasonings, and enough creme fraiche to bind. Fill the well of each cucumber with the scallop mixture, and serve, garnished with a sprig of dill. Yields 2 dozen hors d'oeuvres.

Creme Fraiche:

1   cup heavy cream, room temperature   2   T. buttermilk

Mix cream and buttermilk and pour mixture into a clean, glass jar. Set the jar in a warm place and allow the creme to thicken, for 6 to 8 hours. The creme should be gel-like. Refrigerate.

A faster method: Mix equal parts of sour cream and stiffly beaten, whipped cream. Refrigerate.

Chapter 8

Wedding Adventures

eddings are always adventures. The bride and groom, and their families, step head first into a deluge of details. There are multiple professionals to guide you through the abyss and ultimately create the day of your dreams. After the engagement ring, we highly recommend that you find a wedding coordinator, who assures that all you do on the day of your wedding is "be there." Let this professional handle the glitches, which can cause big headaches, instead of trying to coordinate this yourself. If you've already "been there, done that," you know that a wedding can become a three-ring circus, because even the smallest wedding still requires attention to detail, unless of course, you're eloping to Las Vegas!

Actually, weddings are the joining of two families. We have always told engaged couples that the bottom line is that they marry and live happily ever after. There will always be some hitch, glitch, or sputter on any occasion, but remember that the true importance is their union. The accessories to the wedding are really just trappings. This day should be the happiest of the couple's life. Remember, the excitement of the parties, the planning, and the purchases are just the icing on the cake— (forgive our pun). The real event is their special love for one another.

We're going to start where you should—budget. It is so easy to get caught up in a spending frenzy, but each couple should establish how much they can spend, and not exceed that amount. You might have pressure from parents and friends. Everyone will have an opinion, and every time they open their mouth with a "suggestion," it will cost more money. Use the "put up or shut up" method of communication. Listen to what they have to say, but ultimately, you have the final word, unless of course, you accept financial help. One example might be someone wanting to add six cousins to your guest list that you haven't seen in years, and probably wouldn't recognize if you saw them. These cousins don't fit into your budget, but whoever is adamant about including them could contribute to this extra expense.

Once the budget is established, pick your day, date and time. Sounds easy, doesn't it? The time of day you choose for your reception will greatly impact your budget. If your reception is planned around a time when most people would eat, then you have to feed your guests! It is also mandatory to serve food if you intend to serve alcohol. Your caterer, or hotel event planner, can guide you through your choices.

For those who plan the wedding on your own, without a coordinator, here are a few helpful tips. Keep your budget in mind as you interview vendors—florists, photographers, caterers—making sure you understand the financial details. Ask your friends for referrals, but just because one florist worked for Aunt Betty's daughter, they might not be right for you. Be certain that you have repoire with whomever you select, because their personalities will definitely impact your mood on the day of the wedding. There is already enough stress—why add to it? We have worked with a photographer who thought the wedding day was all about him. One of our brides, who choose her own videographer, was only five minutes into her rehearsal when she told us that he was driving her crazy. It adversely affected her mood, and everyone around her. Yet, he was just trying to do his job. If you are using someone who is not established, be sure you will not be their first "victim." Ask to see pictures and get references, and take that extra step to check all references. We suggest you make a list of all vendors' names, phone numbers, and arrival times, and distribute it to everyone with whom you're working. Coordinate the timing so there will be no surprises. If you are not using a wedding planner, check with your vendors to reconfirm what you expect of them, what their financial requirements are, and if it would be possible to attend an event they are working. If there are any last minute payments, write the checks and designate someone to distribute them after the reception.

There are many books on the market to help you plan your wedding, and although we didn't intend this chapter to be the A-all and B-all of weddings, we have a few more tips that we feel are important, and might not show up in other publications. Tans are beautiful, but for heaven's sake, the bride shouldn't get sunburned before the wedding. Ouch! Brides have a tendency to overextend themselves on the day of the wedding. Everyone is caught up in the excitement of the day. Getting married is exhausting, so keep the day as free as possible, and allow at least three hours to pamper yourself. You should relax while getting your hair and makeup done. If using professionals, it's important to do hair and makeup "dress rehearsals" to avoid any wedding-day disasters and disappointments. Also on our list of do's and don'ts—buy your bridal shoes early; make sure they are comfortable, and wear them around the house to break them in. By the way, be sure to pass this tip on to both mothers as well as anyone with bad feet.

Our next suggestions are for the wedding party on the Big Day. Frequently, eating becomes secondary to the wedding party, so it's important to provide light, non-messy snacks and non-alcoholic beverages at the staging area while getting ready for the ceremony. A tip for the bride—even if you don't feel hungry, be sure you eat some protein an hour before the wedding, but limit liquids. Enough said!

Moving right along, let's talk about the reception. The guests will arrive before the bride and groom; be sure they are greeted with food and beverages. Music is wonderful and adds ambiance, as long as your guests can hear one another. Often the cake cutting is left until the reception is almost over. We suggest, as the new Mr. and Mrs. arrive, they welcome their guests, have the bridal toast, and proceed with cutting the cake. Everyone can enjoy a piece of cake, even if they leave before the bride and groom.

As we were writing this chapter many of our most favorite and least favorite wedding memories came to mind, and we decided to share some of them with you. It's important for couples to understand that "stuff" happens that is totally unforeseeable and uncontrollable. That's okay, however, because it lends character and memories to be shared with grandchildren in years to come, making this wedding day unforgettable.

Cakes are usually the centerpiece of the reception. After so many years and hundreds of weddings we have many wedding cake stories, but have chosen two of our favorites. The first one was a wedding that was a year in preparation. The reception was in the bride's family home, a replica of an old Southern mansion, including a ballroom. The Grecian gardens were breathtaking, filled with statuary and surrounding a lovely, waterfalled pool, which was the setting for the wedding cake. The cake was five-tiered, each layer a different flavor, with hundreds of handmade sugar flowers. We placed it on a magnificent lace-draped table, elevating it on a ring of fresh flowers and pearls. The height of this masterpiece was well over five feet tall. (You know that everything is always bigger in Texas!) It was a perfect month of May, up until that Saturday, the day of the wedding. The morning dawned hot and humid, with no breeze, but by the time the reception began and the 500 guests were arriving, the wind made an appearance. As we were putting the last of the sugar flowers on the cake, a light breeze became gale force gusts that whipped through the statues, and blew the top two layers off the cake onto the table—SPLAT! Trying not to panic—never an option for a caterer—and uti-

lizing the "5-second" rule (since it hadn't exceeded five seconds on the table), back they went. We picked up the layers, one at a time, and placed them back on the cake. It didn't quite look the same (smile), but we reconstructed it (we always carried extra back-up frosting for situations exactly like this) and redistributed the sugar flowers in the nooks and crannies created by the unfortunate fall. It was always our goal to make the food tables appear creative and effortless, as if by magic. However, this time the cake was resurrected before an audience watching with curiosity, awe and admiration.

Another interesting house wedding occurred in the hill country. What really distinguished this wedding in our minds were the unique bridesmaids—the bride's two Great Dane dogs were "dressed" in their finest bows and flowers, matching the color-coordinated decorations. But, this is a cake story, and the "bridesmaid's" interest in the food buffet is another "tail" altogether. Someone unfamiliar with the location of the house, as well as the winding, hilly roads leading to it, delivered the tiered cake at the last minute. The driveway—straight up a 45-degree angled hill, was full of potholes. What can we say—it's the lake region of Central Texas! Up until then the cake had made the journey in perfect condition, but the driveway was too much for it to come through unscathed. When one of the caterers greeted the driver at the top of the driveway, he stopped, gasped, and said, "I'm not touching this cake until you see it!" This lovely wedding cake had taken on the look of the Leaning Tower of Pisa, tilting against the side of the carrying case. The cake layers and frosting were a mashed mess. Once again, though, thanks to the caterers' creativity and the aforementioned back-up frosting and lots of fresh flowers strategically placed, another wedding cake was successfully resurrected.

Spring in the Hill Country is an amazing sight, full of fabulous wildflowers, so it's only natural that many brides want to use the beauty of the area as the background for their special day. Mother Nature's personality is always a factor in outdoor weddings, especially in the spring. Sometimes a wedding day will begin beautifully, and within 45 minutes, it can change drastically. During this April outdoor wedding and reception, everything had come together perfectly—a storybook wedding. The bride and her father arrived at the wedding site in a white, horse-drawn carriage, as the Chamber Ensemble played Mozart. The wedding ceremony went according to plan. It was a joyous time. Under the huge, white tent, seating tables for 300 guests were lavishly adorned with wildflower centerpieces, china and crystal. The main attraction on the heavily ladened food buffet was the shell-shaped ice carving overflowing with shrimp. From out of nowhere, huge, black, billowing clouds appeared in the northern sky. Was the weatherman wrong again? You bet he was! The bride (and everyone there) suddenly felt like we were in Kansas, with Dorothy, from the *Wizard of Oz*. The winds were close to tornado-force and the skies opened their floodgates. That beautiful tent heaved and shook as the caterers, carrying lawn umbrellas, escorted the guests into the nearby ranch house. We managed to get the food, the wedding cake, and naturally, the bar into the house before the tent was picked up by the wind and thrown into a field. The bride and groom, the guests and the caterers were soaking wet, but none the worst for wear, considering the circumstances. Everyone had a wonderful time, making this one of the most unforgettable weddings ever.

Chapter 9

Cows, Cowboys, & Cowpies

ou guessed it! This is the chapter to turn to if you're looking for famous Texas offerings like chicken-fried steak, fajitas, and juicy, flavorful beef. Cowboys, sprawling ranches, and slowly-smoked barbecue are still mainstays in many parts of the state, and we've pleased many a rodeo star and rancher with the sizzling specialties detailed in the following menus. Texas tradition has indeed dictated many of the parties we've organized — rodeo galas, cattle auctions, elaborate ranch weddings, and outdoor dinners under the stars at Texas-styled country estates.

One rodeo gala was particularly memorable. The Travis County Rodeo Association hosts the annual event each April, held in an astro-turf covered dirt-floored arena — a typical rodeo facility lacking luxuries such as air-conditioning and heat. The gala would be a Texas-tuxedo affair, meaning gentlemen come decked out in tuxedo jackets and black ties paired with blue jeans, boots and, of course, the typical, large western belt and buckle. We planned our Texas-sized centerpieces — mammoth stars spilling from 15-foot oil derrick towers — on buffet tables draped in dramatic black and silver mylar.

As usual, April that year had proven a mild month. In fact, for days prior to the party it had been just plain hot. But as we were racing about the arena putting the finishing touches on a lavish buffet, including a life-size boat filled with shrimp, fillets of beef tenderloin, cornbread, beans, and an adult ice cream bar, the wind picked up, chilling things down unexpectedly. Trouble was in the air.

As the guests began arriving in lightweight, though dazzling, western dress, we knew we were in for a long evening. The temperature had plummeted to 40 degrees. Having left home dressed for temperatures in the 90s, the guests were shivering more than their sequins and fringe. It was cold! And although the ice cream bar was popular, what the guests really wanted was coffee. Hot coffee. And lots of it! The evening's special guest was superstar Tom Jones, and despite his reputation as a "hot" performer, even he couldn't generate enough heat to warm the freezing crowd.

Cattle auctions are other events that have consistently challenged us "city gals." Jackie and Jim Leonard introduced us to a whole new concept in entertaining. Auctions are weekend-long events, a combination of business and pleasure for those who come from far and near to buy cattle and, of course, have a good time. For Gourmet Gals & Guys, the auction parties were always an adventure. We literally set up kitchens in the middle of pastures, without electricity or running water. Weather was sometimes a factor. Rain brought seas of mud into the tented party and auction areas, making it necessary to cover the ground with tons of hay. Drought brought dust and dry wells.

At one such party, we were so busy setting up that no one noticed the herd of cattle that had moved in on the tank that supplied the ranch with water. Before we knew it, the cows had heartily quenched their thirst and moved on, leaving behind only mud! We were stuck waiting an hour before the water was replenished. However, nothing ever dampened the ranchers' enthusiasm as they bid, bought, and then partied on menus that ranged from "down-home" to glorious gourmet. In fact, Jim was always pleased with our fare, especially when we included his favorite, Country-fried Steak smothered with our "Forty-Weight Cream Gravy," the latter a name he coined!

So, if it was stereotypical Texas you were expecting from this book, we won't be the ones to disappoint you. Slip into your boots, roll up your sleeves, and start turning out these wonderful Texas recipes.

The North Forty

Cattle Auction on a Texas Ranch

Dinner Buffet:
Country-fried Steak
with Forty-weight Cream Gravy

Chimichangas

Beef and Chicken Fajitas

Black-eyed Pea Salsa

*Sliced Watermelon

Fantasy Fudge Pie

*Recipe not included

COUNTRY-FRIED STEAK

¼ tsp. salt	1 cup buttermilk
½ tsp. granulated garlic	1/8 tsp. Worcestershire
½ tsp. chili powder	Dash of hot pepper sauce
½ tsp. onion powder	1 cup preseasoned flour
½ tsp. finely ground black pepper	(recipe follows)
2 lbs. tenderized round steak	Vegetable oil for frying

Combine salt, garlic, chili powder, onion powder, and black pepper. Season steak with the mixture and place between two pieces of plastic wrap. Using a meat mallet, pound the seasonings into the meat.

Combine buttermilk, Worcestershire, and hot pepper sauce. Dip the steak pieces into the buttermilk mixture, then dredge in the seasoned flour.

Heat ½ inch of vegetable oil in a heavy skillet; fry pieces of coated meat until golden brown on each side. These hold well in a warm oven. Serve with Forty Weight Cream Gravy (recipe follows).

Seasoned flour:

3 cups flour	2 tsp. finely ground black pepper
2 tsp. salt	¼ tsp. dry mustard
1 tsp. paprika	1 tsp. granulated garlic

Combine all ingredients. Store in a tightly covered container.

FORTY WEIGHT CREAM GRAVY

This recipe is dedicated to Jackie and Jim Leonard, as it was served at many of their ranch parties and cattle auctions. The name was coined by Jim. He loves the thick, rich flavor!

5	slices bacon	1	tsp. granulated garlic
1/3	cup flour	2	tsp. chicken bouillon granules
1	cup milk	¼	to ½ tsp. coarsely ground
1	14½-oz. can chicken broth		black pepper

In a heavy skillet, fry bacon until crisp. Drain on paper towels. Add flour to bacon fat and cook until golden brown, whisking constantly. Add milk and chicken broth slowly, continuing to whisk until smooth. Add remaining seasonings and cook until thickened. Crumble bacon and add to gravy, if desired. Gravy will be very thick.

CHIMICHANGAS

3	lbs. ground beef	1	T. sugar
2	cups white onions, chopped	1/3	cup chili powder
2	T. fresh garlic, chopped	¼	cup ground cumin
2	14½-oz. cans chopped tomatoes		Dash of hot pepper sauce
2	tsp. salt	36	6½-inch flour tortillas
1	tsp. cracked black pepper	36	3-inch skewers or toothpicks
2	T. oregano		Oil for frying

In a large skillet, sauté the beef, onions, and garlic until browned. Add tomatoes, salt, pepper, oregano, sugar, chili powder, cumin, and hot pepper sauce. Simmer for 30 minutes. Taste for seasonings. Drain off excess fat. Steam each tortilla so that it is soft and pliable. Place one heaping tablespoon of the meat mixture in the middle of each tortilla and fold, envelope style, securing with a toothpick.* Fry chimichangas in oil over medium heat, until browned on each side, about 2 minutes per side. Chimichangas will hold in a warm oven for 30 minutes. Yields 3 dozen.

*Can be frozen at this point, for up to 3 months. Defrost and allow to come to room temperature before frying.

BEEF AND CHICKEN FAJITAS

Plan 4 to 6 ounces of meat per person. This marinade is delicious for both beef and chicken fajitas.

½ cup vegetable oil
¼ cup soy sauce
⅓ cup Worcestershire sauce
1 12-oz. can Mexican beer
3 T. tequila
2 medium onions, chopped
1 tsp. sugar
Dash of hot pepper sauce

3 T. cumin
1 T. paprika
½ cup cilantro, chopped, packed
¼ cup garlic powder
½ tsp. salt
¼ tsp. pepper
Juice of 3 limes

Blend all marinade ingredients and pour over meat. Refrigerate for at least 12 hours, turning twice.

Bring meat in marinade to room temperature. Remove from marinade and grill until done, brushing with marinade. Slice diagonally into thin strips; serve with warm flour tortillas and traditional condiments, including sour cream, chopped green onions (or grilled onions and green peppers), salsa, sliced black olives, grated cheddar cheese, guacamole, and sliced jalapeño peppers.

BLACK-EYED PEA SALSA

1 15-oz. can black-eyed peas, drained and rinsed
1 medium red bell pepper, diced
3 T. onion, minced
2 T. fresh parsley, minced
1½ T. fresh cilantro, minced
2 tsp. jalapeño pepper, minced

2 T. vegetable oil
2 T. red wine vinegar
Salt and freshly ground pepper
Granulated garlic to taste
Lime juice to taste
Pinch of sugar

Place ⅓ of the black-eyed peas in a food processor and mix until smooth.

Combine the remaining black-eyed peas with the rest of the ingredients. Mix with puréed peas and refrigerate for 6 hours or overnight. Serve with chips. Yields 3–3½ cups.

FANTASY FUDGE PIE

¼ cup unsalted butter
2 oz. unsweetened chocolate
2 eggs
1 cup sugar
¼ cup flour

¼ tsp. salt
1 tsp. white vanilla
1 T. strong coffee
1 T. brandy
¾ cup pecans, chopped

Preheat oven to 350 degrees. Grease a 9-inch pie plate. Melt the butter and chocolate in a double boiler. Remove from heat and allow to cool. In a mixing bowl, beat the eggs and sugar. Add flour, salt, white vanilla, strong coffee, and brandy. Stir in cooled chocolate; fold in pecans. Bake for 30 minutes. The top will appear "cracked." Cool before serving. Garnish with whipped cream and shaved dark chocolate. Serves 8.

The Governor's Barbecue

Political Fundraiser on a Texas Ranch

Chuckwagon Salad Bar
Salad bar with all the trimmings,
presented on an antique chuckwagon

Marinated Sirloin Steaks
with Barbecue Butter

New Potato Salad

Traditional Texas Ranch Beans

Green Chile Cornbread and Butter

Amaretto Bread Pudding

CHUCKWAGON SALAD BAR

An antique buckboard wagon was the showplace for this salad bar. The guests heaped their salad and trimmin's into blue enamelware bowls. The beauty of a salad bar is that all the ingredients can be prepared in advance and refrigerated in airtight containers or plastic bags. Serve a variety of salad dressings, including at least one labeled lowfat. (We have a favorite lowfat dressing, and have included the recipe.) If the ingredients we suggested are not in season, or do not look fresh, be flexible and creative in your choices.

1 cup of lettuce per serving, including Romaine, Butterleaf, Green leaf, Oak leaf, Arugula, Endive and Iceberg

Condiments for Salad Bar:

1	bunch green onions, chopped	1	cup garbanzo beans
1	bunch celery, sliced	2	cups seasoned croutons
8	oz. muhrooms, cleaned and sliced	1	small can mandarin oranges
1	small jar pickled beets	½	lb. snow peas
½	lb. carrots, shredded	1	medium red onion, sliced
1	pint cherry tomatoes	½	lb. fresh green beans, blanched, sliced
2	cups cauliflower flowerettes	2	cucumbers, sliced
2	cups broccoli flowerettes	1	green bell pepper, sliced
1	cup sunflower sprouts	1	red bell pepper, sliced
1	bunch radishes, sliced	1	yellow bell pepper, sliced
	Green and black olives	2	cups cheddar cheese, shredded

Lowfat Salad Dressing (that doesn't taste lowfat!):

¼   cup balsamic vinegar
½   cup buttermilk
½   cup lowfat cottage cheese
½   cup lowfat sour cream
½   cup lowfat mayonnaise
3   T. white onions, chopped

2 garlic cloves, chopped
½   tsp. dill
1   T. honey
1   T. fresh parsley, chopped
Salt and pepper to taste

In a blender, combine all dressing ingredients and mix well. Can be made 48 hours in advance and refrigerated. Yields 2½ cups.

MARINATED SIRLOIN STEAKS
with Barbecue Butter

1   cup red wine
½   cup parsley, chopped
1   oz. olive oil
1   tsp. fresh garlic, minced
½   cup onions, minced
1   tsp. dry mustard

2   T. Worcestershire
Dash of hot pepper sauce
3   to 3½ lbs. lean sirloin steak,
      cut 2-inches thick
Black pepper, coarsely ground

Combine red wine, parsley, olive oil, garlic, onions, mustard, Worcestershire, and hot pepper sauce. Pour marinade over steak; cover and refrigerate 6 to 8 hours.

Remove steak from marinade 1 hour before cooking, and pat dry. Press pepper into both sides of meat. Grill over medium heat for 30 minutes, basting frequently with marinade. Slice and serve immediately with Barbecue Butter (recipe follows). Serves 6.

Barbecue Butter:

½   cup unsalted butter
1   4-oz. can diced green chiles,
      drained
2   T. parsley, chopped
2   tsp. lemon juice

2   tsp. Worcestershire
1   T. brandy
1   tsp. Dijon mustard
1   tsp. granulated garlic
1   tsp. chili powder

Combine all ingredients in a food processor and blend until smooth. Refrigerate. Return to room temperature before serving.

NEW POTATO SALAD

1   lb. new potatoes
¼   cup dry vermouth
½   cup beef bouillon
1/8 cup shallots, chopped
¼   cup green onions, chopped
¼   cup fresh parsley, chopped
¼   cup sour cream
¼   cup mayonnaise

¼   cup celery, chopped
¼   cup red onions, chopped
¼   cup black olives, chopped
1   tsp. horseradish
1/8 cup red wine
2   T. balsamic vinegar
Salt and pepper to taste

Wash, but do not peel, new potatoes and boil until just tender. Drain and cool slightly. Cut into quarters. Combine all remaining ingredients. Gently toss warm potatoes in mixture. This potato salad is best when flavors are allowed to blend, refrigerated, for 12 hours, or overnight.

TRADITIONAL TEXAS RANCH BEANS

2   cups dried pinto beans
Water to cover beans
1   cup onions, chopped
2   cloves garlic, finely chopped
¼   cup oil
2   14½-oz. cans of chopped tomatoes
2   tsp. dry mustard
2   T. Worcestershire

2   tsp. chili powder
¼   tsp. pepper
1   tsp. oregano
¼   tsp. ground ginger
1   T. molasses
Dash of hot pepper sauce
1   tsp. salt

Soak beans overnight in water. Drain and rinse.

Sauté the beans, onion, and garlic in oil until browned. Add remaining ingredients, except salt, and simmer approximately 2 hours, adding salt the last 30 minutes.

These beans get better by the day! Yields 7 cups.

GREEN CHILE CORNBREAD

¾   cup butter, softened
1   cup yellow cornmeal
6   T. sugar
4   large eggs
1½   cups all-purpose flour
1   T. baking powder
1½   tsp. salt
1   15-oz. can creamed corn

1   4-oz. can diced green chiles
1/3   cup packed cheddar
     cheese, grated
1/3   cup packed Monterey jack
     cheese, grated
Dash of dillweed
¼   cup Texas honey
1   T. (heaping) chopped parsley

Preheat oven to 375 degrees. Lightly oil a 9-inch baking pan. Cream butter in a large mixing bowl and add cornmeal and sugar, beating until well blended. Add eggs, one at a time, beating after each addition. Add flour, baking powder, and salt to batter and stir. Mix in creamed corn, green chiles, cheeses, dillweed, honey, and parsley. Pour batter into baking pan and bake for 45 minutes, or until a toothpick comes out clean. Cool slightly. Cut into squares for serving. This is a very moist cornbread. Serves 6-8.

AMARETTO BREAD PUDDING

1   loaf French bread, crust removed
3   eggs, beaten
3   cups milk
1   cup cream
½   cup sugar
2   T. almond flavoring

1/3   cup Amaretto liqueur
1   tsp. vanilla
1   tsp. salt
¼   tsp. cinnamon
¾   cup chopped almonds
¾   cup white raisins (optional)

Topping:
2   T. butter or margarine, melted
½   cup Amaretto liqueur

1   cup powdered sugar
1   egg, beaten

Preheat oven to 350 degrees. Grease a 9x13-inch baking pan. Tear French bread into large bite-sized pieces and place in a mixing bowl. Combine the remaining ingredients; pour over bread pieces and mix well. Bake in pan for 1 hour and 15 minutes. Pudding will be slightly browned around the edges. Combine topping ingredients and pour evenly over the baked pudding while hot. Serves 12.

Somewhere on a Texas Ranch

A Dinner Buffet

Ceviche

Mexican Eggrolls

Cherry Tomatoes Filled with White Corn Salad

Beef Hill Country Rollups

Smoked Chicken Tacos
with Blanco Queso Sauce and Flour Tortillas

*Baskets of Carrots, Fresh Green Beans
and Mushrooms
Served with Dill and Green Onion Dip

Hill Country Peach Cobbler
with Vanilla Ice Cream

*Recipe not included

CEVICHE

A wonderful Mexican tradition – seafood cooked in lime juice. Prepare a day ahead and serve chilled as a starter course, or with tostada chips as an hors d'oeuvres.

There are many different versions of "classic" Ceviche. We have three recipes of our own. We're sharing our favorite one with you.

1   lb. bay scallops
1   cup freshly squeezed lime juice
1   lb. white onions, chopped
1   pt. cherry tomatoes, quartered
1   jalapeño pepper, seeded and finely chopped
1   poblano pepper, seeded and finely chopped

1/3   cup cilantro, chopped
¼   cup fresh parsley, chopped
¼   cup green onions, chopped
1   2¼-oz. can sliced black olives
¼   cup olive oil
Dash of sesame oil
Hot pepper sauce (optional)

Marinate scallops in lime juice for 18 hours prior to assembling Ceviche. (The juice "cooks" the scallops.)

Combine remaining ingredients. Add scallops and lime juice. Add hot pepper sauce for those who like it HOT! Refrigerate.

Drain before serving. Yields 8 servings.

MEXICAN EGGROLLS

1 lb. Monterey jack cheese, grated	Several dashes of hot pepper sauce
8 oz. green chiles, seeds and stems removed	1 tsp. dried oregano
½ cup green onions, chopped	½ tsp. salt
¾ cup black olives, drained and chopped	1 pkg. wonton skins
2 tsp. cumin	1 egg, beaten
	Oil for frying

Filling:

Combine cheese, green chiles, green onions, black olives, cumin, hot pepper sauce, oregano, and salt.

Assembly:

Place a damp towel over wonton skins while working. Place approximately ½ tsp. of filling in center of each wonton skin. Fold in half, diagonally, then fold envelope style, sealing the edges with beaten egg. Place on baking sheet; cover tightly with plastic wrap. Can be made in advance to this point, and refrigerated.

When ready to serve, heat oil, and deep fry until golden brown. Serve with guacamole or salsa. Yields approximately 50 Mexican eggrolls.

WHITE CORN SALAD

½ cup sugar	1 4-oz. jar chopped pimentos, drained
1 cup vinegar	1 medium green pepper, chopped
1 11-oz. can white shoe peg corn, drained	¾ cup onions, chopped
1 16-oz. can red kidney beans, drained and rinsed	¼ tsp. salt
1 14½-oz. can French style green beans, drained	Pepper to taste
	¼ cup salad oil

Combine sugar and vinegar in a medium saucepan and dissolve over medium-low heat. Combine all remaining ingredients, except the salad oil, in a bowl. Pour warm sugar/vinegar mixture over vegetables and toss. Add the salad oil. For best results, prepare recipe at least 24 hours in advance. This unique version of an old favorite will keep, refrigerated, for several days. Drain before serving. Yields 6 cups.

BEEF HILL COUNTRY ROLLUPS

¼ cup teriyaki sauce
2 T. honey
½ tsp. fresh ground ginger
¼ cup vegetable oil
2 T. red wine vinegar
1 garlic clove, crushed

⅛ tsp. pepper
1 sirloin steak,
   approximately 1½ lbs.
10 medium mushrooms, brushed clean
20 4- to 5-inch wooden
   picks or skewers

Combine teriyaki, honey, ginger, oil, vinegar, garlic, and pepper in a 9 x 13-inch baking dish. Add steak; cover and refrigerate for 4 hours, turning meat at least once. Drain meat, reserving marinade. Using a sharp knife, cut the steak across the grain into 10 strips. Roll a strip of meat around each mushroom, securing with 1 or 2 wooden picks. Grill (about 4 inches above the heat) for 3 to 5 minutes on each side, brushing regularly with marinade. Yields 4 servings.

SMOKED CHICKEN TACOS
with Blanco Queso Sauce

1½ lbs. smoked breast of chicken
3 cups onions, sliced
3 T. vegetable oil

½ cup water
1 green bell pepper, sliced

12 flour tortillas

Remove skin and bones from the smoked chicken and slice into thin strips. Sauté the onions in oil over medium heat until they are tobacco brown. Add the water and sliced chicken; cover and steam for approximately 2 minutes. Add green peppers and steam for an additional 2 minutes, or until hot.

To serve, warm flour tortillas. Place 2 oz. meat mixture in each tortilla and top with Blanco Queso Sauce (recipe follows). Yields 6 servings.

Blanco Queso Sauce:
1 12-oz. can evaporated milk
4 oz. Queso Quesadillas Cheese with jalapeño peppers
4 oz. Monterey jack cheese with jalapeño peppers

Melt the cheeses with the milk in a double boiler. Stir until smooth. Serve with Smoked Chicken Tacos. Add your favorite salsa and margaritas — *OLE!* This sauce is also delicious as a warm dip with tostada chips.

DILL AND GREEN ONION DIP

¾ cup sour cream
¾ cup cream cheese, softened
2 tsp. green onions, finely chopped
1 T. white onions, finely chopped
2 T. milk

1 tsp. parsley, chopped
2½ tsp. dill
Salt and white pepper, to taste
Dash of hot pepper sauce
Dash of Worcestershire

Combine all ingredients until smooth, and refrigerate overnight. Serve with baskets of fresh vegetables. Yields 1½ cups.

HILL COUNTRY PEACH COBBLER

This award-winning recipe has been published in Texas Monthly *magazine,* The Austin American-Statesman, *and was picked up by the Associated Press and reprinted in newspapers all around the country. We received calls from coast to coast requesting other recipes of Texas delectables – hence this cookbook!*

¾	cup flour	¾	cup milk
1/8	tsp. salt	½	cup butter
2	tsp. baking powder	3	cups fresh peaches, sliced
1½ + ¼ cups sugar			

Preheat oven to 350 degrees. Sift flour, salt, and baking powder together. Mix with 1½ cups sugar. Slowly stir in milk. Melt butter in 9 x 9 x 2 pan. Pour batter over butter; do not stir. Lay peaches on batter. Sprinkle with ¼ cup sugar or less. Bake for 1 hour. This cobbler freezes well for up to 6 months. Serves 6.

Hill Country Wedding Afternoon Buffet

Mexican Hat Dips Area:

Nacho Mold

Cheese Roll Olé

*Gala Fresh Fruit Display

Marinated Vegetables
(see p. 56)

Southwestern New Potatoes

*Texas Tenderloin
with Black Bean Sauce

Marinated Ranch Chicken

Praline Trifle

*Recipe not included

NACHO MOLD

This recipe was originally shared with us by Artis Schnell. With some strategic changes here and there, Artis' dip has become one of our most popular hors d'oeuvres, often imitated (the finest form of flattery!) but never *quite duplicated.*

1	15-oz. can chili, without beans	1	cup green onion, chopped
3	oz. cream cheese, softened	16	oz. sour cream
2	tsp. chili powder	2	4½-oz. cans chopped black olives, drained
2	tsp. granulated garlic		
2	tsp. cumin	1	4½-oz. can chopped green chiles, drained
¼	tsp. black pepper		
		2	cups cheddar cheese, shredded

1	16-oz. can refried beans	1	tsp. granulated garlic
1	tsp. chili powder		Dash of hot pepper sauce
1	tsp. cumin		

In a medium saucepan, combine the chili, cream cheese, chili powder, granulated garlic, cumin, and black pepper. Cook over medium-low heat, stirring frequently, until hot. Allow to cool.

Blend the refried beans, chili powder, cumin, granulated garlic, and hot pepper sauce in a food processor.

In a 2-quart container (such as a trifle bowl), layer the ingredients in the following order:

Chili
Refried beans
Chopped green onions
Sour cream

Chopped black olives
Chopped green chiles
Shredded cheese

This recipe is at its best if prepared one day prior to serving. Garnish with parsley sprigs and cherry tomatoes, and serve with crisp tortilla chips. (For a festive touch, serve in a large terra cotta plant saucer.) Serves 15 to 20.

CHEESE ROLL OLÉ

2   8-oz. pkgs. cream cheese
4   cups cheddar cheese, grated
½   cup onion, finely diced
1   4½-oz. can chopped green chiles, drained

2   ½ tsp. granulated garlic
3   tsp. chili powder
3   tsp. cumin
2   avocados, mashed
2   cups chopped pecans

Mix cheeses, onions, green chiles, and spices. Line a 15 x 10-inch cookie sheet with plastic wrap. Spread with cheese mixture and top with mashed avocados. Holding the long edge of the plastic wrap, roll the cheese, jelly-roll style; then roll the cheese log in chopped pecans and transfer to serving platter. Garnish with whole green chiles. Serve with crackers. Serves 12.

SOUTHWESTERN NEW POTATOES

2   cups Monterey jack cheese, grated
2   cups cheddar cheese, grated
7   oz. canned chopped green chiles, drained
1   4-oz. can water chestnuts, drained, finely chopped

1   2¼-oz. can chopped black olives, drained
2   T. fresh parsley, chopped
Dash of hot pepper sauce
24 small new potatoes

In a medium bowl, combine the cheeses, chiles, water chestnuts, black olives, parsley, and hot pepper sauce. Cover and refrigerate.

Steam the new potatoes until just tender. Cool. Prepare the potatoes for filling by cutting off the bottom so they will "sit" upright. Cut off tops and scoop out potato, using a small melon baller or potato peeler. Fill with cheese mixture. Bake at 350 degrees for 10-12 minutes. These potatoes are also wonderful when served at room temperature. Yields 8 servings.

BLACK BEAN SAUCE FOR TEXAS TENDERLOIN

1 cup onions, sliced	¼ tsp. black pepper
2 garlic cloves, chopped	1 tsp. chili powder
2 T. vegetable oil	1 cup water
1 cup refried black beans	1 tsp. sesame oil
3 tsp. soy sauce	1 T. cilantro or parsley, chopped
1 tsp. dried cumin	

Lightly sauté onions and garlic in oil until barely translucent, approximately 3 minutes. Stir in all remaining ingredients, except cilantro or parsley. Simmer for 8 to 10 minutes over low heat. Add chopped cilantro or parsley before serving. Serve with Bourbon Beef Tenderloin (p. 142). Yields 2 cups.

MARINATED RANCH CHICKEN

2 whole chickens, cut into pieces	Salt and white pepper
Granulated garlic	Lemon juice

Marinade:

3 oz. tequila	¼ cup soy sauce
¾ cup bottled picante sauce	¼ cup oil
1½ tsp. chili powder	Juice of 1½ limes
3 garlic cloves, chopped	Salt and pepper, to taste
1 T. cumin	Hot pepper sauce, to taste
1 12-oz. can Mexican beer	Worcestershire, to taste
½ bunch cilantro, chopped	
2 T. granulated garlic	

Combine all marinade ingredients in blender until smooth. Wash and pat dry chicken pieces. Marinate, covered, and refrigerate for 24 hours, turning once.

Preheat grill; drain chicken and pat dry. Season with granulated garlic, white pepper, salt, and fresh-squeezed lemon juice. Grill the legs and thighs for 10 minutes. Add breast halves and wings to grill, basting, and cook until done. Serve hot. Serves 6.

PRALINE TRIFLE

Yellow cake recipe (or 1 packaged mix):

½ cup butter or margarine	
1⅛ cups sugar	
2 eggs	
1⅞ cups sifted cake flour	
¾ tsp. salt	
2 tsp. baking powder	
¾ cup milk	
1 tsp. vanilla	

Praline Sauce:

5 12-oz. bags butterscotch chips	
1 14-oz. can sweetened condensed milk	
1 15-oz. can evaporated milk	
1 T. vanilla	
¼ tsp. salt	
¼ cup brandy	
2½ T. Mexican coffee liqueur	
¼ cup white corn syrup	

Whipped cream topping:
1½ quarts heavy cream
4   tsp. vanilla
1   cup powdered sugar

Additional ingredients:
1   cup pecans, chopped
1   cup brickle bits
1½ cups pecan halves

Cake:

Prepare packaged yellow cake mix or make your own with following recipe: Preheat oven to 350 degrees. Grease and flour two round, 8-inch cake pans. Cream butter and sugar until fluffy. Add eggs and beat well. Sift together flour, baking powder, and salt. Stir into batter, alternating flour mixture and milk. Add vanilla. Pour mixture into pans and bake for 25 to 30 minutes or until a cake tester comes out clean. Cool in pan on racks for 10 minutes. Invert pans and remove cake onto racks and cool.

Praline Sauce:

Melt butterscotch chips in a double boiler. Add remaining ingredients, blending thoroughly, and continue cooking for 15 minutes. Makes 9 cups. (Surplus sauce can be stored, refrigerated.)

Whipped cream topping:

Whip cream and vanilla in a chilled bowl, slowly adding powdered sugar until stiff.

To assemble trifle:

Spread 1 cup praline sauce on the bottom of a 14-cup, clear glass trifle bowl. Slice the 8-inch cakes horizontally in half, and place one half in the bowl on top of the sauce. Press cake down so that the sauce comes up to cover the sides of the cake. Spread 1 cup sauce on top of cake, covering it completely. Add pecan halves around the sides of the bowl. Sprinkle ¼ cup brickle bits and ¼ cup chopped pecans on top of the sauce. Top with whipped cream. Add remaining half of cake and cover with 1 cup of the praline sauce. Add pecan halves and repeat until you have three complete layers. Decorate top of trifle with whipped cream and pecan halves. Yields 14 cups.

Wedding Buffet
on the Banks of the Pedernales River

Southwest Seafood Pasta Salad

Orange-Glazed Frog Legs

Beef Fillet
with Pistachios and Port Wine Cherry Sauce

Rosemary Roasted Potatoes

*Sautéed Snow Peas

Monkey Bread

*Halves of Pineapples
with strawberries, kiwi, and papaya

*Chocolate Wedding Cake
with Brandy Sauce

*Recipe not included

SOUTHWEST SEAFOOD PASTA SALAD

½ lb. lump crab
½ lb. shrimp, cooked and peeled
½ lb. bay scallops
8 oz. tri-colored pasta, cooked according to package directions
2 Anaheim peppers, seeded and sliced thin
1 cup red onion, chopped
½ cup cilantro, chopped
½ cup raspberry wine vinegar
½ cup canola oil
½ cup honey
1 cup Italian dressing
1 tsp. salt
1 tsp. white pepper
½ cup fresh parsley, chopped
4 dashes hot pepper sauce
Juice of 1 medium lime
Red and green bell pepper, cut into strips for garnish

Combine crab, shrimp, scallops, cooked pasta, Anaheim peppers, onions, and cilantro in a large mixing bowl. In a blender, mix together vinegar, oil, honey, Italian dressing, salt and pepper. Blend until smooth. Add to seafood/pasta mixture. Add parsley, hot pepper sauce, and lime juice. Add lime juice. Refrigerate for 8 hours. To serve, line plates with leaf lettuce and mound seafood salad in the middle. Garnish with sliced red and green peppers. (Grilled pork or chicken substitute well for the seafood.) Serves 8 1-cup portions.

ORANGE-GLAZED FROG LEGS

Marinade:

1	cup oil	½	tsp. black pepper
4	T. sesame oil	¼	tsp. salt
¼	cup balsamic vinegar		
1	T. Worcestershire	32	pair frog legs
1	cup orange juice concentrate		Oregano
2	tsp. ground ginger		Granulated garlic
2	T. fresh garlic, chopped		

Combine all the marinade ingredients except oregano and granulated garlic in a food processor until smooth. Wash the frog legs and pat dry. In a nonmetal pan, cover frog legs with marinade and refrigerate, covered, for 6 to 8 hours. Remove frog legs from marinade and sprinkle with oregano and granulated garlic. Transfer marinade to a saucepan and reduce by half, over medium heat. Spray cold grill with cooking spray to prevent sticking. Grill frog legs approximately 5 minutes per side. The meat turns slightly pink when done. (Do not overcook or frog legs will be tough and rubbery.) Brush with reduced marinade and serve. Serves 8.

BEEF FILLET WITH PISTACHIOS
and Port Wine Cherry Sauce

This recipe was developed by Gourmet Gals & Guys chef Craig Zrubek.

1	3 to 3½ lb. beef tenderloin, trimmed, rolled, and tied	Fresh cracked black pepper
¼	cup olive oil	½ cup pistachios, crushed

Preheat oven to 325 degrees. Brush beef tenderloin with olive oil and season with black pepper. Sear the meat on all sides in a hot skillet. Press the pistachios into the meat, transfer to a roasting pan and roast, covered, for 45 minutes for medium-rare. Allow meat to rest for 10 minutes before slicing. Serve immediately with Port Wine Cherry Sauce (recipe follows). Serves 8.

Port Wine Cherry Sauce:

1	T. garlic, crushed	1	3-oz. bag dried cherries
4	T. butter	1	T. brown sugar
1	T. flour	2	tsp. Dijon mustard
1	cup Port wine		Salt and pepper, to taste
1	cup beef broth		

Sauté garlic in melted butter for 2 minutes. Add flour, whisking to blend. Stir in the remaining ingredients, cooking for 10 minutes, or until the cherries have plumped. Serve with Beef Fillet with Pistachios.

ROSEMARY ROASTED POTATOES

4   T. olive oil
2   tsp. dried crushed rosemary
1/8 tsp. black pepper

½   tsp. salt
24 small new potatoes, washed
    Parmesan cheese

Mix olive oil, rosemary, salt and pepper in a 9 x 13-inch cake pan. Roll the potatoes in the mixture until they are evenly coated with oil and spices. Cover tightly with foil and bake at 375 degrees, turning potatoes 3-4 times, for 1 hour. Uncover, sprinkle with Parmesan cheese, and return to oven. Continue baking, uncovered, for 15 to 20 minutes. Serve immediately. Yields 8 to 10 servings, depending on the size of the potatoes.

MONKEY BREAD

This recipe is dedicated to a member of the Board of Regents in the University of Texas System, who desperately wanted this recipe and was offended when we politely explained we could not share it with him. And so, "Mr. Regent," this one's for you!

¾   cup butter, melted and cooled
    (1½ sticks)
1   cup Parmesan cheese

2   loaves frozen bread dough
    (slightly defrosted)

Place slightly defrosted bread dough on a lightly floured surface. Cut in half, lengthwise, then cut each half into 6 pieces. (You should have 12 pieces per loaf.)

Preheat oven to 375 degrees. Spray a large bundt pan with cooking spray. Dip each piece of bread first in melted butter, then in Parmesan cheese, and layer in the bundt pan until all bread has been used. Cover pan with a clean, dry towel and allow to rise in a warm, draft-free spot for 1 hour or until doubled in size.

Bake on the middle rack for 25 to 30 minutes, or until golden brown. Remove from pan immediately and cool on wire rack. Yields 1 loaf.

BRANDY SAUCE

1   cup heavy cream
1   T. granulated sugar
1   tsp. vanilla
1   cup softened vanilla ice cream

¼   cup white Creme de Cocoa
    liqueur
1½ T. brandy

Whip the cream until soft peaks form. Beat in the sugar and vanilla. Fold the softened ice cream into the whipped cream; stir in the Creme de Cocoa and brandy. Refrigerate until ready to serve. Serve with your favorite chocolate cake or any dessert of your choice. Use within 8 hours. Yields 2 cups.

Chapter 10

It's A Ball!

s the saying goes, "Everything is bigger and better in Texas." Gala balls are no exception. Planning a ball, from the decorations to menu, begins with selecting a theme. And in Texas, it also means making that theme larger than life. In this chapter we've included menus from three of our favorite extravaganzas.

For one Christmas debutante ball we took the classic Nutcracker theme chosen by the hosts and blew it up to Texas-sized proportions. The young debutantes and their dates, their families and friends mingled in a world of make-believe, eating shrimp off twinkling trees that towered seven feet from the ground. The Sugarland Express train traveled around mountains of meringue on a dessert table that also featured edible marzipan gift packages, and an array of assorted sweets. There were gingerbread houses, intricately decorated Christmas cookies, and tables draped like drums with white tops and red skirts trimmed in gold and black cording.

A summer ball, appropriately named "A Midsummer Night's Dream," was truly an olympic event. Creating both the appropriate foods and the atmosphere in which they were to be served

demanded months of preparation with Susan Richardson, the ball chairman, and her committees. The ordinary setting of a convention hall had to be transformed into the extraordinary. Foods had to inspire awe, and provide something for every palate. Creativity reached new heights in menu planning. When the party-goers entered a glittering, ethereal "forest" of tulle, grapevine branches, and netting created by Ginny and Charles Strong, *"ooh-ing"* in astonishment over the ambiance of the setting and *"aah-ing"* over the food as they filled their plates, we knew we had managed to capture a little bit of the entertaining mystique.

The buffets for the Midsummer Night's Dream Ball included a dozen decorated food stations, each depicting a scene from Shakespeare's famous play, topped with inventive, festive foods. A lavish display of assorted fresh fruit cascaded down in a waterfall effect, and a soaring, fifteen-foot replica of Puck presided over the dessert table, where chocolate lovers were sure they had "died and gone to heaven."

You may never have the chance to prepare for 2,000 guests, but experiment with the flamboyantly festive menus and have a ball of your own!

A Midsummer Night's Dream
The Austin Symphony Ball

A Shakespearean Dinner Buffet

Mushrooms Bourguignon
Caviar Bar and Blue Cornmeal Blinis
Prime Rib of Beef
Pork Diane
Sautéed tableside
Seafood Etouffe on Rice
Breast of Duck
Served with Orange Salsa and Blackberry Sauce
Venison Stew
Vegetable Quesadillas
Garlic Bread Pudding
*Miniature vegetables and dips
*Waterfall of fresh fruits

Chocolate Paradise Desserts:
Chocolate Ribbons
Tres Mocha Brownies
Toffee Bars
Banana Chocolate Truffles
Chocolate Rugelach

*Recipe not included

154

MUSHROOMS BOURGUIGNON

2	T. butter	1	cup tomato sauce
2	T. olive oil	¼	tsp. sugar
4	T. flour	⅛	tsp. mace
2	tsp. sherry	1	bay leaf
1	cup burgundy wine	1	tsp. dill
½	cup beef broth		Salt and pepper, to taste
1	lb. medium mushrooms, destemmed and brushed clean	2	T. olive oil
		4	T. sour cream
½	cup white onions, chopped	¼	cup fresh parsley, chopped

In a large saucepan, heat butter and olive oil. Add flour to make a roux. Cook until roux begins to brown. Add sherry, burgundy, broth, tomato sauce, sugar, mace, bay leaf, dill, salt and pepper. Taste for seasonings. Simmer, covered, for 30 minutes.

Sauté mushrooms and onions in olive oil for 5 minutes. Drain and add to sauce. (Can be refrigerated at this point, for 24 hours.) Add sour cream and sprinkle with parsley before serving. Serve with toast points. Serves 6.

SETTING UP A CAVIAR BAR

Some like caviar; others don't. But most, regardless of their taste buds, will be impressed by a sumptuously laden caviar bar. The key to the caviar bar is presentation. Remember that in serving a caviar bar, you're staging a production. Think beauty and sophistication, and set your stage with intricate cut glass or crystal bowls.

While quality imported caviar such as Beluga should never be removed from its original container, less expensive domestic caviar and caviar substitutes are best served in small containers, presented on a bed of ice. Always serve caviar with a mother of pearl spoon. Use a mix of black, red, and yellow caviars for a festive touch. Presentation of the condiments is what will make your caviar bar memorable. Caviar is luxurious, but a little bit goes a long way. Two 4-ounce jars with condiments will serve 25.

Serve the caviar and condiments from several different levels, using glass blocks. Weave garlands, greenery or flowers around the condiment containers, or drape the blocks with plush velvet, reminiscent of European courts.

Condiments include:　Hard-cooked eggs — whites and yolks
　　　　　　　　　　separated and chopped
　　　　　　　　　Finely chopped red onions
　　　　　　　　　Thinly sliced lemon
　　　　　　　　　Capers
　　　　　　　　　Chopped black and/or green olives

BLUE CORNMEAL BLINIS

¾ cup blue corn pancake mix
¾ cup white cornmeal
3 T. garlic olive oil
1 egg
2 cups buttermilk
½ cup canned corn, drained

¼ cup medium, chunky salsa, drained
1 T. fresh garlic, minced
½ tsp. cumin
Salt and pepper to taste
Olive oil for skillet

Combine pancake mix and cornmeal in a bowl. Add oil, egg, and buttermilk; mix thoroughly. Add corn, salsa, garlic, cumin, salt and pepper and blend well.

Generously brush a nonstick skillet with oil and preheat. Add 1 teaspoon (for each 2-inch blini) and cook completely. Cook until browned. Serve with caviar or smoked salmon.

PRIME RIB OF BEEF

Even in the era of heart-healthy foods, the beef carving station is always a popular spot. But since few will have the opportunity (or desire!) to prepare a 65-pound steamship round of beef, we have adapted this favorite recipe using Prime Rib. Use as a main course or in thin slices, accompanied by miniature rolls for sandwiches and Horseradish Sauce (recipe follows). As always, we recommend the use of a good meat thermometer for accurate doneness.

1 4-6 lb. rib roast, bone-in
4 garlic cloves, slivered
1½ cups flour
1 cup Worcestershire

1 T. oregano
1 tsp. black pepper
½ cup Dijon mustard
¼ to ⅓ cup water

The day before serving, pierce the roast in 10 to 12 places, approximately 1-inch deep, and insert slivers of garlic. Wrap in plastic wrap and refrigerate overnight. Bring to room temperature 1 hour before cooking. Preheat oven to 500 degrees. Make a paste by combining flour, Worcestershire, oregano, pepper, mustard, and water and spread over roast. Spray a heavy roasting pan and rack with cooking spray. Place the roast, fat side up, on rack. Sear meat for 10 minutes in preheated oven, then lower oven temperature to 350 degrees and continue roasting until the meat thermometer inserted into the thickest portion of the meat (without touching the bone) registers 130 degrees for rare (approximately 17- 20 minutes per pound). If the "roasting paste" browns too quickly, tent meat with foil, but do not seal. Remove roast from oven and let rest for about 20 minutes; discard the "roasting paste" before carving.

Horseradish Sauce:

1 cup sour cream
1 cup mayonnaise
1 cup grated Parmesan cheese
½ to ⅔ cup white horseradish, to taste

1 T. granulated garlic
1 T. Worcestershire
Dash of hot pepper sauce

Combine all ingredients. Refrigerate for 4 hours to blend flavors. Yields 3½ to 4 cups.

PORK DIANE

4 lbs. pork tenderloin, cut into cubes

Marinade:

10	garlic cloves, crushed	1	T. sesame paste (from Chinese market)
¼	cup Worcestershire	2	T. black bean sauce
½	cup soy sauce		(from Chinese market)
1½	cups teriyaki sauce	1	T. molasses
10	green onions, chopped	¼	cup ketchup
¼	cup vegetable oil	1	T. black pepper

1	cup clarified butter	Brandy, cognac or rum

Combine all marinade ingredients in blender and mix thoroughly. Transfer marinade to a glass bowl; add cubed pork. Cover and refrigerate for 8 hours. Drain pork 1 hour before serving and allow to come to room temperature.

In a large skillet, heat the clarified butter. Sauté pork until cooked. Add brandy and ignite, carefully. It's wise to try this procedure a few times, until you are comfortable. It's not necessary to flambé to achieve the full flavor of this dish. Serve immediately. Yields 8-10 servings.

SEAFOOD ETOUFFE

⅓	cup olive oil	½	tsp. oregano
3	T. butter	1	T. fresh parsley, chopped
3	tsp. garlic, chopped	1	T. sugar
4	T. green onions, chopped	5	dashes hot pepper sauce
3	T. flour	8	fresh basil leaves
1	cup beef broth	1	bay leaf
½	cup tomato paste	½	tsp. salt
¾	cup white wine		Pepper to taste
¼	cup brandy		
1	fresh jalapeño, seeded and chopped		

Heat the oil and butter in a stock pot. Sauté garlic and onion until translucent. Add flour and cook until brown, stirring frequently. Add beef broth and simmer for approximately 5 minutes. Add remaining ingredients; simmer for 15 minutes.

8	oz. fresh firm white fish	4	oz. shrimp
4	oz. lobster meat (we used one	8	oz. crab
	large lobster tail)	4	oz. scallops

Cut fish and seafood into bite-sized pieces. (If you prefer, use 2 lbs. of fish; or substitute crayfish, chicken, or sausage.) Add to stock pot and simmer, uncovered, until the fish and seafood are cooked. This is not a "spicy" etouffe — add more jalapeños and/or hot pepper sauce if your palate enjoys spicier fare! This is wonderful when made ahead and reheated. Yields 6 servings.

BREAST OF DUCK
with Orange Salsa and Blackberry Sauce

Marinade:

2 cups soy sauce	2 T. fresh garlic, minced
1 cup chicken broth	2 T. orange marmalade
½ cup white wine	1 T. sesame oil
¼ cup sherry	1 T. oil
1 T. fresh ginger	Red pepper flakes, to taste

6 duck breasts	Granulated garlic
Olive oil	White pepper

In a blender, combine all marinade ingredients and mix thoroughly.

Remove skin from duck breasts and marinate for 12 hours.

When ready to grill, remove duck from marinade, reserving marinade, and pat dry. Brush both sides of duck with olive oil and season with granulated garlic and white pepper. Preheat grill to medium heat; grill duck breasts approximately 4 minutes per side. Do not overcook. Serve duck breast on a pool of Duck Sauce, topped with Blackberry Sauce and accompanied by Orange Salsa (recipes follow).

Duck Sauce:

1 cup cornstarch	Reserved marinade
1 cup water	

Bring reserved marinade to a boil for 5 minutes. Combine the cornstarch and water and add to the marinade. Cook until thickened. Serve under the duck breast.

Blackberry Sauce for Duck Breasts:

1 cup blackberry preserves	1 T. sesame oil
1 tsp. Chinese mustard	1 T. teriyaki sauce
1 T. frozen orange juice concentrate	

In a saucepan, melt blackberry preserves. Add remaining ingredients and cook to blend seasonings. Serve warm over duck.

Orange Salsa:

1 large tomato, chopped	2 T. lime juice
1 orange, peeled and chopped	1 T. garlic, chopped
⅓ cup red onion, chopped	½ cup cucumber, peeled, seeded
15 cilantro leaves, chopped	and chopped
⅓ cup green onion, chopped	2 tsp. sugar
⅓ cup green bell pepper, chopped	1 tsp. cumin
Fresh jalapeño, seeded and chopped, to taste	Salt and pepper to taste

Combine all ingredients at least 6 hours prior to serving. Refrigerate.

VENISON STEW

This recipe was contributed by Midsummer Night's Dream Ball chairman Susan Richardson, and although we did not serve it at the ball, we wanted to include it for you to enjoy.

¼ lb. sliced bacon, cut into ½-inch pieces	2 T. currant jelly
2 lbs. venison, cut into 1-inch pieces (rump roast works well)	2 tsp. dried or fresh thyme
Black pepper, coarsely ground	8-10 small potatoes, halved (do not peel)
6 carrots, peeled, cut into thirds	6-8 garlic cloves, minced
2 T. sugar	1 head of elephant garlic, coarsely chopped
2 cups beef broth	10 Roma tomatoes, quartered
2 cups burgundy wine	½ cup parsley

Cook bacon in a large skillet until browned. Remove bacon, leaving rendered fat, to a large ovenproof casserole. Brown venison in bacon fat, sprinkling liberally with pepper. As venison browns, remove the pieces to the casserole with the bacon. Sauté carrots in the same skillet, sprinkling with sugar. Set carrots aside in a separate bowl.

In the same skillet, combine beef broth, wine, jelly, and thyme. Scrape pan thoroughly and bring to a boil. Pour over the venison and bacon; add potatoes, garlic, and elephant garlic. Bake in 350-degree oven for 45 minutes, covered. Remove from oven and add tomatoes, carrots, and parsley. Return to oven for an additional 45 minutes, uncovered.

This venison is best served as a juicy stew or soup with crusty French bread. The recipe doubles or triples easily, for a crowd. Serves 6-8.

VEGETABLE QUESADILLAS

Filling:

1 T. basil, chopped	3 T. olive oil
2 tsp. mint, chopped	½ of a medium white onion, sliced
¾ cup feta cheese	1 head roasted garlic, puréed
½ cup pine nuts, toasted	1 medium zucchini, sliced thin
	Salt and pepper to taste

8 6-inch flour tortillas

Mix together the basil, mint, feta cheese, and pine nuts. In a skillet, sauté onions in olive oil until soft. Add roasted garlic and sliced zucchini. Cook until crisp-tender. Salt and pepper to taste. Remove from heat. Combine cheese mixture and vegetables.

Spread 4 flour tortillas with cheese/vegetable mixture and top each with remaining tortillas. Lightly brush a skillet or griddle with olive oil; brown quesadillas on both sides. Remove to a cutting board and cut into quarters. Yields 16 hors d'oeuvres-sized portions.

GARLIC BREAD PUDDING

2	cups milk	1	tsp. rosemary
8	garlic cloves, chopped	¾	tsp. salt
2	egg yolks		Pepper to taste
2	whole eggs	2½	cups Italian bread,
3	T. fresh parsley, minced		cut into ½-inch cubes

Preheat oven to 350 degrees. In a saucepan, scald the milk with the garlic. Remove from heat and set aside for 15 minutes. Strain the milk through a sieve and discard the garlic. Whisk together the egg yolks and whole eggs. As you whisk add milk in a stream. Stir in parsley, rosemary, salt and pepper. Divide the bread cubes among 8 well-buttered 1/3 cup muffin tins. Ladle the custard mixture over the bread, dividing equally, and allow puddings to stand for 10 minutes.

Bake puddings in preheated oven for 45 minutes, or until golden brown and puffed. Allow to cool for 10 minutes. Run a thin knife around the puddings and lift out carefully with a fork. Serve while warm. Serves 8.

SNOWBALL DIP

2	6½-oz. cans minced clams, drained	1	T. Worcestershire
8	oz. cream cheese		Juice of ½ lemon
8	oz. fresh Brie, rind removed		Dash of hot pepper sauce
2	tsp. garlic, chopped		Salt and pepper to taste
	Chopped parsley or paprika for garnish		

Combine all ingredients. Garnish with chopped parsley and/or paprika for color. Serve with bagel chips or pita chips. Yields 2 cups.

GARDEN CUCUMBER DIP

2	large cucumbers, peeled, seeded and finely chopped	2½	T. fresh dill, chopped
		¼	cup green onions, chopped
1	cup mayonnaise	½	tsp. salt
1	cup sour cream	1	T. Dijon mustard
1	T. lemon juice	¼	tsp. pepper
	Several dashes hot pepper sauce		

Combine all ingredients. Cover and refrigerate overnight. Serve with assorted vegetables. Yields 3 cups.

PESTO DIP

1	cup mayonnaise	½	cup walnuts, chopped
1	cup sour cream	1	tsp. dried basil
1	10-oz. pkg. chopped spinach, defrosted and squeezed dry	4	garlic cloves, minced
			Dash of dried red peppers
1/3	cup Parmesan cheese		Salt and pepper to taste

Combine all ingredients in food processor until almost smooth and refrigerate. Yields 2 cups.

CHOCOLATE RIBBONS

3   large eggs
2/3 cup heavy cream
4   T. sugar
1/8 tsp. salt
1   scant cup sifted flour

6   T. unsweetened cocoa
1   cup clarified butter
Chocolate sauce (recipe follows)
Whipped cream (recipe follows)
Strawberry for garnish

Mix the eggs, cream, sugar, salt, flour, and cocoa in the blender until smooth. Refrigerate batter for 45 minutes.

Spray a crepe pan with cooking spray; heat to medium heat and brush with clarified butter. Pour ¼ cup crepe mixture into the pan and swirl, coating the pan completely. Cook for approximately 1 minute. Flip out onto wax paper and allow to cool. Continue until all batter is used. Once cooled, the crepes can be stacked with wax paper. Wrap well and store in refrigerator.

When ready to serve, slice each crepe into thin ribbon strips. Allow one to two crepes per serving.

Drizzle chocolate sauce lightly on top of sliced crepes. Add a dollop of sweetened whipped cream and top with a long-stemmed strawberry. A surprisingly light dessert! Serves 6-8.

Sauce for Chocolate Ribbons:

1   cup semisweet chocolate chips
2   T. butter
¾   tsp. instant espresso coffee granules

1   tsp. Mexican coffee liqueur
4   tsp. heavy cream
1   tsp. vanilla

Melt the chocolate chips and butter in a double-boiler. Whisk constantly until smooth. Remove from heat and whisk in remaining ingredients.

Sweetened Whipped Cream:

1   pt. heavy cream
1   T. brown sugar

1   tsp. vanilla

Chill mixing bowl and beaters. Whip the cream until slightly thickened. Add the sugar and vanilla. Continue to whip until soft peaks form.

TRES MOCHA BROWNIES

Brownies:
1 21½-oz pkg. brownie mix
½ cup water
¼ cup oil
1 large egg
4 tsp. instant espresso coffee granules
1 tsp. vanilla
1 tsp. Mexican coffee liqueur

Filling:
½ cup dark brown sugar, firmly packed
¼ cup butter, softened
1 large egg
3 tsp. instant espresso coffee granules
1 tsp. vanilla
1 cup pecans or walnuts, coarsely chopped
12 oz. mini chocolate chips

Topping:
1 cup semisweet chocolate chips
2 T. butter
½ tsp. instant espresso coffee granules
2 to 4 tsp. heavy cream

Preheat oven to 350 degrees and grease a 9 x 13-inch baking pan. Combine all brownie ingredients and beat by hand, approximately 50 strokes. Spread mixture in baking pan and bake on the middle oven rack for approximately 20 minutes.

For filling, beat together the brown sugar and butter until light. Add egg, espresso, and vanilla and blend well. Mix in pecans and chocolate chips. Spread mixture over the partially baked brownies and return to oven for 10 additional minutes, or until lightly browned.

For the topping, slowly melt the butter and chocolate chips in a double-boiler, whisking smooth. Remove from heat; add espresso and enough cream for a glaze consistency. Drizzle the topping over the brownies. Cool and refrigerate for 24 hours before slicing and serving. These brownies freeze well. Yields 3 to 4 dozen.

TOFFEE BARS

15 chocolate graham crackers
1 cup brown sugar, firmly packed
1 cup butter
1 cup chocolate chips
2 tsp. Mexican coffee liqueur
2 tsp. vanilla
½ cup chopped almonds, divided in half

Preheat oven to 400 degrees. Spray a large cookie sheet with cooking spray and line with foil. Cover the bottom of the cookie sheet with chocolate graham crackers, filling in any cracks with crushed crumbs.

In a saucepan, bring the brown sugar and butter to a boil. Continue to boil for 3 minutes. Pour over the graham crackers; bake for 5 minutes or until the mixture bubbles. Melt chocolate chips; add Mexican coffee liqueur, vanilla, and half of the almonds. Remove cookie sheet from the oven and immediately pour the chocolate mixture over the crackers, spreading the chocolate mixture evenly. Sprinkle with remaining almonds. Allow the cookies to cool for a few minutes, but cut into bars while still warm. Yields 2 dozen bar cookies.

BANANA CHOCOLATE TRUFFLES

A great flavor combination – and very, very rich!

Miniature muffin paper cups
12 oz. semisweet chocolate
4 egg yolks
1/3 cup Mexican coffee liqueur
2/3 cup unsalted butter

1 T. banana extract
½ tsp. vanilla
¼ tsp. cinnamon
Pinch of salt
¼ lb. dried banana chips

Place paper liners in miniature muffin tins. Melt chocolate in a double boiler. Remove from heat and allow to cool. Beat egg yolks and slowly add to chocolate, stirring until well blended. Add liqueur. Again, warm chocolate/egg mixture in a double boiler for 3 minutes, stirring constantly. Pour chocolate mixture into a mixing bowl and beat in butter, 1 tablespoon at a time. Add remaining ingredients (except banana chips) and beat until light and fluffy. Immediately fill each of the paper liners with 1 teaspoon of the mixture. Top each truffle with a piece of dried banana chip. Refrigerate, covered, for 48 hours or longer before serving. Yields 2 dozen truffles.

CHOCOLATE RUGELACH

Sour Cream Pastry:
2 cups flour
½ tsp. salt
1 cup unsalted butter
¾ cup sour cream
1 large egg yolk

For rolling dough:
¼ cup sugar
1 T. cinnamon

Chocolate-nut filling:
1/3 cup mini semisweet chocolate chips
½ oz. unsweetened chocolate, coarsely chopped
1/3 cup walnuts, chopped
3 T. sugar
½ tsp. cinnamon

Blend the flour, salt, butter, sour cream, and egg yolk in food processor with a metal blade until the dough comes away from the sides. Divide the dough into four sections, and wrap each quarter well in plastic wrap. Refrigerate overnight.

Combine all the filling ingredients and chop finely in a food processor.

When ready to roll, sprinkle work surface with sugar/cinnamon mixture. Remove one section of dough and roll dough into a 9-inch circle. Sprinkle and pat 3 T. of filling into dough. Using a pizza cutter, cut the circle into 12 wedges. Place ½ tsp. filling at the wide end of each wedge and roll tightly. Place each crescent, point side down, on an ungreased, insulated cookie sheet and refrigerate for 20 minutes.

Preheat oven to 350 degrees. Bake on the middle rack approximately 20 minutes. Remove immediately to a wire rack to cool. These cookies freeze well — and taste just like Grandma used to make! Yields 48 cookies.

December Debutante Ball

Dinner Buffet:

Bourbon Beef Tenderloin
A Twinkling Shrimp Tree
Wreaths of Bread
Served with Roquefort Brie Ball
Christmas Caviar Cane
Caviar Cheesecake
Salmon Mousse
Monte Cristos
Reuben Rollups

Dessert Sugarland Express:

Pavlovas with Black Forest Mousse
*Gingerbread House
*Petit Fours in shapes of Christmas presents
Christmas Cookies
Eggnog Buttons
Chocolate Covered Cherries
Sunburst Lemon Bars
Butter Thumb Cookies

*Recipe not included

BOURBON BEEF TENDERLOIN

1   large beef tenderloin, trimmed   Granulated garlic
    (approximately 3 lbs.)   Black pepper

Marinade:

1   cup soy sauce   1   cup orange juice
1   cup bourbon   4   garlic cloves, minced
1   cup brown sugar   1   cup onions, chopped
¼   cup red wine vinegar   1/8 tsp. Worcestershire
2   T. molasses

Combine all marinade ingredients. Pour over tenderloin. Cover, seal well, and refrigerate for 24 hours, turning meat twice.

When ready to roast or grill, remove tenderloin from marinade and pat dry. Season with garlic and pepper.

For roasting: Preheat oven to 450 degrees. Cook for 12 minutes. Lower temperature to 325 degrees; for an additional 20 minutes, or until medium rare. (Rare meat is soft to the touch. Well-done does not "give" at all when touched.) Allow the meat to rest for 15 minutes before slicing.

For grilling: Preheat the grill to hot; sear the meat on each side. Lower the heat, and cook for 15 minutes more on each side. Serves 8.

A TWINKLING SHRIMP TREE

The Gourmet Gals & Guys Shrimp Tree is a relatively simple way to add glitz and glitter to any affair. You will need:

Hot glue/glue gun   Waterproof twinkle lights
1   24-inch Styrofoam cone with   Paper towels
    a base diameter of 6-inches   5   dozen large shrimp, boiled
1   16-inch by 1-inch Styrofoam circle   and peeled
Floral tape   Frilly toothpicks
4-5 heads leaf lettuce, washed   Parsley, for garnish
    and dried   Cherry tomatoes, for garnish
Floral pins

Begin construction of the tree by hot-gluing the Styrofoam cone to the circular base. Secure the tree to a serving tray with floral tape for stability. Test the twinkle lights.

Assemble the tree by attaching washed and fully dried leaf lettuce to the base of the cone using floral pins. Layer the lettuce upward to the top of the cone, completely covering the Styrofoam. Attach the waterproof twinkle lights to the tree with floral pins, beginning at the tip of the cone and circling downwards to the tree's base. If you choose to decorate the top of your tree, do so now. Cover with damp paper towels and place the tree in a cool place. (The damp paper towels will keep the lettuce leaves crisp.)

One hour before serving, attach the boiled, peeled shrimp to the tree with frilly toothpicks, beginning at the top of the cone and working downward, following the line of twinkle lights. Intersperse with parsley and cherry tomatoes to cover any holes and add additional color. Reserve any remaining shrimp. Again, cover the tree with damp paper towels until guests arrive. Prepare a serving bowl for cocktail sauce (see p. 86) and a bowl for serving remaining shrimp, and place alongside the Shrimp Tree.

DECORATIVE WREATHS OF BREAD

This is an easy but effective way to decorate your holiday buffet table. The bread doubles as a vehicle for spreads.

Ask your baker to make a braided egg bread wreath with a 10-12-inch center. Use the center of the wreath to hold the Roquefort Brie Ball. Order three bread wreaths of various sizes to cluster on the buffet. Fill the centers with spreads, vegetables, or crackers and decorate the edges with parsley and cherry tomatoes.

ROQUEFORT BRIE BALL

8 oz. Brie cheese, rind removed and cut into chunks	¼ cup unsalted butter
½ cup white wine	¼ cup Roquefort cheese
	1 cup walnuts, finely chopped

In a small bowl, pour wine over Brie. Refrigerate overnight, covered.

Drain and discard the wine. Combine Brie, butter, and Roquefort cheese in a food processor and blend until almost smooth. Chill slightly; form into a ball and roll the ball in chopped walnuts. Refrigerate. The cheese ball can be refrigerated for one week and the flavor improves with age. Serve at room temperature. Yields 1½ cups.

CHRISTMAS CAVIAR CANE

This is an outstanding spread to use any time of the year. Serve with your favorite crackers.

2 oz. Parmesan cheese	½ tsp. garlic, finely chopped
8 oz. cream cheese, softened	2 oz. red caviar, drained well (you could substitute minced red pepper)
2 T. sour cream	
3 drops hot pepper sauce	
2 T. green onions, whites only, chopped	½ cup green onions, whites and green, chopped
¼ tsp. pepper	Parsley for garnish

Combine the Parmesan cheese, cream cheese, sour cream, hot pepper sauce, whites of onions, pepper, and garlic in food processor and mix well. Chill mixture for 24 hours allowing flavors to blend.

Mold the cheese mixture into the shape of a candy cane or log. Score the design into the mold and decorate, alternating the caviar and chopped green onions. Garnish with parsley. Serves 12.

CAVIAR CHEESECAKE

This recipe was contributed by Mary Lou Morrison. It's a mistake-proof recipe that makes a wonderful impression.

2	8-oz. pkgs. cream cheese, softened	4	dashes hot pepper sauce, or to taste
3	T. sour cream	3	2-oz. jars black lumpfish caviar
3	T. mayonnaise	2	bunches green onions, greens only, chopped
	Juice of 1 lemon	2	hard-cooked eggs, chopped
	Dash of Worcestershire		Toast rounds

Blend cream cheese, sour cream, and mayonnaise with lemon juice, Worcestershire, and hot pepper sauce until smooth. Lightly spray or grease an 8-inch round cake pan. Evenly spread cream cheese mixture in the cake pan. Refrigerate overnight.

Unmold, and flatten top, if necessary. Decorate with caviar, chopped green onions, and chopped eggs. Serve with toast rounds.

SALMON MOUSSE

1	16-oz. can salmon	1	tsp. dried dill
1	6-oz. can tuna, drained	¼	tsp. pepper
2	envelopes unflavored gelatin	4	hard-cooked eggs, finely chopped
2	cups mayonnaise		
½	cup chili sauce	½	cup pimento stuffed olives, finely chopped
2	T. lemon juice		
1	T. Worcestershire	¼	cup onion, finely chopped

Drain the salmon, reserving the liquid. Add water if necessary, for a total of ½ cup liquid. Bone and flake salmon; add tuna. Set aside.

In a heatproof measuring cup, combine gelatin and reserved liquid. Place the cup in a saucepan of hot water and stir to dissolve the gelatin. Transfer dissolved gelatin to a mixing bowl; gradually blend in the mayonnaise. Stir in the chili sauce, lemon juice, Worcestershire, dill, and pepper. Fold in salmon, tuna, egg, olives, and onion. Turn into a 6-cup fish shaped mold sprayed with cooking spray. Cover with plastic wrap and refrigerate. When chilled, unmold on a serving tray and garnish with lemon slices and sprigs of fresh dill. Serve with cocktail rye bread or crackers. Serves 24 as an hors d'oeuvres spread.

MONTE CRISTOS

24 slices of very thin white bread	Herb Butter (recipe follows)
	Honey Mustard (recipe follows)
10 oz. sliced ham, rectangular shape, halved	Pancake Batter (recipe follows)
	Oil for frying
8 oz. sliced cheddar cheese	Powdered sugar for garnish

Lay out 24 bread slices. Spread 12 slices with Herb Butter and 12 slices with Honey Mustard. Place a slice of ham and a slice of cheese on the buttered slices. Cover with mustard slices. Cut into quarters. (Cover with a damp towel to prevent drying.)

Heat oil in a deep skillet. Dip each sandwich quarter into prepared batter; fry until browned on each side. Drain on paper towels and hold in warm oven. Sprinkle with powdered sugar before serving. Yields 48 pieces.

Herb Butter: Mix together.
4 T. butter
¼ tsp. fine herbs

Honey Mustard: Mix together.
¼ cup Dijon mustard
1 T. honey

Pancake Batter: Combine all ingredients and mix well.

2	cups complete pancake mix	⅛	tsp. ginger, ground
1½	cups club soda	1	tsp. fine herbs
⅛	tsp. dry mustard	2	tsp. granulated garlic

REUBEN ROLLUPS

4	oz. Swiss cheese, grated	¼	cup Dijon mustard
1	cup sauerkraut, drained well	15	slices pastrami, halved

Combine Swiss cheese, sauerkraut, and mustard. Heap a generous spoonful of the mixture on each piece of pastrami. Roll tightly; skewer through the center with a toothpick. Yields 30 hors d'oeuvres.

BLACK FOREST MOUSSE

3	16-oz. cans pitted Bing cherries	¼	cup water
1	cup cherry flavored liqueur	½	cup granulated sugar
2	cups semisweet chocolate	4	egg yolks, beaten
½	cup half and half	1	cup heavy cream, whipped
2	envelopes unflavored gelatin		

The day before, drain the cherries and marinate overnight in cherry liqueur.

In a double boiler, melt the chocolate in the half and half, stirring to mix. Remove from heat and allow to cool slightly. Drain the cherries, reserving 8 to 10 for garnish.

Dissolve the gelatin in the water. Add gelatin, sugar, and egg yolks to the chocolate mixture. Stir until smooth and creamy. Fold the whipped cream into the chocolate mixture. Add cherries, stirring only enough to mix. Refrigerate for at least 2 hours.

Serve in Pavlovas (recipe follows), garnished with whole cherries. Serves 10-12.

PAVLOVAS

8 egg whites
1 tsp. baking powder
¼ tsp. salt
2 cups sugar
2 tsp. white vinegar
2 tsp. vanilla
½ tsp. almond extract

Parchment paper

2 qts. whipping cream

Black Forest Mousse (previous recipe)

Cut 3 circles of parchment paper — 10-inches, 9-inches, and 8-inches in diameter. Spray baking sheet with vegetable spray and line with wax paper. Preheat oven to 250 degrees. Beat egg whites until frothy. Add baking powder and salt, beating until stiff. Beat in sugar, 1 tablespoon at a time, until the mixture is stiff and glossy. Slowly add vinegar, vanilla, and almond extract, continuing to beat on high speed.

Place parchment circles on baking sheets and cover with 1-inch of meringue mixture, making a slight indentation in the middle. Bake Pavlova shells for 30-40 minutes, or until crisp but not browned. Turn off heat, but do not remove the shells until the oven is cool. Remove parchment paper and cool meringues on wire racks. Store in airtight containers.

Assembly:
Whip 2 qts. whipping cream to stiff peaks. Place 10-inch meringue shell on a serving platter. Fill the indentation with one-third of the Black Forest Mousse, spreading evenly, to within ½-inch of the edge. Pyramid the 9-inch and 8-inch meringues on top, filling each as above. Frost the Pavlova with prepared whipped cream. Using a large star pastry tip and tube, pipe a decorative border of whipped cream around the base. Serve accompanied by a bowl of Whoopie Sauce. (see p. 57).

EGGNOG BUTTONS

Cookies:
½ cup powdered sugar
1 cup butter or margarine, softened
1 tsp. rum extract

2 cups flour
1 cup ground almonds
¼ tsp. salt

Glaze:
½ cup powdered sugar
½ tsp. rum extract

3-4 tsp. milk
Ground nutmeg

Preheat oven to 325 degrees. In a large bowl, beat powdered sugar, butter, and rum extract until light and fluffly. Stir in flour, almonds, and salt; mix well. (Dough will be crumbly.) Lightly grease your hands to prevent the dough from sticking. Shape heaping teaspoons of dough into balls and place 1-inch apart on an ungreased cookie sheet. Bake for 12-15 minutes. Immediately remove from cookie sheets. Cool on wire racks.

In a small bowl, combine powdered sugar, rum extract, and enough milk for glaze consistency. Drizzle over cooled cookies and sprinkle with nutmeg. Store in loosely covered container. Yields 5 dozen cookies.

CHOCOLATE COVERED CHERRIES

Cookie:
½   cup butter, softened (1 stick)
1   cup sugar
1   egg
1½ tsp. vanilla
1½ cups all-purpose flour
½   cup cocoa
¼   tsp. salt
¼   tsp. baking soda
¼   tsp. baking powder
36 miniature paper baking cups
36 stemmed maraschino cherries

Glaze:
6   oz. semisweet chocolate chips
¼   cup light corn syrup
2   T. water

Preheat oven to 350 degrees. In a large mixing bowl, cream butter and sugar. Beat in the egg. Add vanilla and mix well.

Sift flour, cocoa, salt, baking soda, and baking powder together. Add dry ingredients to butter/sugar and mix thoroughly. Line a miniature muffin tin with paper baking cups, and fill each half full. Insert one stemmed maraschino cherry into the center of each cup. Bake for 15 to 18 minutes. Remove from muffin tin and cool on a wire rack. Glaze. Yields 36 cookies.

Glaze:
Heat all ingredients in a double boiler until chips are melted, whisking until smooth. Drizzle over cherries.

SUNBURST LEMON BARS

The Sunburst Lemon Bars are dedicated to the man from Houston who assured us he could not live through the week if we did not send him home with a doggy-bag filled with these tasty creations!

Crust:
2   cups all-purpose flour
½   cup powdered sugar

1   cup butter or margarine,
      softened

Filling:
4   eggs, slightly beaten
2   cups sugar
¼   cup all-purpose flour
1   tsp. baking powder

¼   cup fresh squeezed lemon juice
2   tsp. lemon extract
1 T. grated lemon peel
Powdered sugar

Heat oven to 350 degrees. To make the crust, use a large mixing bowl and combine flour, powdered sugar, and butter. Mix at low speed, until crumbly. Line a 9x13-inch baking pan with foil and spray with baking spray. Press mixture evenly on the bottom of the baking pan. Bake for 20 to 30 minutes, or until light golden brown.

In a large mixing bowl, combine eggs, sugar, ¼ cup flour, and baking powder. Blend well. Stir in lemon juice, lemon extract, and lemon peel. Pour mixture over the warm crust and return to oven. Bake 25 to 30 minutes, or until top is golden brown. Cool in refrigerator. Remove from pan; remove foil. Sprinkle with powdered sugar and cut into bars. Yields 54 bars, cut into 1¼-inch squares.

BUTTER THUMB COOKIES

4	T. butter, softened	½	tsp. baking powder
3	T. sugar	1	cup flour
4	tsp. heavy cream	2	tsp. vanilla or almond extract
2	egg yolks, lightly beaten		Favorite jam or preserve for filling

Preheat oven to 325 degrees. Spray a cookie sheet with cooking spray. In a small mixing bowl, cream the butter and sugar until fluffy. Add the cream and egg yolks. Mix the baking powder and flour together and add to batter. Add vanilla and mix until dough holds together.

With oiled hands roll the dough into 1½-inch balls and place on cookie sheet. Using your thumb, make an indentation in the dough and fill with ½ tsp. of jam. Bake for 8-10 minutes. Do not allow cookies to brown. Remove from cookie sheet and cool on rack. Yields 3 dozen cookies.

December Debutante Ball

After The Ball Breakfast Buffet

Spiced Pancakes:
Pecan

Chocolate

Blueberry

Apple

Toppings:
*Maple Syrup

*Fresh Strawberries

Amaretto Whipped Butter

*Cinnamon and Sugar

Cantina Cafe:

Terry's Cappuccino for a Crowd

Nancy Payne's Holiday Nog

Cappuccino Brownies

*Recipe not included

SPICED PANCAKES

3 cups complete buttermilk pancake mix

1 pkg. each, Instant Apple and Cinnamon Oatmeal and Cinnamon and Spice Oatmeal*

1 tsp. cinnamon

4 cups milk

Pinch of nutmeg

Mix all the ingredients until combined. Allow batter to rest for 20 minutes. Preheat skillet; make pancakes using 1/3 cup batter for each. Serve pancakes immediately. Yields approximately 36 pancakes. Add chopped pecans, chocolate chips, blueberries, or sliced apples for varying flavors.

*You can substitute any of the instant oatmeal flavors.

AMARETTO WHIPPED BUTTER

1½ cups butter, softened
3 T. honey
1 T. heavy cream
¼ cup Amaretto liqueur

2 T. powdered sugar
Pinch of nutmeg
Orange slices for garnish

Mix butter, honey, cream, Amaretto, powdered sugar, and nutmeg until well blended. Serve at room temperature with Spiced Pancakes. Garnish with fresh orange slices. Yields 1½ cups.

TERRY'S CAPPUCCINO FOR A CROWD

15 cups strong coffee
"Cappuccino" base (recipe follows)

Cream base (recipe follows)
1 pt. whipped cream for topping

"Cappuccino" base:

3 sticks cinnamon, broken into pieces
¼ tsp. whole cloves
¼ tsp. whole allspice
Cheesecloth
1 oz. light creme de cocoa

1 oz. dark creme de cocoa
1 oz. gin
1 oz. vodka
1 oz. rum
1 oz. brandy

Wrap cinnamon, cloves, and allspice in cheesecloth. Combine in a saucepan with creme de cocoas, gin, vodka, rum, and brandy and bring to a boil. Remove from heat and let cool. The base can be refrigerated for 5 days.

Cream base:

2 cups whipping cream
½ cup powdered sugar

1 cup cocoa
½ cup instant espresso granules

Whip cream and add remaining ingredients. Refrigerate. Can be made 4 hours before serving.

To serve:

Combine strong coffee with the "Cappuccino" base and fill demitasse cups half full. Stir in ½ T. of cream base. Top with a dollop of whipped cream. Yields 25 servings.

NANCY PAYNE'S HOLIDAY NOG

This delicious eggnog became a tradition at Bauer House, the chancellor's residence at the University of Texas Austin, for the annual holiday Open House. Although this favorite is definitely not fat-free, remember that Christmas comes but once a year!

Eggnog base:

2 oz. Tia Maria
2 oz. brandy
2 oz. bourbon

2 oz. vodka
6 eggs, separated
¼ lb. powdered sugar

At least 24 hours in advance, combine the liquors, egg yolks, and powdered sugar. Cover and refrigerate. Reserve the egg whites and refrigerate.

173

2	cups whipping cream	6	reserved egg whites
1	T. vanilla		Nutmeg for garnish
2	cups half and half		Candy canes

Whip cream until thick. Add vanilla and half and half. Whip egg whites until they form soft peaks. Fold egg whites into cream. 2 hours before serving, combine the eggnog base with cream mixture; refrigerate until serving. Sprinkle with nutmeg, and decorate the sides of the punch bowl with candy canes. Yields 16 4-oz. servings.

CAPPUCCINO BROWNIES

Brownie base:

1	box brownie mix	2	tsp. vanilla
4	T. instant espresso mixed with 2 T. boiling water	¼	cup oil
		½	cup water
2	large eggs		

Preheat oven to 350 degrees. Grease a 9 x 13-inch pan. Mix all the brownie base ingredients and bake for 20 minutes or until done. Remove from oven and allow to cool.

Cream Cheese Filling:

8	oz. cream cheese, softened	1	tsp. cinnamon
6	T. unsalted butter, softened	¼	tsp. nutmeg
1½	cups powdered sugar	4	T. Mexican coffee liqueur
1	tsp. vanilla		

Mix the filling ingredients in a mixer. Spread on cooled brownies.

Glaze:

6	oz. fine quality chocolate	3	T. Mexican coffee liqueur
2	T. unsalted butter		Dash of nutmeg
½	cup heavy cream	1	tsp. vanilla
1½	T. espresso, dissolved in 1 T. boiling water		

Melt chocolate and butter in double boiler. Add remaining ingredients, stirring until smooth. Spread over cream cheese mixture. Refrigerate for 48 hours. (Good luck! Ours didn't last for 6 hours!) Yields 18 brownies.

Lara's Theme

A Debutante Ball

Estaffado
(Mexican Stew)

Pecan-Crusted Catfish
with Cumin Tartar Sauce

*Grilled Zucchini

Laredo Chicken

Monterey Salsa

Dessert Table:
Praline Cheesecake

*Recipe not included

ESTAFFADO (MEXICAN STEW)

We usually make a large pot of Estaffado, because it is a wonderful winter meal for a crowd, and if there are leftovers, it freezes well. This recipe will serve 20 to 24 guests.

¼ cup oil
10 cloves garlic, chopped
5 cups onions, sliced
6 14½-oz. cans chopped tomatoes
1 12-oz can tomato paste
6 cup water
¾ cup chili powder (start with ¼ cup and add to taste)

⅓ cup granulated garlic
¼ cup oregano
2 4-oz. cans chopped green chiles
½ cup cumin
1 tsp. salt
1 tsp. pepper

In a large, heavy stock pot, sauté the garlic and onions in oil. Add next 10 ingredients; simmer and taste for seasonings. In a large bowl, combine the flour, salt, and pepper.

3 cups flour
3 tsp. salt
2 tsp. pepper
5 lbs. stew meat, cut into large pieces
3 cups oil
5 sweet potatoes, cut in large, bite-sized pieces
8 zucchini, sliced

5 yellow squash, sliced
5 green peppers, roasted, chopped
16 oz. corn
⅓ cup fresh parsley, chopped
⅓ cup green onions, chopped
3 dashes hot pepper sauce
Jalapeños (optional)
Red pepper flakes (optional)

Dredge the stew meat in seasoned flour. Using ½ cup of oil per batch, sauté the meat in 6 batches in a large skillet. Add meat to stock pot and simmer for 1 hour. Add sweet potatoes; simmer for 30 minutes. Add zucchini, squash, green peppers, and corn and simmer for 30 more minutes, or until the vegetables are cooked, adding more water if necessary. Before serving, add the parsley, green onions, and hot pepper sauce.

PECAN-CRUSTED CATFISH
with Cumin Tartar Sauce

1½ lbs. catfish pieces	Seasoned Cornmeal (recipe follows)
2 eggs, beaten	Canola oil for frying

Dip fish in beaten eggs and roll in seasoned cornmeal. Cover and chill for 2 hours. In a heavy skillet, heat 1 inch of oil. Fry the catfish, turning once, until tender. Drain on paper towels. Keep warm in low oven until ready to serve, no longer than 45 minutes. The catfish can be dipped, fried in advance, and reheated. Serve with Cumin Tartar Sauce (recipe follows). Serves 4.

Seasoned Cornmeal:

1 cup white cornmeal	1½ cups pecans, finely chopped
2 tsp. taco seasoning (or more, if you like it spicier!)	1¼ tsp. salt
	¾ tsp. black pepper

Cumin Tartar Sauce:

1 T. capers, drained	½ cup sour cream
3 T. dill pickles, finely chopped	1 T. chili powder
1 T. parsley, chopped	1 T. cumin
1 T. cilantro, chopped	1 tsp. sugar
½ cup mayonnaise	2-3 T. milk
	Salt and white pepper, to taste
	Dash of hot pepper sauce, to taste

Combine all ingredients, blending until smooth. Add more milk, if necessary, for desired consistency. Refrigerate. Yields 1¾ cups.

LAREDO CHICKEN

8 boneless, skinless chicken breast halves	1 10-oz. can Ro-tel tomatoes
Taco seasoning	8 oz. shredded Velveeta Mild Mexican Cheese
Granulated garlic	8 oz. mushrooms, sliced
4 T. butter	1 cup seasoned croutons, crushed
4 T. flour	1 cup ranch flavored tortilla chips, crushed
2 cups milk	Olive oil
Salt and pepper to taste	
8 oz. Swiss cheese slices	

Preheat oven to 325 degrees. Pound and season the chicken breast halves on both sides with taco seasoning and granulated garlic.

In a saucepan, melt the butter and add flour, mixing well, and cook over medium heat; slowly add the milk, stirring constantly, until slightly thickened. Add salt and pepper.

Spray a 9 x 13-inch baking pan with cooking spray; place the sliced Swiss cheese on the bottom. Arrange the chicken breasts in a single layer over the cheese and top with the white sauce. Layer the remaining ingredients in the following order: Velveeta cheese, Rotel tomatoes, and mushrooms. Sprinkle with the crushed croutons and tortilla chips; brush lightly with olive oil.

Bake in the upper half of the oven, uncovered, for 1 hour. Allow to sit for 20 minutes before serving. Serves 8.

MONTEREY SALSA

This is a fun dish to serve, because most of your guests have probably never eaten cactus!

2-4	cactus pads, to equal 1 cup when processed	4	green onions, finely chopped
2	oranges, peeled, seeded, broken into segments	1	tsp. salt
		1	T. fresh lime juice
2	T. fresh orange juice	¾	tsp. hot pepper sauce (more or less, to taste)
¾	cup fresh pineapple, cut into small pieces	1	large, ripe avocado, peeled and cut into small pieces
¾	cup fresh tomatoes, chopped		

Carefully remove any thorns from the cactus pads. Peel the edges. Steam cactus for approximately 1 minute. Cool and dice.

Combine cactus with remaining ingredients. Refrigerate. Serve with chips. Yields approximately 4 cups.

PRALINE CHEESECAKE

This recipe was adapted from THE COLLECTION — A Cookbook, *published by the Junior League of Austin.*

Crust:		*Pie Filling:*	
1	cup graham cracker crumbs	3	8-oz. pkgs. cream cheese
3	T. sugar	1	cup dark brown sugar
3	T. butter, melted	2	T. flour
Pinch of nutmeg		3	eggs
Pinch of cinnamon		1½	tsp. white vanilla
Topping:		1	T. lemon juice
Maple syrup		1	tsp. salt
Whole pecans for garnish		½	cup finely chopped pecans

For crust: Combine graham cracker crumbs, sugar, butter, nutmeg, and cinnamon. Press into the bottom of a 9-inch springform pan. Bake at 350 degrees for approximately 7 minutes.

For filling: In a large mixing bowl, cream together cream cheese, brown sugar, and flour. Add eggs, one at a time, mixing well. Add vanilla, lemon juice, salt, and chopped pecans. Pour the mixture into the pie crust.

Bake at 350 degrees in the top half of oven, for 50 to 55 minutes, or until the blade of a knife comes out clean. Brush the pie with maple syrup and garnish with whole pecans.

Chapter 11

Traveling Texas and Beyond

his chapter features some of our favorite road menus. Off-premise catering, of course, always involves packing up the kitchen and setting it up again elsewhere. But occasionally, parties literally require us to "take the show on the road."

One special event we organized in Houston turned out to be a "trip" in itself. We left Austin before dawn on the morning of the party with three Gourmet Gals & Guys vans overflowing with food, props, and staff. Our task? To transform an empty warehouse into a setting that would carry the guests along the road from "rags to riches."

The guests, in the spirit of the party, arrived in inventive costumes ranging from a French maid to an alleycat. They began the evening in a re-created alley where the hobo-costumed caterers served Corny Dogs, Red Beans and Rice and Gumbo in hundreds of sterilized tin cans (the contents of which had been removed and donated to the Salvation Army). As the evening progressed, so did the party goers, ending their escapade before a backdrop of the twinkling Houston skyline, sipping champagne and enjoying Bananas Foster, flamed tableside from a vintage limousine.

One spring, we hit the road in the direction of Nevada to handle a Las Vegas Luau in honor of a couple's wedding anniversary. We had catered their wedding and each of their annual anniversary parties, so even though they had moved from Austin, they couldn't imagine the celebration without us. An abundance of Polynesian skewered meats, grilled fish, fresh tropical fruits, and lavish decorations transported everyone into the island paradise we created in their palm tree-lined backyard.

Gourmet Gals & Guys food has traveled by plane to Annapolis and California, and one of our famous White Chocolate Wedding Cakes even helped mark one couple's fifth year together. Preparing their duplicated wedding cake for travel was an expensive project, but our Washington, D.C. client assured us our efforts were appreciated!

We've often taken our road show closer to home, into the Texas Hill Country. At one event, guests visiting Texas' own Fall Creek Vineyards, in Tow, were presented with grapevine baskets filled with a gourmet lunch to enjoy during the bus trip from Austin. Following a tour of the winery, we served a formal dinner, showcasing wines from the vineyard. Our fare has made it across state lines to Oklahoma and fed hundreds of wedding guests up the road in Dallas. But we've also experienced our fair share of pitfalls in traveling. Food-filled vans have broken down, making it necessary to rent replacement vehicles. Heavy rains have flooded low water crossings, waylaying both caterers and guests. And a steep hill once wreaked havoc on a wedding cake being delivered to a reception, though quick thinking, extra frosting, and fresh flowers came to its rescue. The bride never knew that her cake was a near-disaster.

As we've said before, catering is always an adventure! Often we're asked, "How do you do that?" We often wonder ourselves. . .

Rags to Riches
In a warehouse somewhere in Houston

"Rags Area"
decorated as an alley

Soup Line
Served out of sterilized tin cans
Red Beans and Cajun Rice
Gumbo
*Po'Boy Sandwiches
World's Best Corny Dogs
Franks a la Gourmet
*Large Pretzels and Mustard

"Riches Area"
decorated as the twinkling night skyline of Houston
Bananas Foster flamed tableside

Old-fashioned desserts:
*Ice Cream Drumsticks
*Popsicles
*Fudgsicles
*Ice Cream Bars
*Ice Cream Sandwiches
And served from a vintage limousine:
Champagne
Cigars
including tobacco, chocolate, and bubblegum
*Cascading Champagne Grapes, Strawberries

*Recipe not included

RED BEANS AND CAJUN RICE

1	lb. red beans	1	T. Worcestershire
2	T. oil	1	tsp. salt
1	medium onion, chopped	½	tsp. black pepper
3	cloves garlic, chopped	¼	tsp. ginger
1	lb. ham hocks		Dash of hot pepper sauce, to taste

Soak beans overnight. Drain and rinse.

Sauté the onion and garlic in oil until brown. Add the beans and enough water to cover. Add the ham hocks, Worcestershire, salt, pepper, ginger, and hot pepper sauce. Bring to a boil; reduce heat and simmer for 3½ to 4 hours. Adjust seasonings while cooking. When done, the beans will be soft and the cooking liquid thick. Serve with Cajun Rice (recipe follows). Serves 8.

Cajun Rice:

2	T. olive oil	1	10-oz. can Ro-tel tomatoes
2	cups Basmati rice	1	tsp. chili powder
1	large onion, chopped	1	tsp. paprika
2	cloves garlic, chopped	1	bay leaf
1	green pepper, chopped	1	tsp. black pepper
2	cups chopped tomatoes and juice	1	tsp. salt
4	cups chicken stock (or chicken broth)		

In a large, deep pot, sauté the rice, onions, garlic, and green peppers in olive oil. Add remaining ingredients and bring to a boil. Simmer over medium-low heat until cooked. Serve with Red Beans (previous recipe). Serves 8-10.

GUMBO

1	cup oil	1	lb. okra, cleaned and sliced
1	cup flour	2	cups chicken broth
8	stalks celery, chopped	½	cup Worcestershire sauce
3	large onions, chopped	4	dashes hot pepper sauce
1	bunch green onions, chopped	½	cup ketchup
2	garlic cloves, chopped	2	bay leaves
½	cup fresh parsley, chopped		4 to 6 allspice seeds
1	green pepper, chopped	½	tsp. thyme
2	16-oz. cans chopped tomatoes		Salt and pepper to taste
2	lbs. smoked link sausage, cut into rounds *	1	T. brown sugar
2	lbs. ham, cubed *		Lemon juice to taste
	4½ lbs. chicken, cut into pieces *		File for garnish

Heat oil in a large stew pot. Gradually add the flour to make a roux, stirring constantly, until chocolate brown. Be patient. This is an important step. Add celery, onions, green onions, garlic, and parsley and cook for 45 minutes, stirring occasionally. Add remaining ingredients, except the salt, pepper, brown sugar, and lemon juice. Simmer for approximately 2½ hours. Add remaining ingredients. Remove the bay leaves and allspice, and taste for seasonings. Serve with file. Serves 8–10.

For Seafood Gumbo, substitute shrimp, crab, and crawfish.

WORLD'S BEST CORNY DOGS

Better than at the Texas State Fair!

⅔	cup cornmeal		Dash of hot pepper sauce
1	cup flour	¾	cup milk
2	T. sugar	8	hot dogs
1½	tsp. baking powder	1	can beer
1	tsp. salt	1½	cups water
2	T. oil	8	wooden sticks or skewers
1	egg, slightly beaten		Oil for frying
1	T. chili powder		

Combine cornmeal, flour, sugar, baking powder, salt, oil, egg, chili powder, and hot pepper sauce. Add milk and mix well.

Cook the hot dogs in beer and water for 3 minutes. Remove hot dogs and allow to cool. Insert a wooden stick in each hot dog.

Dip each hot dog in the batter and deep fry at 360 degrees until browned. Naturally, kids like these, but adults love them too! Serves 8.

FRANKS A LA GOURMET

This recipe was contributed by Mrs. Eugene McDermott of Dallas. It's a favorite of hers for luncheons, served with garlic French bread and a fresh green salad.

1	pkg. frankfurters		Juice of 1 lemon
3	T. Dijon mustard	2	tsp. Worcestershire
½	cup green onions, chopped	2	tsp. sweet basil
½	cup green bell pepper, chopped	2	tsp. parsley, chopped
2	garlic cloves, minced	1	tsp. Beau Monde
1	cup sharp cheddar cheese, grated	1	tsp. dill
½	cup chili sauce	½	tsp. black pepper
½	cup white wine		Celery seed, to taste

Preheat oven to 350 degrees. Slice frankfurters in half lengthwise and place flat in a single layer in an 8x12-inch Pyrex casserole dish, sprayed with cooking spray. Spread each frank with Dijon mustard and sprinkle with chopped green onions, chopped bell eppper, garlic and grated cheese.

Mix chili sauce, white wine, lemon juice, and Worcestershire in a bowl. Blend in basil, parsley, Beau Monde, dill, pepper, and celery seed.

Pour the seasoned mixture over each frankfurter and bake, covered with foil, for 30 minutes. Serves 4.

BANANAS FOSTER

½ cup sugar
2 T. butter
2 tsp. cinnamon
1 T. banana extract
¼ tsp. nutmeg

1 tsp. vanilla
6 bananas
3 T. white rum
Vanilla ice cream

Heat the sugar, butter, cinnamon, banana extract, nutmeg, and vanilla in a large pan and stir until well melted.

Cut the bananas into chunks. Add to sauce and toss gently to coat.

Pour rum over the bananas and heat for 15 seconds. Carefully ignite the mixture and swirl the pan until the flame dies.

Scoop ice cream into individual dessert bowls* and top with sauce and bananas. Serve immediately. Serves 6.

*For easier serving, scoop ice cream into dessert bowls earlier in the day and store in freezer.

Fourth of July Party on Lake Travis

"Hill Country Chic"

Cheese Roll Olé
(see p. 124)

*Fabulous Fireworks Fruit Display
Watermelon balls, strawberries, blueberries
and white chocolate-dipped strawberries

Miniature Party Burgers
Served with
Guacamole, chili, chopped red onions, bleu cheese, sour cream,
chopped bacon, sliced tomatoes, dill pickle slices, hickory smoked
mustard, mayonnaise, shredded cheddar cheese and corn chips

Grilled Vegetable Kabobs

Chicken and Mushroom Spirals

Firecracker Shrimp

*Adult Ice Cream Bar:
Vanilla, Chocolate and Strawberry Ice Creams,
Candy-coated Chocolate Candies, Brickle Bits,
Chopped Pecans, Crushed Pineapple, Sliced Bananas,
Red, White, and Blue Coconut
Whipped cream, Cherries with stems,
Creme de Menthe, Irish Cream, Coffee-flavored Liqueur,
Peach Schnapps, Coconut Cream Liqueur

Fresh Peach Sauce (see p. 34)
"Whoopie" Chocolate Sauce (see p. 57)

*Red White and Blue Jelly Beans
Supreme Sugar Cookies
decorated as American flags

*Recipe not included

MINIATURE PARTY BURGERS

5	lbs. finely ground hamburger meat	3	T. + 1 tsp. granulated garlic
2	white onions, coarsely chopped	3	T. Worcestershire
1	tsp. salt	2½	tsp. coarse ground black pepper

Combine all the ingredients and mix well. Pat the hamburger meat out to ½-inch thickness. Using a biscuit cutter with a 2½-inch diameter, cut out miniature patties. (These can be refrigerated or frozen.)

Broil or grill the patties, until cooked, 3 minutes per side. (The patties can also be baked in a 375-degree oven for 10 to 12 minutes.) Serve with miniature hamburger buns (2 to 2½ inches) ordered from your favorite bakery, and a medley of condiments. Yields 50 miniature hamburgers — 2 per person for 25 guests.

CHILI

Everyone has their favorite chili recipe, and naturally so do we. We reduced it from 30 pounds to 1 pound, but if you decide to make it for a crowd, or to freeze some for a future occasion, it multiplies well. A word of caution – if you make a large amount, do not add salt until you are ready to serve the chili.

1	T. oil	1	tsp. sugar
1	cup onions, chopped	1	tsp. oregano
2	garlic cloves, crushed	¼	tsp. granulated garlic
1	lb. beef, ground for chili	1	T. chili powder (or to taste)
1	cup tomato paste	2	tsp. cumin
1	15-oz. can chopped tomatoes	1	cup water
½	tsp. coarse ground black pepper	1½	tsp. salt

In a large pot, brown the onions and garlic in oil. Add the chili meat and cook until browned. Add remaining ingredients and simmer, uncovered, for 1 hour. Taste and adjust the seasonings, if necessary. Chili is best when made at least 24 hours prior to serving. It freezes well for up to 3 months. Yields 1 quart.

GRILLED VEGETABLE KABOBS

The choices of vegetables to grill are limited only by the grocer's selection. Use an array of fresh seasonal vegetables and be flexible. Cut the vegetables into equal pieces to assure even cooking. When deciding the amounts to prepare, plan two skewers for each guest, and approximately 3 ounces of vegetables per skewer.

Wooden skewers, soaked in water for one hour
Assorted fresh vegetables, cut into bite-size pieces
Basting Sauce (recipe follows)

Basting Sauce:

1	cup olive oil	1	T. fresh parsley, chopped
¼	tsp. salt	½	cup balsamic vinegar
½	tsp. pepper		Juice of 1 lemon
			Sprigs of fresh herbs for garnish

Blend all ingredients for Basting Sauce and set aside.

Skewer vegetables, alternating by color, and grill over medium heat, rotating and brushing with Basting Sauce until done. Serve immediately.

CHICKEN AND MUSHROOM SPIRALS

2	cups soy sauce	1	tsp. black pepper
1	cup honey	3	whole boneless, skinless
1¼	tsp. ground ginger		chicken breasts
2	cups vegetable oil	1	lb. medium mushrooms,
1	cup vinegar		brushed, stems removed
5	garlic cloves, minced		Salt to taste

Combine the soy sauce, honey, ginger, oil, vinegar, garlic, and black pepper in a blender until smooth.

Cut the chicken breasts into 5/8-inch strips. Wrap strips around the circumference of the mushrooms, securing with a long toothpick. Place the chicken rolls in a glass bowl; cover with marinade. Refrigerate for 4 hours, turning rolls 3 to 4 times. Remove from marinade and grill over high heat, 3 to 4 minutes per side. Sprinkle with salt and pepper and serve immediately. Makes approximately 24 rolls.

FIRECRACKER SHRIMP

½ cup butter, melted
2 T. olive oil
Juice of 2 large lemons
6 lbs. raw jumbo shrimp (15-18 per lb.), shelled, deveined, and butterflied
Parsley Sauce (recipe follows)
Assorted bottles of hot sauce

Preheat grill. Combine butter, olive oil, and lemon juice for a basting sauce. Grill shrimp for 4 to 5 minutes, basting with butter sauce until the shrimp turns pink. Do not overcook. Serve with an assortment of your favorite hot sauces and Parsley Sauce (recipe follows). Serves 10.

Parsley Sauce:

1	cup fresh parsley, chopped	6	T. onions, finely chopped
6	garlic cloves, chopped	4	T. flour
1	cup dry white wine	1	cup tomatoes, chopped
6	T. olive oil		Salt and pepper to taste

Chop parsley and garlic in food processor. Add wine and blend until smooth. Set aside. Sauté onions in olive oil in a large skillet until onions are translucent. Add flour and whisk until smooth. Slowly add chopped tomatoes, salt, pepper, and parsley/garlic mixture and simmer until hot. Adjust seasonings to taste. Serve hot or cold with Firecracker Shrimp.

SUPREME SUGAR COOKIES

4	cups flour	1½	cups sugar
1	tsp. baking powder	1	egg
½	tsp. baking soda	½	cup sour cream
½	tsp. salt	1	tsp. vanilla extract
½	tsp. nutmeg	½	tsp. almond extract
1	cup unsalted butter, softened		

Sift together the flour, baking powder, baking soda, salt, and nutmeg.

Cream butter and sugar until light and fluffy. Mix in the egg. Beat in sour cream, vanilla and almond extract. Add flour mixture, 1 cup at a time, blending thoroughly after each addition. Form dough into a ball; wrap with plastic wrap and refrigerate for 12 hours.

Preheat oven to 375 degrees. Divide dough into fourths, using ¼ at a time. Roll dough ¼-inch thick on a floured surface. Cut dough, using cookie cutters to suit the occasion. Place cookies ½-inch apart on a greased cookie sheet and bake on the middle oven rack for 12 minutes, or until the cookies just begin to brown. Decorate with colored sugars or frosting. These cookies freeze well. Yields 4 dozen cookies.

You can create a cookie flower arrangement, with various flower-shaped cookies, sticks baked in, decorated and secured in florist foam, and arranged in a flowerpot. It's a unique edible centerpiece!

Las Vegas Luau
Dinner Buffet

Guests were greeted with
King Kamehameha Cocktails

Pupu:
Several individual miniature hibachis were available
for guests to grill their own:
Polynesian Skewered Meats
with Hukilau Mustard, Thai Peanut Sauce, and Brandied Plum Sauce
Teriyaki Sirloin Strips
Glazed Baby Pork Ribs
Coconut Chicken

Big Island Buffet:
Charbroiled Fish with Ginger Glaze
Mushrooms Lelani
Sweet Potato Chips
Maui Treasure Bowl
Vegetable Wontons

Paradise Desserts:
Tropical Pineapple Tikis
Rum Broiled Pineapple
Glazed Pineapple Cookies
*Assorted Tropical Fruit

*Recipe not included

KING KAMEHAMEHA COCKTAIL

1	cup pineapple juice	1	cup white rum
1	cup orange juice	½	cup coconut milk
¼	cup triple sec	½	cup half and half
¾	cup dry gin	¾	cup brandy
		2	small bananas (optional)

Combine all ingredients in a blender and mix well. Chill until ready to serve. Yields 8 8-oz. servings.

We have served this out of cored pineapples, coconut shells or tall glasses, but always with a long straw and a gardenia or fruit garnish! It is a great way to start a Luau.

HUKILAU MUSTARD

7	oz. prepared honey mustard	1	tsp. sesame oil
4	T. teriyaki sauce	½	tsp. granulated garlic
½	tsp. ground ginger		

Combine all ingredients and mix until smooth. Yields approximately 1 cup.

This will keep in the refrigerator for up to 3 weeks. Use to baste the Glazed Baby Pork Ribs (recipe follows) and as an accompaniment with other Luau meats. Serve at room temperature.

THAI PEANUT SAUCE

½	cup onions	1	tsp. cayenne pepper
1	cup coconut milk	1	T. + 2 tsp. teriyaki sauce
½	cup smooth peanut butter	1	T. sesame paste
2	tsp. light brown sugar	2	T. fresh lime juice

Mix all the ingredients in a food processor until smooth. (Add more cayenne pepper if you like it really spicy!) Refrigerate. Serve with Luau meats. Yields approximately 2 cups.

BRANDIED PLUM SAUCE

2	T. peach chutney	¼	tsp. salt
¼	cup chili sauce	2	T. honey
¼	cup plum preserves	½	cup brown sugar
½	cup apricot preserves	½	cup cider vinegar
1	tsp. brandy	¼	tsp. granulated garlic

In a medium saucepan over medium-low heat, combine all ingredients and bring to a boil. Reduce heat and simmer for 10 minutes, stirring constantly. This can be make in advance and stored in the refrigerator. Serve at room temperature or heated. If sauce is too thick, add a small amount of club soda to thin. Yields 2½ cups.

TERIYAKI SIRLOIN STRIPS

3 lbs. top sirloin steak, cut 1½-inch thick
36 wooden skewers

Marinade:

½ cup soy sauce
4 T. brown sugar
1 T. honey
½ cup teriyaki sauce

1 garlic clove, minced
2 slices fresh ginger, minced
1 T. sesame oil

Combine all marinade ingredients and set aside.

Trim fat from the sirloin and freeze for approximately 30 minutes, for easier slicing. Remove meat from freezer and thinly slice across the grain. Weave the steak strips on the skewers and marinate for 3-4 hours, refrigerated. When ready to serve, remove the skewered meat from the marinade and arrange on a service platter. Locate the platter on the buffet near table-top hibachis, if available, to allow your guests the fun of grilling their own meats. If hibachis are not used, grill skewered meats 1½ minutes per side before serving.

GLAZED BABY PORK RIBS

1 cup soy sauce
⅓ cup club soda
2 T. sherry

1 slice fresh ginger root, minced
2 garlic cloves, minced
2 racks of baby pork ribs

The day before serving, combine the soy sauce, club soda, sherry, ginger root, and garlic. Pour over ribs and refrigerate for 24 hours, turning occasionally.

On the day of serving, preheat oven to 375 degrees. Place ribs in a heavy roasting pan. Pour marinade over ribs and bake, covered, for 1 hour. Then transfer to a hot grill. Cook until tender. Baste on both sides with Hukilau Mustard Sauce (previous recipe) during the final 10 minutes. Cut into individual pieces and serve with remaining Mustard Sauce.

Number of servings will vary, but keep in mind that even those guests watching their fat intake will eat at least four of these delicious ribs!

The ribs can be prepared ahead and refrigerated after oven baking. Return to room temperature before grilling.

COCONUT CHICKEN

6 4-oz. boneless, skinless
   chicken breasts
2 green onions, finely chopped
2 slices of fresh ginger root,
   finely chopped
3 T. rum
¼ cup soy sauce

1 tsp. sugar
2 cloves garlic, finely chopped
1½ T. sesame oil
1 cup coconut milk
Dash of hot pepper sauce
Wooden skewers for grilling

Cut chicken into strips approximately ½-inch wide and 2 to 2 ½ inches long.

Combine remaining ingredients in a glass bowl; add chicken strips. Marinate for 24 hours, turning several times.

Drain and reserve the marinade. Pat chicken dry. Weave chicken strips onto wooden skewers that have been soaked in water. Chicken can be refrigerated at this point, and grilled later. Boil reserved marinade for 10 minutes. Cool and refrigerate.

When ready to serve, cook on a hot grill or hibachi, basting with reserved marinade. The chicken will cook very quickly, so use caution not to overcook! Serve with Thai Peanut Sauce, Hukilau Mustard, and Brandied Plum Sauce (see previous recipes). Serves 6.

CHARBROILED FISH WITH GINGER GLAZE

1 cup chicken broth, reduced to half	1 T. ginger root, minced
1/3 cup light soy sauce	1 tsp. fresh garlic, minced
2 T. orange marmalade	¼ tsp. cayenne pepper
1 T. + 1 tsp. sugar	Salt and pepper to taste
4 tsp. molasses	2½ lbs. firm whitefish
1 T. + 1 tsp. lemon juice, freshly squeezed	Sherry

Combine reduced chicken broth, soy sauce, marmalade, sugar, molasses, lemon juice, ginger root, garlic, cayenne, salt and pepper in a saucepan and simmer for 15 minutes. Remove from heat and cool. Place fish in a glass dish and cover with marinade. Refrigerate for 4 hours, turning fish once.

Preheat grill. Remove fish, reserving the marinade. Grill fish, basting with sherry, until fish flakes easily. Meanwhile, make a glaze for the fish by simmering the reserved marinade for 10 minutes. Serves 6.

MUSHROOMS LELANI

1½ lbs. medium mushrooms, brushed clean and destemmed (reserve stems)	1 cup mozzarella cheese, shredded
	1 T. parsley, minced
	¼ tsp. ground ginger
½ cup green onions, finely chopped	½ tsp. granulated garlic
¼ cup mushroom stems, chopped	2 T. soy sauce
2 T. rum	1 tsp. sesame oil
6 oz. cooked shrimp, chopped	¼ cup water chestnuts, diced
1 cup cheddar cheese, shredded	Salt and pepper to taste

Mix together the green onions, mushroom stems, rum, shrimp, cheeses, parsley, ginger, garlic, soy sauce, sesame oil, water chestnuts, salt and pepper. Fill the mushrooms with mixture. Bake in a 375-degree oven for 10-12 minutes. Serves 6-8.

SWEET POTATO CHIPS

¼ cup ground cinnamon	2 lbs. sweet potatoes, peeled and sliced into ¼-inch thick pieces
3 cups granulated sugar	
1 tsp. ground ginger	
Oil for frying	Salt

Combine the cinnamon, sugar, and ginger. Heat oil and fry the sweet potatoes until lightly browned. Drain on paper towels. Sprinkle lightly with salt, then with the cinnamon/sugar/ginger mixture. Yields approximately 100 chips.

MAUI TREASURE BOWL

This wonderful array of marinated vegetables presents beautifully when served in a glass trifle bowl or salad bowl.

Marinade:
1   cup sour cream
1   cup mayonnaise
¼   cup white horseradish
2   tsp. dry mustard
2   tsp. fresh lemon juice
¼   tsp. salt
1/8 tsp. pepper
2   tsp. Worcestershire
½   tsp. soy sauce
3   garlic cloves, crushed
1   tsp. sesame oil
4   green onions, sliced

Salad:
2   cups broccoli flowerettes
2   cups cauliflower flowerettes
2   zucchini, sliced
2   yellow summer squash, sliced
1   pt. cherry tomatoes
1   6-oz. can pitted black olives
1   8-oz. can sliced water chestnuts, drained
8   oz. fresh button mushrooms
2   cups celery, julienned

Combine all the marinade ingredients in a large bowl. Set aside. Slightly steam the broccoli, cauliflower, zucchini, and squash. Chill.

Combine the cherry tomatoes, black olives, water chestnuts, mushrooms, and celery and toss in the marinade. (This can be done 24 hours prior to serving.) Just before serving, add the chilled broccoli, cauliflower, zucchini, and squash. Serve in a glass bowl. Serves 15.

VEGETABLE WONTONS

1   T. sesame oil
1   T. vegetable oil
1   cup coarsely grated carrots
1   T. soy sauce
3   garlic cloves, minced
1   T. ground ginger
6   green onions, finely chopped
1   cup mushrooms, chopped
2   cups shredded cabbage
2   cups thin noodles, cooked and drained
1   T. sugar
1   tsp. bean paste
½   cup cilantro, chopped
¼   cup mint leaves, chopped
Salt and pepper to taste
3   dashes of hot pepper sauce
1   egg, beaten
1   pkg. wonton skins
Vegetable oil for frying

Prepare the vegetable filling the day before making the wontons. Heat the oils in a sauté pan or wok. Add the carrots, soy, garlic, ginger, green onions, mushrooms, and cabbage. Cook over medium heat for several minutes. Remove from heat. Add the noodles, sugar, bean paste, cilantro, mint, salt, pepper, and hot pepper sauce. Cover and refrigerate overnight.

To make the Wontons: Remove 6 skins from the package and lay them out on wax paper. Cover remaining skins with a damp towel to prevent them from drying out. Place approximately 1 tsp. of filling in the middle of each skin. Brush the upper edges of the skin with the beaten egg. Fold in half, bring the edges together, forming a triangle. Press down the edges to seal. Bring the outer tips together, using the beaten egg to hold the seal. This forms the wonton shape. Repeat with remaining ingredients; cover finished wontons with a damp towel.

To fry Wontons: Heat about 2 inches of oil in a heavy skillet. Fry wontons for 2 to 2½ minutes per side. Drain on paper towel. Hold in a warm oven until serving. Can be frozen and reheated in a 400-degree oven for 10 to 15 minutes. Yields approximately 5 dozen Wontons.

TROPICAL PINEAPPLE TIKIS

1¼ cups orange juice	2 T. brandy
1¼ cups pineapple juice	1 T. rum flavoring
2 envelopes unflavored gelatin	3 cups crushed pineapple
½ cup sugar	Whipped cream for garnish (optional)
6 egg yolks	Wedges of fresh pineapple for
2 T. Galliano liqueur	garnish (optional)

Combine the orange juice, pineapple juice, gelatin, and sugar in a saucepan. Stir over medium-high heat until the gelatin dissolves and the mixture comes to a boil. Remove from heat.

In a separate bowl, beat the egg yolks on high for 5 minutes. Stir half of the gelatin mixture into the yolks, then return to the saucepan. Whisk constantly over medium-high heat until the sauce boils. Reduce heat and simmer for 5 minutes.

Remove from heat and allow to cool. Stir in the Galliano, brandy, rum flavoring, and crushed pineapple. Refrigerate for 2 hours, whisking every 30 minutes. When the mixture begins to thicken, pour into individual serving containers (we used crystal stemmed sherbet glasses). Refrigerate until firm.

Garnish with whipped cream or wedges of fresh pineapple. Serve with Glazed Pineapple Cookies (recipe follows). Yields 8 to 12 servings, depending on your choice of glass.

RUM BROILED PINEAPPLE

1 whole, ripe pineapple	¼ cup rum
1 cup dark brown sugar	¼ cup unsalted butter
	Chopped macadamia nuts

Prepare pineapple for grilling by removing frond, coring and slicing vertically, making each slice approximately ½-inch thick. Pat dry.

Combine the brown sugar, rum, and butter and spread the mixture over each pineapple slice. Broil until hot and bubbly. Sprinkle with chopped macadamia nuts. Can be served warm or at room temperature. Serves 6-8.

GLAZED PINEAPPLE COOKIES

Cookie:

½ cup butter, softened
½ cup granulated sugar
½ cup brown sugar, packed
1 egg, slightly beaten
1 cup crushed pineapple, drained
½ cup almonds, chopped

2 tsp. vanilla extract
2 tsp. rum flavoring
2 cups flour
½ tsp. baking soda
1 tsp. baking powder
¼ tsp. salt

Glaze:

½ tsp. rum extract
2 cups powdered sugar

4 T. pineapple juice

Cream butter and sugars until light and fluffy. Add egg, pineapple, almonds, vanilla and rum flavoring, mixing well. Combine the dry ingredients and add to mixture.

Combine the glaze ingredients and set aside.

Preheat oven to 325 degrees. Drop 1 tsp. of batter on a cookie sheet sprayed with cooking spray, and bake in the upper half of the oven approximately 12 minutes, or until the cookie edges begin to brown. While warm, spoon the glaze on the cookies and transfer to a wire rack to cool. These cookies can be frozen. Yields 48 cookies.

A Spring Trip to Fall Creek Vineyards

The guests were transported to Tow, Texas, by bus,
and each was presented with a woven grapevine basket filled with:

Liver Paté glazed with Jalapeño Jelly
Texas Goat Cheese with Poblano Pepper Wafers
*Seedless Grapes
Parmesan Pretzels
Sugared Texas Pecans and assorted nuts (the caterers!)
Packets of Texas bluebonnet seeds

After a tour of the winery and a wine tasting,
the guests were served a seated dinner, featuring Fall Creek Wines

*Assorted field greens salad
tossed with Hill Country Vinaigrette Dressing and
garnished with edible flowers

Shrimp Butter on toasted French bread
Wine: Fall Creek Vineyards Chardonnay

Spring Chicken with asparagus
Wine: Fall Creek Vineyards Sauvignon Blanc

Beef Tenderloin stuffed with Tomato Cilantro Paste
Wine: Fall Creek Vineyards Cabernet Sauvignon

Potato Waffles
Minted Julienne Carrots
*Dinner Rolls and Butter

Joey's Sour Cream Apple Pie
Wine: Fall Creek Vineyards Sweet Johannisberg Riesling

*Recipe not included

LIVER PATÉ WITH JALAPEÑO JELLY

¼ cup olive oil
4 shallots, minced
1½ lbs. chicken livers,
  washed and trimmed
2 garlic cloves, minced
¼ tsp. cayenne pepper
½ tsp. black pepper
¼ tsp. nutmeg
¼ tsp. mace

8 oz. fresh mushrooms, sliced
2 T. butter
2 T. brandy
8 oz. cream cheese
2 T. fresh parsley, chopped
1 tsp. salt
1 tsp. basil
1 jar jalapeño jelly

Heat olive oil in a medium skillet over medium-low heat. Add shallots and chicken livers and sauté until livers are completely browned. Stir in garlic, cayenne, black pepper, nutmeg, and mace. Remove from pan and cool. In the same skillet, sauté the mushrooms in butter and brandy. Set aside. In a large mixing bowl, combine cream cheese, parsley, salt, and basil. Reserve. Combine chicken liver mixture and mushrooms in a food processor then add to cream cheese mixture, mixing well.

Line a small bread loaf pan with plastic wrap. Fill with liver paté, spreading evenly. Cover with plastic wrap and refrigerate for at least 24 hours before serving. To remove, invert loaf pan onto a serving platter. Melt jalapeño jelly in a saucepan over medium heat and spoon over paté. Serve with your favorite cracker or cocktail rye bread. Serves 12-15 as an hors d'oeuvres.

POBLANO PEPPER WAFERS

½ cup unsalted butter, softened
¼ cup sugar
1 poblano pepper, seeded and
  chopped
4 sun-dried tomatoes, chopped
Whites of 2 large eggs, at room
  temperature

½ tsp. salt
¼ tsp. pepper
½ cup flour
¼ cup Parmesan cheese
¼ cup pecans, chopped
Pesto Sauce (recipe follows)
Parmesan cheese for garnish
Texas Goat Cheese

Cream butter and sugar until light and fluffy. Add poblano pepper, sun-dried tomatoes, egg whites, salt, pepper, flour, Parmesan cheese, and pecans and mix, blending well. Form dough into a ball; wrap with plastic wrap and refrigerate overnight.

Preheat oven to 400 degrees. Place quarter-size balls of dough on a greased baking sheet and press a thumbprint into the middle of each ball, flattening slightly. Fill indentation with Pesto Sauce. Bake for 8 to 10 minutes, on the middle rack. Do not brown. Sprinkle baked wafers with Parmesan cheese and cool on wire racks. Yields 12 wafers. Serve with your favorite goat cheese.

Poblano Pepper Pesto Sauce:

1   garlic clove
1   cup fresh basil leaves, washed and torn
1   cup cilantro leaves, washed and torn
¾   cup Parmesan cheese
½   cup pine nuts, toasted
2   poblano peppers, seeded and sliced, or to taste
⅓   cup olive oil
Salt and pepper, to taste

Combine garlic, basil, cilantro, Parmesan cheese, pine nuts, and poblano pepper in a food processor until blended. With the food processor running, slowly add the olive oil in a steady stream until the mixture is well mixed. Salt and pepper as desired. This Pesto Sauce will keep, refrigerated, for 5 days. Use for Poblano Pesto Wafers. Yields approximately 1½ cups.

PARMESAN PRETZELS

1   box large, salted pretzels
1   cup Parmesan cheese
2   T. granulated garlic
1   tsp. oregano

½   tsp. cayenne pepper
6   T. butter
¼   cup olive oil

Combine the Parmesan cheese, garlic, oregano, and cayenne pepper. Melt the butter with the oil. Dip one side of each pretzel in the butter/oil mixture, then dip in Parmesan mixture. Repeat, until all ingredients are used.

Place on a large cookie sheet. Bake at 275 degrees for 20 to 25 minutes. Allow to cool. These wonderful pretzels store well in a tightly covered container. Serves 10.

SUGARED TEXAS PECANS

1½ cups blanched almonds
1   cup walnut pieces
1   cup pecan halves
2   egg whites
1   cup sugar
½   tsp. salt

¼   tsp. nutmeg
1   tsp. cinnamon
1   tsp. chili powder
1/8 tsp. curry powder

½   cup butter

Combine the nuts and bake in a 325-degree oven, stirring twice, until lightly browned. This takes about 20 minutes.

Beat the egg whites until they form stiff peaks. Gradually add the sugar and seasonings, beating constantly. Toss in the toasted nuts, taking care that all the nuts are evenly coated.

Melt the butter in a heavy-bottomed jellyroll pan; add coated nuts and spread out evenly over the pan. Bake at 325 degrees in the upper 1/3 of the oven, for approximately 30 to 40 minutes, stirring every 10 minutes. Turn out onto wax paper to cool. Yields 4 cups.

HILL COUNTRY VINAIGRETTE

1 cup olive oil	½ cup balsamic vinegar
1 cup vegetable oil	½ cup garlic vinegar
1 cup Romano cheese, grated	1 cup sour cream
½ cup Parmesan cheese, grated	1 tsp. sugar
6 garlic cloves	1½ tsp. salt
1½ tsp. dry mustard	Dash of pepper
1 cup mayonnaise	

Combine all ingredients in a food processor and mix well. This can be prepared several days in advance. Yields approximately 5 cups.

SHRIMP BUTTER

This recipe was contributed by Susan Auler, co-owner of Fall Creek Vineyards. Susan suggests that Fall Creek Vineyard Chardonnay is a perfect wine match for salad, accompanied by Shrimp Butter.

2 T. butter	1 T. tomato paste
½ lb. medium shrimp, shelled and chopped	2 tsp. lemon juice
	1 tsp. fresh basil, minced
1 tsp. garlic, minced	Salt and pepper, to taste
3 T. butter, softened	French Bread

Sauté shrimp in 2 T. butter until the shrimp turn pink. Transfer contents of the sauté pan to a food processor and add remaining ingredients, blending until smooth. Chill and serve on toasted French bread rounds, with salad.

SPRING CHICKEN WITH ASPARAGUS

6 oz. mozzarella cheese, shredded	1 red bell pepper, cut into thin strips
1 green bell pepper, seeded and finely chopped	18 fresh asparagus spears, trimmed, blanched, and seasoned with lemon butter
½ cup green onions, chopped	
6 5-oz. boneless, skinless chicken breasts, pounded thin and seasoned with salt, pepper, and garlic powder	4 T. butter
	1 T. olive oil
	3 shallots, chopped

Combine cheese, green peppers, and green onions and mix well. Place a heaping teaspoon of the cheese mixture in the middle of each seasoned breast. Add 2 strips of red bell pepper and 2 to 3 asparagus spears on top of the cheese. Roll the chicken tightly, making sure that the tips of the asparagus peek out one end. Secure with a toothpick.

Heat the butter, oil, and shallots in a skillet. Brown the chicken on each side and place in a greased baking pan. Bake in a 350-degree oven for 20 to 25 minutes, or until cooked through. Serve with Spring Chicken Glaze (recipe follows). The chicken can be prepared and assembled the day before serving and refrigerated. Serves 6.

Spring Chicken Glaze:

4   shallots, finely chopped
1   garlic clove, finely chopped
1/3 cup olive oil
1/3 cup white wine
1½ cups chicken broth

¼   cup fresh parsley, chopped
2   T. carrots, finely chopped
½   cup sour cream
Salt and pepper to taste

Sauté the shallots and garlic in olive oil until soft. Add the wine and broth; simmer for 5 minutes. Remove from heat and add parsley, carrots, and sour cream. Whisk until sauce is smooth. Add salt and pepper to taste.

BEEF TENDERLOIN STUFFED WITH TOMATO CILANTRO PASTE

Susan and Ed Auler, co-owners of Fall Creek Vineyards, contributed this recipe, and suggest either Fall Creek Vineyards Cabernet Merlot or Cabernet Sauvignon as a wine match for this delectable beef tenderloin.

½   cup olive oil
2   T. balsamic vinegar
3½ to 4 lbs. beef tenderloin, free of
    fat and sinew, at room temperature

Salt and pepper, to taste
Tomato Cilantro Paste (recipe
    follows)

Whisk oil and vinegar together and pour over tenderloin. Marinate for 1-2 hours.
   Pour off marinade and cut a deep slit in the center, down the length of the tenderloin. Preheat oven to 400 degrees and season the meat with salt and pepper. Stuff the slit with Tomato Cilantro Paste. Roast tenderloin, uncovered, on a rack in a roasting pan for approximately 35 minutes for medium rare. Serves 8.

Tomato Cilantro Paste:

1   T. unsalted butter
3   tsp. garlic, minced
6   T. tomato paste

4   T. chicken broth
¼   tsp. salt
4   T. cilantro, minced

Sauté garlic in butter. Add tomato paste, broth and salt and cook, stirring frequently, until sauce thickens. Remove from the heat and stir in cilantro.

POTATO WAFFLES

2/3 cup flour
4   tsp. baking powder
2   tsp. salt
1   tsp. white pepper
1   tsp. sugar
1   tsp. dill
4   large eggs

½   cup oil
½   cup onions, chopped
2   T. lemon juice
Pinch of nutmeg
3   lbs. baking potatoes, shredded
    and squeezed dry

Preheat waffle maker according to manufacturer's directions and grease the grids. Combine dry ingredients except nutmeg in a large mixing bowl. Add eggs, oil, onions, lemon juice, and nutmeg; mix well. Add squeeze-dried potatoes. Spread 1 cup of batter per waffle evenly over the grids and cook for approximately 10 minutes. These waffles freeze very well. Reheat in toaster. Yields 5 potato waffles, or 10 servings.

MINTED JULIENNE CARROTS

2¼ cups sugar
2¼ cups raspberry vinaigrette
¼ cup fresh mint, chopped

2 lbs. carrots, peeled and julienned
Whole mint leaves for garnish

Combine sugar, raspberry vinaigrette, and fresh mint and stir until the sugar is completely dissolved.

Blanch the carrots; drain and immediately add the mint vinaigrette. Refrigerate for 24 hours before serving. Drain the carrots before serving and garnish with whole mint leaves. Serves 8.

JOEY'S SOUR CREAM APPLE PIE

Pie filling:
1 cup sour cream
¾ cup sugar (more, if apples are very tart)
2 T. flour
1 egg, beaten
½ tsp. vanilla
½ tsp. rum extract
¼ tsp. salt
2 cups Granny Smith apples, sliced
1 pie shell, prebaked

Streusel topping:
2 T. butter
4 T. flour
4 T. sugar
Pinch of cinnamon
Pinch of nutmeg

Preheat oven to 350 degrees. Mix the sour cream, sugar, flour, egg, vanilla, rum extract and salt together in a mixing bowl. Fold in sliced apples. Pour into prebaked pieshell and bake for 25 minutes.

For streusel topping: Combine all streusel ingredients and mix until crumbly.

Remove pie from oven and cover with topping. Return to oven for 25 minutes. Cool before serving. Yields 8 generous servings.

Chapter 12

The Russians Are Coming!

ecause of our location in Austin, the capital of Texas, we have been fortunate to find ourselves at the center of "big events." The city is not only the state's administrative headquarters, but also home to one of the United States' largest universities, The University of Texas.

Many of the events we've planned have been for visiting scholars and philanthropists. One of our most memorable weeks was the arrival of more than 100 Russian and American delegates to the prestigious Kettering Foundation's Dartmouth Conference, an unofficial, bilateral, ongoing exchange between the Russians and Americans. Because of the delicate issues discussed at the conference and the high-level profile of its civilian delegates, the location of the conference was never publicized in advance and the security measures were even more intense than the usual Secret Service precautions.

We wined and dined these impressive guests for days, surprising them with things new and different in addition to serving some of their favorite native Russian dishes, and making lasting friendships along the way. The Russian visitors were a boisterous, demonstrative bunch when they weren't discussing bilateral communication. Their warmth was par-ticularly apparent at the LBJ Ranch party, lending a campy atmosphere filled with laughter and song. The Russian guests were, in a word, fun! They enthusiastically embraced the Texas atmosphere at the ranch, experiencing for the first time meals off a chuckwagon, Tex-Mex treats, bandannas, and ten-gallon hats.

The simplest things seemed to please these visitors the most, like the fresh bananas we set out as part of a cascading fruit centerpiece for the formal dinner party, our first evening together. So thrilled were the Soviet power brokers by the ripe yellow fruit, not readily available in their home country, that the centerpiece ended up as dessert, and from that first taste forward through the duration of their stay, we served bunches of bananas at every meal.

We never expected this academic contingent to become like family, though by the end of their stay we had grown accustomed to the sound of the men's guitars playing native Russian folk songs, and the bear hugs and kisses that were their trademark.

The menus in this chapter (sadly lacking in bananas) feature recipes that are Tex-Mex, Russian, and some of our signature personal specialties. In honor of one of our all-time favorite weeks of catering, this chapter is dedicated "To Russia With Love" from us.

A Texas Welcome

Cocktail buffet to welcome participants of the Kettering Foundation Dartmouth Conference at Bauer House, The University of Texas

Zakooska — Appetizer Table:
*Smoked Salmon and Absolut Vodka
Herring in Mustard Sauce
*Fresh Gulf Shrimp

Entrees:
Stuffed Pork Tenderloin
Grilled Lamb Rib Chops
Marvelous Meatballs
Ravioli with Marinara Sauce

Desserts:
*Huge Stemmed Strawberries
*Ice Cream
with Blackberry Ambrosia
Vatrushki (Cottage Cheese Tartlettes)

*Recipe not included

ZAKOOSKA SEL YODKA I GARCHICHJ SOUS
Salt Herring in Mustard Sauce

24	oz. herring filets in wine sauce	2	tsp. Dijon mustard
2	cups sour cream	3	T. sugar
1	green apple, peeled, cored and chopped	1	tsp. black peppercorns
		1	T. dry mustard

Lemon to taste

Drain the herring, reserving the liquid. Cut the herring filets into bite-sized pieces. Combine the remaining ingredients; add the herring and the reserved liquid. Chill for at least 24 hours. Serve with cocktail rye bread. Serves 24 as an hors d'oeuvres.

STUFFED PORK TENDERLOIN
with Apple Sausage and Calvados Sauce

2   T. olive oil, divided
12 oz. chicken apple sausage,
    no casing   (available at
    specialty markets)
1   T. breadcrumbs
½   egg, slightly beaten

2   12-oz. pork tenderloins, silver
    skin removed
Salt
White pepper
Granulated garlic

Heat 1 T. olive oil in sauté pan. Cook sausage until done, stirring constantly. Remove from heat and let cool. Pulse mixture in a food processor until finely chopped. Mix in breadcrumbs and egg. Set aside.

Cut pork tenderloins in half, at an angle. Cut a slit into the center of each piece. Stuff with sausage mixture until completely filled and pork is firm. Fold edges over opening and secure with long toothpicks.

Preheat oven to 350 degrees. Season pork with salt, white pepper, and granulated garlic. Heat 1 T. olive oil in sauté pan. Sear pork pieces until brown on all sides. Place meat on roasting rack and bake for 15-20 minutes, or until done. Prepare sauce while pork is in oven.

Calvados Sauce:

1   T. butter, clarified
2   T. shallots, chopped
1   cup Calvados apple liqueur

1   tsp. sugar
1   cup heavy cream
Salt and white pepper

In a saucepan heat butter and shallots until translucent. Add liqueur and reduce by half. Add sugar and cream and whisk until reduced to sauce consistency. Season with salt and white pepper. Serves 4.

GRILLED LAMB RIB CHOPS
with Artichoke Heart Glaze

12 rib lamb chops
Black pepper, finely ground

6   garlic cloves, minced
Worcestershire

Trim fat from lamb chops, sprinkle with black pepper and Worcestershire and press minced garlic into the meat. Cover and refrigerate for 12 hours.

Preheat grill to medium-high. Grill lamb chops 4 minutes per side for medium-rare. Serve hot with Artichoke Heart Glaze (recipe follows). (The lamb chops can also be broiled or sautéed.) Serves 4.

Artichoke Heart Glaze:

4   garlic cloves, minced
6   green onions, sliced
2   tsp. olive oil
2   tsp. unsalted butter
4   tsp. flour

2   14½ oz. cans beef broth
2/3 cup burgundy
36 artichoke hearts, drained, halved
Freshly squeezed lemon juice, to taste
Salt and pepper, to taste

Sauté garlic and onions in olive oil and butter until soft. Add flour and cook until lightly brown. Add beef broth and burgundy, stirring until sauce thickens; add the artichoke hearts, lemon juice, salt and pepper. Serve hot with Grilled Lamb Chops.

MARVELOUS MEATBALLS

1   lb. finely ground sirloin
2   8-oz. cans water chestnuts, drained and chopped
1   bunch green onions, finely chopped
3   T. soy sauce
1   tsp. salt

½   tsp. pepper
½   cup fine breadcrumbs
1   tsp. ground ginger
1   T. granulated garlic
1   T. Worcestershire
Cornstarch
Oil

In a large bowl, combine the ground sirloin, water chestnuts, green onions, soy sauce, salt, pepper, breadcrumbs, ginger, garlic and Worcestershire. Chill for 1 hour. Roll the meat mixture into 1½-inch balls and roll each ball in cornstarch, coating completely.

Using a heavy skillet, heat 1 inch of oil to medium-high temperature. Fry the meatballs, a few at a time, turning until well browned. Drain on paper towel. (The meatballs can be frozen at this point.) Toss the meatballs in the Marvelous Meatball Glaze (recipe follows) and serve in a water-based chafing dish. Yields 50 1½-inch meatballs.

Marvelous Meatball Glaze:

2   T. butter
1   cup + ½ cup chicken broth
¼   cup white vinegar
¾   cup pineapple juice
½   cup granulated sugar
½   tsp. salt
1   T. ground ginger
1   T. sesame oil
½   tsp. white pepper
2   tsp. granulated garlic

4   dashes of hot pepper sauce
½   cup plum preserves
½   cup ketchup
¼   cup white wine
2   T. cornstarch
¼   cup soy sauce
1   20-oz. can pineapple chunks, drained
1   green pepper, seeded, cut into chunks

In a medium saucepan, bring the butter and 1 cup chicken broth to a boil. Add the vinegar, pineapple juice, sugar, salt, ginger, sesame oil, white pepper, garlic, hot pepper sauce, plum preserves, ketchup, and white wine. Remove from heat and set aside.

In a separate bowl, combine the cornstarch, ½ cup chicken broth, and soy sauce.

Return the glaze sauce to the heat. To thicken the sauce add the cornstarch mixture and simmer for 5 minutes. Pour over the meatballs; garnish with pineapple chunks and green pepper chunks. Yields 4 cups.

RAVIOLI WITH MARINARA SAUCE

2 T. olive oil	2 T. sugar
2 T. vegetable oil	Pinch red pepper flakes
½ cup onions, chopped	1 T. salt
2 tsp. fresh garlic, chopped	2 tsp. black pepper
1 12-oz. can tomato paste	2 14½-oz. cans crushed tomatoes
¼ cup carrots, finely chopped	1 16-oz. can tomato sauce
1 lbs. mushrooms, sliced	2 cups water
2 T. fresh parsley, chopped	1 cup red wine
3 T. oregano	
3 T. basil	

In a large stockpot, heat oils and sauté onions and garlic until soft. Add tomato paste and cook for 10 minutes. Add carrots and mushrooms and cook for an additional 10 minutes. Add parsley, oregano, basil, sugar, red pepper, salt, black pepper, crushed tomatoes, tomato sauce, and water and simmer for 1 hour. Check consistency after 30 minutes, adding more water if sauce is too thick. Add red wine for the final 15 minutes. Freezes well. Yields 5 cups.

Ravioli:

Fresh ravioli is available in a variety of flavors in most grocery stores. We offer at least three flavors, allowing 10 ravioli per person (3 oz.). Serve with Marinara Sauce (recipe above).

BLACKBERRY AMBROSIA

1 tsp. cinnamon	¼ cup raspberry liqueur
6 T. sugar	¼ cup dark rum
¼ cup fresh lime juice	1 lb. frozen blackberries
¼ cup bitters	

In a medium saucepan, heat the cinnamon, sugar, lime juice, and bitters over medium heat. Add the liqueur, rum, and frozen berries. Heat thoroughly. Serve, either hot or cold, over your favorite ice cream.

VATRUSHKI
Cottage Cheese Tartlettes

Dough:

2 cups flour	8 T. butter, softened
2 T. sugar	2 egg yolks
½ tsp. salt	¾ cup sour cream

Mix all ingredients together in a food processor until the dough pulls away from the edges of the bowl. Press dough into ungreased miniature tart pans. Set aside.

Filling:

1½ lbs. small curd cottage cheese, well-drained	6 T. sugar
	6 T. sour cream
3 egg yolks	2 tsp. vanilla extract
¼ tsp. salt	6 T. raisins

Mix all filling ingredients together and fill tart dough with mixture. Preheat oven to 375 degrees.

1 egg yolk	1 T. cold water

Beat egg yolk and water and brush tops of the tartlets with egg mixture. Bake approximately 25 minutes. Cool on wire racks.

Chuck Wagon Barbecue Buffet at the LBJ State Park in Stonewall, Texas

*Grilled Texas Hot Sausage

Spinach Queso
with tortilla chips

Sour Mash Barbecued Brisket
with miniature potato rolls

Texas Grilled Chicken

Catfish Burritos
with Tomato Dill Salsa and Avocado Mayonnaise

Trio Mustard Potato Salad

*Condiments:
Jalapeño peppers, pickles, olives and sliced white onions

*Homemade white bread and whipped butter

Strawberry Shortcake Bar

*Recipe not included

SPINACH QUESO

2	T. oil		8	oz. cream cheese
1	4-oz. can green chiles		2	cups grated Monterey jack cheese
2	jalapeños, seeded and chopped		1¼	cups half and half
1	cup onions, chopped		½	tsp. granulated garlic
3	garlic cloves, chopped		¼	tsp. cumin
1	14½-oz. can chopped tomatoes with garlic		1	T. taco seasoning
1	10-oz. pkg. frozen chopped spinach, defrosted and squeezed dry		2	dashes hot pepper sauce
			1	tsp. salt
1	T. red wine vinegar		½	tsp. black pepper

Heat the oil in a large saucepan and sauté the green chiles, jalapeños, onion, and garlic until soft. Remove from the heat; add remaining ingredients and mix well. Return to medium heat and cook for 20 to 25 minutes, or until hot and bubbly. Serve with tortilla chips. Yields 4 cups.

SOUR MASH BARBECUED BRISKET

1   **cup vegetable oil**
1   **cup sour mash bourbon**
1   **cup beer**
4   **T. black pepper, freshly ground**
2   **T. garlic powder**
2   **bay leaves**
1   **tsp. dry mustard**
1   **tsp. minced basil**
Liquid smoke (optional)
1   **large beef brisket, trimmed (approximately 6 lbs.)**

Combine oil, bourbon, beer, pepper, garlic powder, bay leaves, dry mustard, basil, and liquid smoke. Pour marinade over the brisket; cover with plastic wrap and refrigerate for 24 hours, turning meat twice.

Preheat oven to 250 degrees. Cook brisket in the marinade, covered, for 8 hours. Remove meat from marinade and grill, basting frequently, for 1 to 2 hours, or until the brisket is tender. Allow the meat to rest 20 minutes before slicing across the grain. Serve with Sour Mash Barbecue Sauce (recipe follows) and all the "fixin's."

SOUR MASH BARBECUE SAUCE

1	**1-lb. bottle ketchup**	1	**tsp. red pepper flakes, or to taste**
¼	**lb. butter**	1	**tsp. ground cinnamon**
2/3	**cup sugar**	1	**tsp. ground allspice**
2/3	**cup white vinegar**	1	**tsp. celery salt**
¾	**cup Worcestershire**	1	**T. lemon juice**
1	**cup strong brewed coffee**	1	**tsp. black pepper**
6	**garlic cloves, minced**	1	**tsp. mace**
3	**T. chili powder**	½	**cup sour mash bourbon**
1	**tsp. salt**		

Combine all ingredients and bring to a boil for 5 minutes. Reduce heat to low and simmer, covered, for 1 hour; add water, if necessary, for desired consistency. Best when made 5 days ahead and refrigerated, allowing the flavors to "marry." Yields approximately 6 cups.

TEXAS GRILLED CHICKEN

Marinade:

1   14½-oz. can chicken broth
3¼ cups dry white wine
¾   cup white wine vinegar
1/3 cup lemon juice
13 garlic cloves, minced

2   bay leaves
2/3 cup vegetable oil
2   T. chili powder
1   tsp. black pepper
Pinch of salt
Hot pepper sauce, to taste

6   lbs. chicken, cut-up
Salt and pepper, to taste
1   cup barbecue sauce, your favorite

Combine all marinade ingredients. Reserve 3 cups. Pour the remaining marinade over chicken and refrigerate, covered, for 6 to 8 hours, turning chicken twice.

Combine the reserved marinade and barbecue sauce in a saucepan and bring to a boil. Set aside to use as a sauce for the chicken.

Preheat grill to medium-high. Remove chicken from the marinade, pat dry, season with salt and pepper and grill, basting frequently with marinade, until thoroughly cooked. Serve immediately with warmed sauce. Serves 4 to 6.

CATFISH BURRITOS
with Tomato Dill Salsa and Avocado Mayonnaise

This recipe was contributed by Susan Auler, co-owner of Fall Creek Vineyards, Tow, Texas. Susan recommends serving Fall Creek Vineyards Sauvignon Blanc as the perfect accompaniment to this unique catfish preparation.

8   catfish filets
Salt and pepper, to taste

8   flour tortillas
Garlic chives, minced, for garnish

Marinade:

1   T. brown sugar
2/3 cup canola oil

1   T. red wine vinegar
1   tsp. balsamic vinegar

Combine marinade ingredients and marinate catfish filets 30 minutes to 1 hour. Season catfish with salt and pepper and grill. Wrap in flour tortillas and pan sauté in butter or oil until crisp. Serve with Tomato Dill Salsa and Avocado Mayonnaise (recipes follow). Sprinkle with chives before serving. Serves 8.

Tomato Dill Salsa:

1   tsp. garlic, minced
1   large tomato, minced
2   tomatillos, minced
1   T. green onions, minced

1   T. fresh dill, minced
2   T. extra virgin olive oil
2   tsp. balsamic vinegar
2   jalapeño peppers, seeded and
    finely minced

Combine all salsa ingredients and chill before serving.

Avocado Mayonnaise:

1	ripe avocado	1	T. garlic, minced
1	T. lime juice	1	tsp. Dijon mustard
½	tsp. salt	2	egg yolks + 1 egg
2	T. balsamic vinegar	1	cup safflower oil
2	T. fresh basil, minced		

Purée avocado, lime juice, and salt in a food processor. In a saucepan, simmer vinegar, basil and garlic until the liquid is reduced to one-half. Transfer contents of saucepan to a blender and add mustard, egg yolks, and egg. Blend on high until mixture is smooth. With motor running, add safflower oil slowly while the mixture continues to thicken. Add avocado mixture and blend. Serve warm or cold with Catfish Burritos.

TRIO MUSTARD POTATO SALAD

½	cup mayonnaise	1	tsp. celery salt
¼	cup yellow mustard	1	4½-oz. can black olives,
¼	cup Dijon mustard		sliced (optional)
1/3	cup smoked mustard	4	lbs. potatoes, boiled, peeled,
¼	cup dill pickle, chopped		cut into bite-size pieces
¾	cup onion, chopped	3	eggs, hard-cooked and sliced
1	cup celery, chopped		Salt and pepper, to taste

Combine mayonnaise, mustards, pickles, onion, celery, and celery salt in a large bowl. Fold in black olives, potatoes, eggs, and salt and pepper. Serve chilled. Serves 6.

FRUIT SHORTCAKE

Shortcake:

2¼	cups flour	¼	cup buttermilk
1/3	cup sugar	1	T. vegetable oil
1½	tsp. baking powder	1	tsp. vanilla extract
¾	tsp. baking soda	¼	tsp. almond extract
¼	tsp. salt	1	T. skimmed milk
2	T. cold, unsalted butter, diced	¼	to ½ cup chopped almonds
		1	T. sugar

Preheat oven to 375 degrees and spray a cookie sheet with baking spray.

In a medium bowl, stir together the flour, sugar, baking powder, baking soda, and salt. Cut the butter into the flour mixture until crumbly. In a separate bowl, combine buttermilk, oil, vanilla and almond extracts. Make a well in the flour mixture and pour in buttermilk mixture. Stir until dough is only slightly sticky. Do not overmix.

On a floured surface, pat out the dough to 1-inch thickness. Using a biscuit cutter, cut out 2½ to 3-inch circles and place on cookie sheet. Brush shortcakes with milk and sprinkle with chopped almonds and sugar. Bake for 10 to 15 minutes or until golden. Remove from cookie sheet and allow to cool on racks.

Fruit filling:

1 pt. fresh strawberries, hulled, washed and halved	1/3 cup granulated sugar
	1 pt. whipping cream
1 pt. fresh raspberries, washed	¼ cup rum
2 ripe peaches, peeled and sliced	

Toss the prepared fruit in the sugar. Whip the cream slowly until it forms soft peaks. Add the rum.

Split shortcakes in half. Spoon fruit and whipped cream into the bottom half; top with shortcake lids. Garnish with fruit and whipped cream. Serves 8.

Hillside Box Lunch
on Texas-shaped trays

Doozie Sandwiches
Black Bean and Cabbage Salad
Gazpacho
Black-eyed Susan Deviled Eggs
Texas Turtles

DOOZIE SANDWICHES

The Doozie Sandwich is wonderful either as a main course, as in this box lunch, or cut smaller for hors d'oeuvres. Prepare the triple-decker sandwiches early in the day, wrap in damp paper towels, and seal tightly with foil or plastic wrap to maintain freshness.

Herbed Mayonnaise:

1	cup mayonnaise	1	tsp. Worcestershire
2	tsp. fine herbs	½	tsp. garlic powder
			Several dashes of hot pepper sauce

Combine all ingredients and mix well. Refrigerate.

Honey Mustard Sauce:

3	T. cider vinegar	1	T. onion, chopped
3	T. honey	1½	T. fresh parsley, chopped
6	T. Dijon mustard		Salt and pepper, to taste

Heat vinegar and honey on low heat, stirring until the honey dissolves. Set aside to cool. Whisk in remaining ingredients. Refrigerate.

Horseradish Sauce:

½	cup sour cream	2	T. fresh horseradish
½	cup mayonnaise	2	tsp. garlic powder
1	cup Parmesan cheese	2	tsp. Worcestershire
			Dash of hot pepper sauce

Combine all ingredients and mix well. Refrigerate.

Assembly:

1 (½ lb.) loaf bread, thin-sliced horizontally	1 lb. roasted turkey breast, thinly sliced
1 lb. Swiss cheese, thinly sliced	1 lb. cooked roast beef, thinly sliced
1 lb. smoked ham, thinly sliced	1 lb. Cheddar cheese, thinly sliced

Our baker makes marbled rye bread, using light rye and dark rye swirled together. It provides a unique appearance as well as a wonderfully delicious taste. He then slices the loaves horizontally, allowing us to build one large sandwich, which we later slice into portion sizes, depending on whether we want main course sandwiches or cocktail-sized hors d'oeuvres. If marbled bread is not available to you, alternate two different types of bread.

Place one horizontally sliced piece of bread on a work surface and layer the ingredients as follows:
Spread with Honey Mustard Sauce
Swiss cheese
Ham
Spread Honey Mustard Sauce
Bread
Spread Herbed Mayonnaise
Turkey
Spread Herbed Mayonnaise
Bread
Spread Horseradish Sauce
Roast beef
Cheddar cheese
Spread Horseradish Sauce
Final piece of bread

Score the top of the sandwich with the appropriately sized portions and cut with a sharp, serrated knife. Secure the layers with a decorative frilled toothpick. Serves 4 for lunch, or 8 for cocktails.

BLACK BEAN AND CABBAGE SALAD

½ cup sesame oil	2 16-oz. cans black beans, drained and rinsed
¾ cup vegetable oil	2 15-oz. cans kernel corn, drained and rinsed
3 tsp. granulated garlic	1 cup celery, chopped
½ tsp. salt	1 cup green onions, chopped
2 tsp. sugar	Salt and pepper
½ tsp. black pepper	3 cups fresh green cabbage, shredded, packed
½ cup white wine vinegar	
¼ tsp. ginger	
¾ tsp. cumin	
½ cup red onions, chopped	

Combine all ingredients, except the cabbage. Add cabbage and mix well. Refrigerate for 6 hours. This salad will hold for 3 days. Serves 10.

GAZPACHO

4 cups ripe tomatoes, chopped (about 4 tomatoes)
1 large cucumber, peeled, seeded and diced
½ cup red onion, chopped
2 garlic cloves, minced
¼ cup watercress, chopped
1 medium green pepper, chopped
½ cup scallions, chopped

1 T. fresh basil, chopped
3 T. olive oil
2 T. red wine vinegar
2 cups cold tomato juice
1 tsp. salt
¼ tsp. cumin
3 to 4 drops hot pepper sauce
1 T. honey
Dash of cayenne pepper
Fresh ground black pepper, to taste

Put tomatoes, cucumber, onion, garlic, watercress, green pepper, scallions, and basil into a large bowl and mix well. Purée half of the mixture in a blender or food processor. Return to the bowl and mix thoroughly. Whisk in olive oil, vinegar, tomato juice and remaining ingredients. Chill for several hours. Serve cold. Serves 6.

BLACK-EYED SUSAN DEVILED EGGS

1 dozen large eggs, hard-cooked, peeled
½ cup fine breadcrumbs
2 T. green onions, finely chopped
¼ cup sour cream

1 T. Dijon mustard
Salt and pepper, to taste
2 2-oz. jars black caviar, drained
2 2-oz. jars red caviar, drained

Cut the eggs in half and remove the yolks. Reserve the whites.

In a bowl, mix the yolks, breadcrumbs, green onions, sour cream, Dijon mustard, salt and pepper. Fill the egg whites with yolk mixture. Make a small indentation in the yolk mixture using the back of a melon baller. Cover tightly and refrigerate.

When ready to serve, fill the indentations with black and/or red caviar. Place eggs on a serving platter, garnished with large, fresh flowers. Yields 24 deviled eggs.

Alternative:

1 dozen eggs, hard-cooked, peeled
½ cup fine breadcrumbs
¼ cup sour cream
2 T. fresh parsley, chopped

1 T. capers
1 tsp. lemon juice
½ tsp. anchovy paste
Salt and pepper, to taste

Follow instructions as above.

TEXAS TURTLES

Crust:
½ cup powdered sugar
½ cup butter or margarine, softened
1 T. whipping cream
1 cup all-purpose flour

Filling:
24 vanilla caramels
1/3 cup whipping cream
2 cups pecan halves

Topping:
1 tsp. butter or margarine
½ cup milk chocolate chips
2 T. whipping cream

Preheat oven to 325 degrees. Grease a 9-inch square pan.

In a medium bowl, combine powdered sugar, butter and whipping cream; blend well. Add flour to butter mixture and mix until crumbly. With floured hands, press crust evenly into the greased pan. Bake for 15 to 20 minutes, or until firm to touch.

For filling:

Combine caramels and whipping cream in a saucepan and cook over low heat, until caramels are melted and mixture is smooth, stirring occasionally. Remove from heat. Add pecans; stir well to coat evenly. Immediately spoon over baked crust, covering it completely.

For topping:

In a double boiler, melt butter and chocolate chips, stirring constantly. Add whipping cream. Drizzle over filling. Refrigerate Turtles 1 hour or until filling is firm. Cut into bars. Yields 24 bars.

Farewell to Our Kettering Friends
A Mexican Buffet

Texas Sushi

Mexican Salad
with Border Dressing

Acapulco Avocados with Chicken

Lady Bird Johnson's Shrimp Squash Casserole

Sweet Potato Tamales

Vegetable Burritos

Pico de Gallo

Dessert:
Apple Chimichangas

TEXAS SUSHI

Rice Filling:

1½ cups short-grain rice	1 tsp. cumin
2 cups water	1 tsp. fresh parsley, chopped
3 T. distilled white vinegar	Salt and freshly ground pepper
2 T. sugar	⅓ cup Monterey jack, grated

Place rice and water in medium saucepan. Bring to boil. Reduce heat and simmer, covered, for 20 minutes, or until all liquid is absorbed. While rice is cooking, combine vinegar, sugar, cumin, parsley, salt and pepper in a separate saucepan. Bring to a boil, stirring constantly. When sugar dissolves, remove from heat. Stir vinegar mixture into cooked rice and set aside until liquid is absorbed. When rice mixture has cooled, add cheese and stir. Adjust seasonings, if needed.

Sushi Wrapping:

1 lb. lean, rare roast beef, cut ⅛ to ¼-inch thick
2 cups salsa
1 cup refried beans
¼ tsp. cumin
1 green bell pepper, cut into 3/8 inch strips

1 red bell pepper, cut into 3/8-inch strips
1 bunch fresh cilantro, chopped
2 bunches fresh chives

Cut roast beef into 1½-inch wide by 3-inch long rectangles and marinate in salsa for 5 to 10 minutes. Drain and pat dry. Combine refried beans and cumin in food processor and blend until smooth. Spread beef slices with bean mixture. Top with a layer of Rice Filling and place strips of peppers (jalapeños can be added, if desired) in a vertical line across the rice. Sprinkle with cilantro. Roll, jellyroll fashion, and refrigerate until firm, at least 1½ hours. Before serving, cut each roll into 3 1-inch pieces. Tie each Sushi with a chive. Serve with salsa or guacamole. Yields 20 hors d'oeuvres.

MEXICAN SALAD WITH BORDER DRESSING

Border Dressing:

¾ cup oil
¼ cup red wine vinegar
⅛ cup sherry wine vinegar
¾ cup mayonnaise
1 cup sour cream
1 T. oregano
2½ tsp. cumin

2½ tsp. granulated garlic
1½ tsp. taco seasoning
½ tsp. salt
¼ tsp. black pepper
3 dashes hot pepper sauce
3 T. chopped green chiles
¼ cup milk

Combine all ingredients in a blender and mix until thick and emulsified. Thin with additional milk, if necessary. Refrigerate for 3 hours before serving. Yields 3 cups.

Mexican Salad:

2 heads iceberg lettuce, washed and torn into bite-sized pieces
½ cup green cabbage, shredded
½ cup red cabbage, shredded
1 red onion, sliced into rings
5 green onions, chopped

1 pt. cherry tomatoes, halved
3 ripe avocados, sliced or chunks
1 cup garbanzo beans
1 2½-oz. can sliced black olives, drained
3 cups crushed tortilla chips

In a large salad bowl, toss the lettuce, green cabbage, and red cabbage together. Layer the remaining ingredients in the listed order. Accompany with a bowl of Border Dressing. Serves 8.

ACAPULCO AVOCADOS WITH CHICKEN

1 T. vegetable oil	2 T. chopped green chiles
½ cup onions, chopped	½ tsp. cumin
2 garlic cloves, chopped	1 cup canned chopped
1 lb. boneless, skinless	tomatoes, with juice
chicken breasts	Salt and pepper, to taste
½ cup raisins	
½ cup pecans, chopped	12 ripe avocados
¼ tsp. cinnamon	Sauce (recipe follows)
1 tsp. sugar	Cilantro leaves for garnish

Heat oil in a large skillet and sauté onions and garlic until soft. Add chicken and cook until browned. Remove the chicken breasts from the pan and dice into small pieces. Return the diced chicken to the skillet; add the raisins, pecans, cinnamon, sugar, green chiles, cumin, chopped tomatoes, salt and pepper and simmer for 10 minutes. (Can be made ahead to this point and refrigerated or frozen.)

Acapulco Sauce:

½ cup green onions, chopped	2 T. green chiles, chopped
½ cup green bell peppers, chopped	½ tsp. salt
1 T. fresh garlic, chopped	1 T. tomato paste
2 T. oil	1 14½-oz. can diced tomatoes

Sauté the onions, green onions, green pepper, and garlic in oil until soft. Add remaining ingredients and simmer for 15 minutes. (Can be made ahead and refrigerated or frozen.) Yields 2½ cups.

Assembly:

Preheat oven to 375 degrees. Cut the ripe avocados in half, lengthwise, and remove the seed. Do not peel. Cut ⅛ inch off the bottom of each avocado half so they will sit flat.

In a large casserole, place 1 heaping tablespoon of the chicken mixture in the middle of each avocado and pack tightly. Top with enough sauce to cover. Bake for 15 to 18 minutes, or until hot. Garnish with cilantro leaves. Serves 12.

LADY BIRD JOHNSON'S SHRIMP SQUASH CASSEROLE

This recipe was contributed by the late Lady Bird Johnson, wife of former President of the United States, the late Lyndon Baines Johnson. It was frequently served to family and friends at the Johnson Ranch in Stonewall, Texas.

2 T. margarine	¾ cup raw shrimp, peeled,
2 T. flour	deveined, rinsed and drained
½ tsp. salt	3 cups yellow squash, cut
1/8 tsp. pepper	crosswise into ¼-inch slices
1 cup chicken broth	½ cup coarse breadcrumbs
1 T. onion, finely minced	¼ cup Parmesan cheese
½ cup heavy cream	1 T. margarine, melted

Heat margarine in a saucepan and blend in flour, salt and pepper. Cook until mixture bubbles. Remove from heat and gradually add chicken broth, stirring constantly. Bring to a boil for 1-2 minutes. Blend in cream and onions; stir in raw shrimp. Set aside.

Preheat oven to 400 degrees. Layer squash in 1½-quart casserole dish. Spoon half of shrimp sauce over squash. Repeat with remaining squash and shrimp sauce. Cover tightly and bake for 30 minutes.

Meanwhile, toss crumbs and Parmesan cheese with melted margarine. After 30 minutes of baking, remove casserole from oven, top with breadcrumbs, reduce heat to 350, and return the casserole to the oven for 15 additional minutes, or until crumbs are golden brown. Serves 6-8.

SWEET POTATO TAMALES

3 lbs. sweet potatoes, baked and peeled	1 tsp. salt
½ tsp. ginger	½ cup heavy cream
4 egg whites, beaten	1 cup mangoes, drained, diced
1½ tsp. cinnamon	1 cup apples, peeled, chopped
½ tsp. nutmeg	1 pkg. dried corn husks, soaked in water overnight

Combine sweet potatoes, ginger, egg whites, cinnamon, nutmeg, salt and heavy cream in a food processor. In a bowl, combine sweet potato mixture with mangoes and apples. Chill for 2 hours.

Place one softened corn husk on a flat surface and pat dry. Spread ⅓ cup of the sweet potato mixture in the center of the husk and roll cigar-style, tying the ends with thin strips of softened corn husks. Repeat until all ingredients have been used.

Steam for 25 minutes. The tamales can be made ahead, refrigerated, and steamed 25 minutes prior to serving. Yields approximately 3 dozen tamales.

VEGETABLE BURRITO

1 cup onions, chopped	2 T. ripe olives, sliced (optional)
1 tsp. fresh garlic, minced	1 red pepper, sliced into strips
2 T. olive oil	1 T. cilantro
1 15-oz. can black beans, drained and rinsed	½ tsp. marjoram
	½ tsp. thyme
1½ cups fresh Roma tomatoes, diced	½ tsp. oregano
1 medium zucchini, sliced into strips	½ tsp. chili powder
2 yellow squash, sliced into strips	¾ tsp. salt
1 yellow bell pepper, sliced into strips	¼ tsp. pepper
4 oz. green chiles, chopped (optional)	

Condiments:

8 10-inch flour tortillas, heated in foil	2 cups sour cream
	4 oz. shredded cheddar cheese
½ cup green onions, chopped	¾ cup fresh tomatoes, chopped
½ cup jalapeño peppers, seeded, sliced	1 cup Pico de Gallo (recipe follows)

Sauté onions and garlic in olive oil, in a large skillet, until lightly brown. Add remaining ingredients and simmer for 15 minutes or until crisp-tender. Serve with condiments. Serves 4.

PICO DE GALLO

This is a Pico de Gallo for tender mouths. Using the freshest ingredients assures perfect results. For a spicier version, add additional peppers.

8 tomatoes, chopped
1 cup white onions, chopped
1 Serrano chile pepper (or more to taste)
1 green bell pepper, seeded and chopped
½ cup green onions, chopped

1 cucumber, seeded and chopped
1 red bell pepper, seeded and chopped
2 T. fresh lime juice
1 tsp. sugar
2 tsp. salt
Dash of hot pepper sauce
Black pepper, to taste

Combine all ingredients. Refrigerate for several hours. Serve chilled. Yields 8 cups.

APPLE CHIMICHANGAS

4 cups apples, peeled and chopped
Juice of 1½ lemons
2 T. sugar
2 T. brown sugar
2 T. honey
1½ tsp. cinnamon
1 T. white vanilla

Pinch of nutmeg
18 thin flour tortillas
18 long toothpicks
Oil for frying
Cinnamon-sugar mixture
Powdered sugar

As you peel and chop apples, add them to the lemon juice and toss. Add sugars, honey, cinnamon, vanilla, and nutmeg and mix well.

Heat flour tortillas, four at a time, in the microwave for 20 seconds, until soft. Place a heaping tablespoon of filling down the center of each tortilla, and roll, cigar style, securing with a toothpick. As you roll the chimichangas, place a damp towel over them to prevent their drying out.

Heat oil to 375 degrees. Fry chimichangas, seam side down, taking care not to crowd. Turn once when bottoms are lightly browned. (Overcooking will cause toughness.) Drain on paper towel. While still hot, sprinkle chimichangas with cinnamon-sugar mixture and/or powdered sugar.

An alternative cooking method: Preheat oven to 400 degrees. Lightly brush cookie sheet with oil. Place rolled chimichangas, seam side down, on the cookie sheet. Brush with oil and bake for 10 to 11 minutes, turning once when the bottoms are light golden brown. Remove from oven and sprinkle with cinnamon-sugar mixture and/or powdered sugar. Yields 18 chimichangas.

Spring Chicken with Asparagus, page 198.
Photo by *Austin American Statesman*

Texas Sushi, page 216
Photo by *Austin American Statesman*

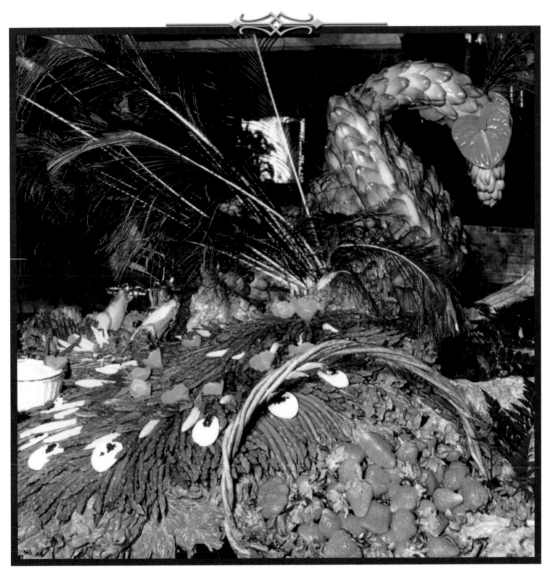

Edible Vegetable Peacock Centerpiece created for
His Royal Highness, Prince Charles.

Photo by Carol Felauer

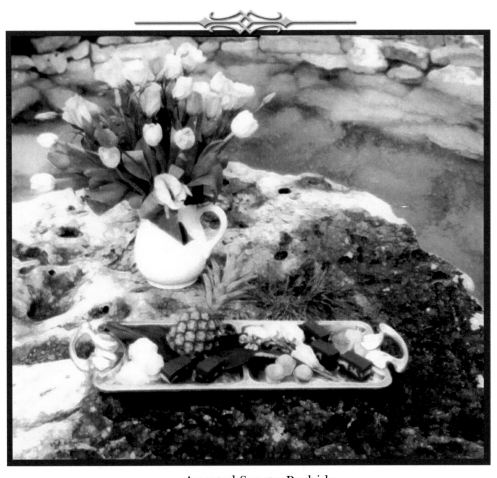

Assorted Sweets, Poolside
From left to right: Glazed Pineapple Cookies, page 194;
Cream Cheese Brownies, page 57; Almond Butter Cups, page 51.
Photo by *Austin American Statesman*

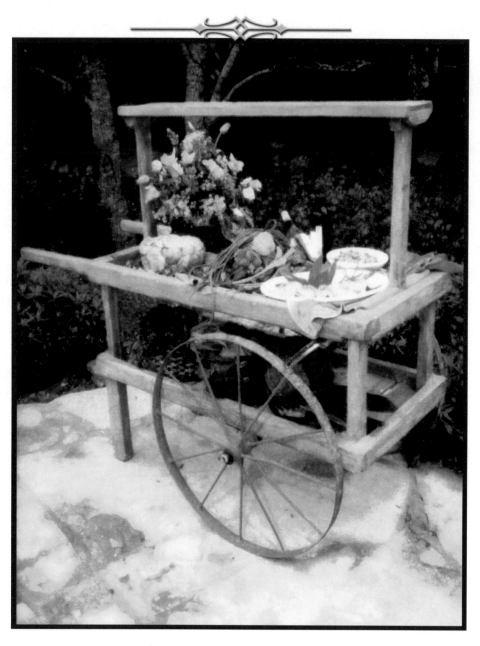

Appetizers at Fall Creek Winery, page 195.
Photo by *Austin American Statesman*

Chapter 13

Our Royal Touch

here's a time each year that those in the catering business generally refer to as "Christmas Chaos." It's that countdown to Christmas when parties fill every day and chefs and their elves forego sleep, working around the clock to serve mouthwatering holiday cheer.

With this in mind, imagine the scene at Gourmet Gals & Guys on December 18 when, with dozens of holiday parties behind us and our sights set on the fast-approaching and much needed New Year break, we received a late afternoon call from Dorothy Territo, our contact from the LBJ Library and Museum, seeking a bid on a gala dinner party. The February event was to be no ordinary affair, she assured us. The guest of honor? None other than England's Prince Charles (formerly known as Princess Diana's husband)!

For months, Austin had been buzzing with news of the Prince of Wales' imminent visit. The heir to the British throne was coming to town to participate in a gala fundraising drive. Like everyone in our industry, we, too, were looking forward to the visit, having high hopes of serving the future King.

And then out of the blue, the bid we'd been waiting for! That golden opportunity to dazzle a man whose list of scrupulously planned meals was undoubtedly longer than the tree-lined drive leading up to Windsor Castle.

But with opportunity came challenge. How to make a lasting impression? What to serve a man who has been entertained around the world's most prestigious tables? How to woo the Prince's silver-lined palate? And equally — if not more — challenging, how to handle the logistics of serving 500 guests, each of whom had paid a hefty $2,500 for a dinner ticket, in a severely restricted amount of time? Scheduling was tight, the event planner explained. His Royal Highness and escort, Mrs. Lady Bird Johnson, would have to greet all the guests in a formal receiving line, then leisurely "eat and run" in order to make it to a special concert engagement by Texas' own Willie Nelson. Adding to our "catering crazies," the bid had to be submitted by the following day.

Battling seasonal burnout, we summoned our remaining energy and got those creative juices flowing. In the wee hours of the morning, a lavish menu was conceived, and the logistical complications resolved. Later that day, a call was made, the bid turned in, and in no time, the dinner of the year was in our hands.

We were off and running! Twenty-five buffet tables in the Great Hall of the LBJ Library were to be laden with Continental specialties. More than 100 pounds of fresh asparagus would be marinated to form the "tails" for three magnificent peacock centerpieces. The evening's elegant buffet was to feature seafood and poultry, lamb and beef, in addition to an array of tantalizing accompaniments. Given the restricted time period and number of guests expected, it was out of the question that dessert be served by the wait staff. Our solution? Graceful, custom-made, white chocolate swans would be filled with miniature sweets and placed on each dining table, doubling as centerpieces. Guests would serve themselves.

February was soon upon us, and although the menu was filled with extravagant entrees, something about the menu didn't seem right. What was missing? The Prince had seen his share of culinary feats, and we wanted our offerings to be memorable to him. After all, the man had been around.

And then it came to us. Prince Charles was coming to Texas! We Texans declare proudly that our home is like a country of its own. Why not serve something to prove it? And so it was decided. The missing menu link was, quite simply, our state's specialty: something Tex-Mex. The dish we would present had to be authentic and straightforward, but extraordinary nonetheless. So into the spotlight came our Cheese and Spinach Enchiladas with Verde Sauce. We called to inform the coordinator of our ingenious addition, and in a strained, if amiable voice, she acquiesced, with a huge sigh, replying half-heartedly, "If you must."

The fairytale had begun. Prince Charles flew into town on a balmy February day. A media blitz reported the man's every move, and the local news-paper, the *Austin American-Statesman,* even published the menu that we would serve His Royal Highness.

If television anchors and the print media scrutinized each of the Prince's activities, local radio host Bob Cole had a different approach to the royal hoopla. During his popular morning show, Mr. Cole revealed with his usual charm that "for a mere $2,500 you, too, can meet Prince Charles, shake his hand and dine on Cheese and Spinach Enchiladas . . . " Our Tex-Mex menu addition had taken center stage!

At 6:00 P.M. Prince Charles arrived at the LBJ Library and Museum, to visit with Mrs. Johnson in her private suite. At 7:00 P.M. the two moved to the Great Hall to greet all 500 guests personally. By the time Prince Charles was seated, the evening's schedule was already twenty minutes behind. After going through the buffet tables and scanning the offerings, to our surprise, His Royal Highness, the Prince of Wales, chose one single enchilada! Not that we were watching, mind you, but we noticed that he savored it down to the very last bite.

Soon, our part of the show would be over. Months of preparation and anticipation were coming to a close. The time had come for the Prince to depart for an earful of Willie's crooning. But in a move that marked a crowning success (no pun intended) for us, His Royal Highness requested another serving of enchiladas. And like a winning royal flush, a second helping of our Texas offering was laid down on the table before him.

Fit for a King

Cocktail Buffet honoring
His Royal Highness,
Charles, the Prince of Wales

In the Great Hall of the LBJ Library/Museum

Royal Seafood Salad

Gourmet Gals and Guys Famous
Vegetable Peacock
Ladened with Fresh Marinated Asparagus

Chicken Cachet

Tawny Beef Tenderloin Royale
Broiled Salmon

Cheese and Spinach Enchiladas

Dessert:
*White Chocolate Swans
Filled with assorted sweets

English Raspberry Tarts

Nonnie's Pecan Crescents

Chocolate Cherry Surprises

*Recipe not included

ROYAL SEAFOOD SALAD

Basil Sauce:

2 T. fresh garlic, chopped	1 T. dried basil
1/3 cup white wine vinegar	2/3 cup olive oil
2 cups sour cream	Salt and pepper, to taste
6 T. fresh parsley, chopped	Freshly squeezed lemon juice, to taste
1 T. fresh basil, chopped	

Mix garlic, white wine vinegar, sour cream, parsley, and basil in a food processor until well blended. Slowly add the oil until the mixture is thick. Add salt, pepper and lemon juice. Refrigerate for 24 hours.

Seafood Salad:

2 cups celery, thinly sliced	½ lb. large shrimp, cooked, shells removed and deveined
1 cup onion, chopped	
1½ T. olive oil	1 cup artichoke hearts, finely sliced
½ lb. sea scallops	
2 cups cooked lobster, cut in chunks	1 8-oz. can water chestnuts, chopped

Sauté celery and onions in olive oil until crisp and translucent. Add the scallops, lobster, and shrimp and cook for 3-4 minutes. Remove from heat and let cool. Toss the seafood with Basil Sauce and stir in the artichoke hearts and water chestnuts. Refrigerate and serve chilled. Serves 6.

ARTICHOKE AND ASPARAGUS PEACOCK

The Artichoke and Asparagus Peacock is a show-stopper originally designed for the buffet tables in the LBJ Library Great Hall for the reception honoring His Royal Highness, the Prince of Wales. Since then, it has become our "Coat of Arms" for other fabulous parties. The peacocks are constructed specifically for each party, and often include additional vegetables for color and variety. The leaves are removed from cooked artichokes and secured with floral pins to a Styrofoam base forming the head and body of the peacock. The tail consists of artfully placed asparagus and an array of other vegetables. The following ingredients, when processed into cocktail-size pieces, are enough to serve 150 guests on a dinner buffet.

30 lbs. asparagus, trimmed and blanched	2 dozen hard-cooked eggs, sliced (used to create the "eyes" on the peacock's tail)
8 lbs. snow peas, blanched	
2 lbs. baby yellow squash	2 oz. black caviar, garnish for hard-cooked eggs
2 lbs. baby carrots	

CHICKEN CACHET

This is a wonderful chicken dish, indeed fit for a King! But it takes some care in preparation. If you are unaccustomed to working with Fillo dough, carefully read and follow the directions on the Fillo dough box. An important thing to remember when working with Fillo is to keep the dough covered, preventing the pastry from drying out.

4   whole chicken breasts, cut in half
Salt and pepper
2   10-oz. pkgs. frozen chopped spinach, defrosted and squeezed dry
¾   cup Parmesan cheese
1   cup Swiss cheese, shredded
¾   cup mayonnaise
½   tsp. granulated garlic
3   dashes hot pepper sauce

2   T. Worcestershire
½   cup green onions, chopped
¼   cup white wine
1   lb. mushrooms, cleaned, chopped and sautéed in 1 T. butter
1 to 2 boxes of Fillo dough, defrosted at room temperature
½   cup butter, melted
3   T. Dijon mustard

Pound and season the chicken breasts with salt and pepper. Cover and refrigerate.

Combine the spinach, cheeses, mayonnaise, seasonings, onions, wine, and sautéed mushrooms.

Prepare the pastry by layering 7 sheets of Fillo dough in this order: 1 sheet of Fillo, brushed with butter; 2nd sheet of Fillo, brushed with butter; 3rd sheet (no butter); 4th sheet (no butter); 5th sheet, brushed with butter; 6th sheet, brushed with butter; and the 7th sheet, brushed with butter.

Place 4 breast halves overlapping on the lower third of the Fillo rectangle, leaving a 1-inch margin on the sides. Brush the chicken with Dijon mustard and spread 1 cup of spinach mixture over the chicken.

Fold the Fillo over the chicken and spinach, folding in the 1-inch side margins. Continue to roll until it is a log. Brush all sides. Repeat procedures with the remaining ingredients. You will have two Chicken Cachets. Cover and refrigerate for 24 hours.

To bake: Preheat oven to 350 degrees. Bring the Chicken Cachet to room temperature and place on a wire rack on a baking sheet. Bake for 30-35 minutes, rotating the baking sheet after 15 minutes.

Allow to cool. Slice into 1-inch rounds, approximately 18 per roll. Serve at room temperature with Chicken Cachet arranged domino-style on a silver platter. Serves 8.

TAWNY BEEF TENDERLOIN ROYALE

This recipe was contributed by the Texas Beef Council, and was their 1993 entry in the Texas Beef Recipe Contest. An elegant yet simple entree that will impress your guests with its regal flavor and will become one of your favorites because of its ease in preparation.

1 T. olive oil	1 cup beef broth
½ tsp. salt	10 juniper berries, crushed
½ tsp. black pepper, crushed	¼ cup seedless raspberry
4 beef tenderloin steaks, cut	preserves
1-inch thick	2 tsp. cornstarch mixed with
¼ cup red onion, diced	2 tsp. water
4 garlic cloves, minced	Sprigs of basil, rosemary, or fresh
1 T. fresh rosemary, crushed	raspberries for garnish
1 cup tawny port wine	

Preheat oven to 200 degrees, or "warm." Pour olive oil in a pie pan and tilt to coat bottom. Sprinkle salt and pepper on top of oil. Dredge both sides of steaks in mixture. Brown steaks in a large nonstick skillet over medium heat and cook 8 to 10 minutes for rare to medium, turning once. Remove steaks to an ovenproof platter, cover with foil, and place in oven to stay warm while making sauce.

Sauté onions in drippings in skillet until translucent, about 2 minutes. Stir in garlic, crushed rosemary, wine, beef broth, and juniper berries. Bring liquid to a boil and cook until volume is reduced by half, about 10 minutes. Strain liquid through a fine sieve and return to skillet. Discard pulp. Stir in raspberry preserves and cornstarch/water mixture over medium heat until preserves are dissolved and sauce is thickened. Spoon sauce over steaks and serve immediately, garnished with sprigs of fresh herbs and fresh raspberries. Serves 4.

Note: If tawny port wine isn't available, use any port wine or red burgundy, though it will alter the flavors a bit.

BROILED SALMON

2½   lbs. fresh salmon filets,
    deboned

Marinade:

½ cup dry vermouth	½ tsp. basil
½ cup olive oil	1 tsp. sugar
2 T. lemon juice,	½ tsp. rosemary
freshly squeezed	½ tsp. thyme
½ tsp. salt	1 T. fresh parsley, minced
1/8 tsp. black pepper,	½ cup green onions, chopped
freshly ground	

Combine all marinade ingredients in a blender and mix well. Pour marinade over salmon and refrigerate in a glass dish for 4 to 6 hours, turning fish twice.

Remove salmon, reserving marinade, and broil on a greased rack, basting with reserved marinade, for approximately 6 to 8 minutes per side, or until the salmon flakes easily. Serves 6.

CHEESE AND SPINACH ENCHILADAS

Dedicated to our friend, Bob Cole.

Enchilada Sauce:

2	cups onions, chopped		1	2-oz. can Ro-tel tomatoes, chopped
2	T. vegetable oil		4	oz. green chiles, chopped
2	T. garlic, chopped		2	cups milk
¼	lb. butter		2	cups chicken broth
¾	cup flour		½	tsp. salt

Sauté the onions in oil. Add the garlic and cook for 1 minute. Add butter and melt; stir in flour and cook for approximately 2 minutes. Slowly add remaining ingredients, stirring after each addition. Simmer for approximately 10 minutes.

Filling:

½	lb. cheddar cheese, grated		1	bunch green onions, chopped
½	lb. mozzarella cheese, grated		1	16-oz. pkg. chopped, frozen spinach
1	4-oz. can chopped ripe olives			(defrosted and squeezed dry)

Combine ingredients. Set aside.

Assembly:
16 corn tortillas

Spray a large casserole dish with cooking spray. Pour a small amount of the sauce on the bottom of the dish. Dip each side of the tortillas in the warm enchilada sauce. Spoon 1 heaping tablespoon of filling into each of the tortillas; roll cigar-style, and place seam down in the casserole. Pour the remaining sauce over the top of the enchiladas. Cover and bake in 350-degree oven for approximately 40 minutes. Uncover, and bake additional 10 minutes. Allow to sit for 15 minutes before serving. This can be made ahead and baked just before serving. Garnish with sour cream, chopped green onions, shredded cheese. Yields 8 servings.

ENGLISH RASPBERRY TARTS

Dough:

1½ cups flour
2 T. sugar
¼ tsp. salt
½ cup butter
1 egg yolk
2 to 2½ T. ice water

Filling:

1 egg
½ cup sugar
½ cup almond paste
1 cup almonds, finely chopped

6-8 tsp. seedless red raspberry preserves

For dough: Combine flour, sugar, salt, and butter in a food processor and mix well. Add egg yolk and ice water and mix until the dough forms a soft ball. Refrigerate.

For filling: Combine egg, sugar, and almond paste and blend well.

Preheat oven to 350 degrees. Line miniature muffin tins with 24 mini-muffin paper baking cups. Press dough into paper cups. Spoon ¼ tsp. raspberry preserves into each tart shell. Top with 1 tsp. of the almond mixture and sprinkle with chopped almonds. Place muffin tins on baking sheets to prevent the bottoms of the tarts from scorching, and bake for 15 to 20 minutes. Cool the tarts slightly in the tins, then remove, and cool on wire racks. May be frozen. Yields 24 tarts.

NONNIE'S PECAN CRESCENTS

2   cups all-purpose flour, sifted
½   tsp. salt
1   cup butter, softened
6   T. powdered sugar

1   tsp. vanilla
1   cup pecans, finely chopped
Powdered sugar

Preheat oven to 350 degrees. Sift flour and salt together. In a medium mixing bowl, cream the butter until soft. Add powdered sugar and vanilla, blending well. Add flour in small amounts. Fold in finely chopped pecans. Chill dough slightly. Roll a heaping tablespoon into the shape of a pencil. On an ungreased cookie sheet form the "pencil" into a crescent. Bake for 10 to 15 minutes or until lightly browned on edges. While still warm, dust with powdered sugar. Remove from cookie sheet while warm. Yields 4 dozen.

CHOCOLATE CHERRY SURPRISES

40 Maraschino cherries, well-drained
¼   cup brandy
½   cup butter, softened
¼   cup powdered sugar

½   tsp. vanilla extract
½   tsp. almond extract
1   cup flour

Glaze:

6   oz. semisweet chocolate chips
¼   cup light corn syrup

2   T. water

Soak the cherries overnight in brandy.

Preheat oven to 350 degrees. Cream the butter, powdered sugar, vanilla and almond extracts. Add the flour, mixing on low speed until fully combined. Drain cherries then wrap 1 tsp. of dough around each cherry, covering completely. Place on a cookie sheet and bake for 8 to 10 minutes or until lightly browned. Cool on wire racks.

While the cookies are baking, heat glaze ingredients in a double boiler until the chips are melted and the sauce is smooth. Place wax paper beneath cookie racks.

Spoon the glaze over each cookie and allow to cool completely. Yields 40 cookies.

Chapter 14

On the Road

SHE SAID, SHE SAID ...

fter a year of writing our stories, a year of recipe testing, and a year of publishing, we finally "birthed" *Texas Tuxedos to Tacos*. We thought our jobs were over, but weren't we surprised! Book signings. That was when the fun really started. The more signings we did, the busier we became. It snowballed! It wasn't enough for us to only sign books, but organizations and groups of all sizes and shapes, women and even men's groups, wanted us to tell more of our stories. Did we have more stories to tell—you bet! Before we knew it, we developed our "Dog and Pony" show, bought our plane tickets, and hit the road. We found that these presentations were as much fun as writing the book, and it gave us the opportunity to expound and express what we really wanted to say but couldn't print. This chapter (darn it!) isn't an expose, but will tell more of our "catering crazies" that we divulged during our road shows.

The extent of our travels amazed us. The mystique of Texas is always "in," and forgive us for bragging, but these two Texas gals with a cookbook were in great demand. Who knew? Sometimes we were cheap dates, as we never turned down an opportunity to help an organization with fund raising. Anything for charity.

We traveled from one end of Texas to the other, and packed our bags for Atlanta, Chicago, New York, Washington, D.C., Oklahoma, Arizona, and California. How thrilling for "two little gals from Austin" (the nickname our publisher, the late Ed Eakin, had for us). If working closely together for 30 years wasn't enough of a "marriage," traveling together taught us more about each other than we really needed to know.

The format for our theatrical presentations took several guises. Our favorite one was to play off each other. The more we did it, the better we got, and the more fun we had. We had great audiences that we amused, and they usually amused us right back during the question and answer periods. We would often begin by describing what happened while writing the book. During that time we had a broken leg, three new grandchildren, and one of us learned excellent computer skills. We also realized that we were going to have to test all the new recipes for the cookbook, because chefs are notorious for only listing ingredients without amounts in their recipes. Besides, who wanted a recipe to serve 1,200 people? For your information, during the recipe-testing time, our families and all our neighbors ate well, and we each gained twenty pounds that year. We enjoyed our own cooking so much, that instead of "taste-testing" the huge popovers, in the chapter named "Austintatious," the two of us ate all 8!

There were so many things to say and tell. There's a story in the book about a cattle auction, where the cows drank the "tank" dry, putting us completely out of water. It took over an hour to replenish the water supply. What we didn't tell you before was that because of the lack of water, the kitchen faucets stopped flowing and the bathrooms were out of order—and because this was a beer-drinking crowd, most of the guests sat with their knees crossed or stood with their legs together for the better part of an hour. In the meantime, our staff was fighting a constant battle with the client's cats, trying to keep them out of the tented catering kitchen and the garbage, to no avail. As an exasperated caterer came around the corner of the house with another bag of garbage, she heard a noise and yelled, "Caught you!" to frighten away the guilty cats. What she actually "caught" was one of the male guests, trying to relive himself in what he thought was an inconspicuous spot.

At one point, our largest event was the grand opening of a regional mall, for 10,000 guests. We had been planning it for six months. Each wing of the mall featured different food areas highlighting Academy Award winning movies. "Rhett" and "Scarlett" served southern foods in front of "Tara," from *Gone With the Wind*, and there was a rock and roll station featuring John Travolta and Olivia Newton John look-alikes from *Grease*. Desserts were served in Casablanca, with the piano in the background, and "Humphrey Bogart" serving champagne. It was a particularly exciting event, because Faith Hill was the headliner, just as she was becoming Faith Hill. Besides coordinating 275 in staff, the biggest problem of the night was keeping our love-sick chef in the kitchen with his mind on the food, and not on Faith's performance.

The directors of a new hospital complex hired us for their grand opening. It was a huge undertaking, as it spanned three days of intricate events. The first night, Friday, was for 1,500 VIPs, and Saturday evening was a black-tie dinner, for 500 guests, with 75 food choices on the extensive buffets. The final event, open to the public, was on Sunday afternoon, where we were told to expect about 2,000 people. All well and good, until Sunday's newspaper had a full-page ad, extending an invitation to the entire community—"Come One; Come All"—and they did! At least 10,000 people showed up for ice cream sundaes on that notorious Sunday. Always keeping our sense of humor, however, we served the ice cream in the Labor and Delivery area, naturally accompanied by dill pickles.

Prince Charles—our piece de resistance! What you don't know is the rest of the story. In the first printing of *Texas Tuxedos to Tacos*, we told you that His Royal Highness, Prince Charles, came to Austin to help raise funds for the restoration of the Texas Capitol. Being a vegetarian, he absolutely loved our Spinach and Cheese Enchiladas. In fact, he asked for a second helping. We also told you about the local radio disc jockey, ignoring the wonderful extensive menu, who jokingly said that anyone can eat Spinach and Cheese Enchiladas with the future King of England for a mere $2,500 per plate. Shortly after the book was published, we decided to send the disc jockey a copy of the book, with the said enchiladas. We asked our chef to prepare the dish, exactly from the book's recipe. Imagine our chagrin, and humiliation, to discover that the main ingredient—the spinach—had been left out of this featured recipe in our wonderful, new cookbook! With all the proofreading and editing, it remains a mystery where the spinach went. Those early books are now collector's items.

Our audiences loved our personal stories, some of which weren't in the least bit funny when they actually occurred, but became humorous after the fact. Our "Swan Songs" were a favorite. Swans were one of our special forms of food presentation. We used them in different styles and designs, sometimes as centerpieces, but most of the time, we used them for dessert. We often made them of pate-choux or chocolate. In either case, they were very labor intensive, as well as weather-sensitive. One April evening, while serving dinner on a veranda, we served pate-choux swans filled with a creamy chocolate mousse, sitting on a pool of raspberry anglaise and garnished with orchids—the crowning glory to the fabulous dinner party. As the waiters served these masterpieces, we overheard the guests' laughs and giggles, instead of oooh's and ahh's. Because of the high humidity that night, as the plates were placed in front of the guests, the little heads and necks of our fabulous swans took a nose-dive into the pool of raspberry sauce.

Our chocolate swans, and fabulous chocolate baskets, didn't fare any better when we took them on a three-hour early morning trip to a Texas Hill Country ranch. It was dark and cold the morning we left for the party, and we were early, so we decided to stop along the way for a hearty breakfast, knowing that the next chance for a meal could be twelve hours away. Imagine our surprise, when we left the restaurant and were greeted by the blistering spring sun! The temperature in the car had risen 30 degrees in the short time we were inside, and all the fabulous, handmade, chocolate "serving pieces," including the swans, had been reduced to puddles. Only one of the woven chocolate baskets survived! The moral to this story is no pate-choux or chocolate desserts without checking with the weatherman first.

Shopping is an art, and no less in the life of a caterer. The freshest fruits and vegetables reflect the quality of the food we served, so every day was a shopping day at the market. In the early days of Gourmet Gals and Guys, the commercial kitchen was in a neighborhood home. The staff, at that time, was all women, mostly in their thirties, who were all very attractive. We were a fun group, who shared all the working tasks happily, except for the daily shopping chore. Then there was Arlys, who was definitely "born to shop." She didn't care what she shopped for, she just loved going to the store, so she was a natural. Arlys is 5' 6", 120 pounds with long, platinum blonde hair, and always wore three-inch heels—even at twelve-hour parties. (The rest of us hobbled around in tennis shoes.) One day, while Arlys was shopping, a gentleman from the neighborhood walked up to her in the store, and started a conversation. It was obvious that his curiosity had gotten the better of him as he remarked to her, "I often see you and other women coming and going from the house down the block, at all times of the day and night. Just what IS it you all do there, and what's going on?" What was going on indeed! Shortly after that experience, we moved out of the neighborhood and into a commercial kitchen.

There's a special bond between the caterer and the client as their event is being planned. The client trusts that the caterer will make it happen, even perform miracles if necessary, by using all of their skills and knowledge (remember Chapter One "And What Are You Doing About the Weather?") Organization, checks and balances are the key words here. What would be a client's worst nightmare? The caterers showing up at the wrong time or date? It could never happened to us, because we double-checked the final details constantly with the client, and gave precise times when the rentals, flowers, and caterers would arrive. However, there was a Saturday graduation brunch, beginning at 11:00 A.M. We had been in contact with the hostess all week, which was our usual business practice. She had picked out the colors for the floral centerpieces, given us the deposit, and her final guest count. We were ready to go—and we did. We arrived punctually at 7:00 A.M., as

planned, ready to begin setting up the table and chairs, which had been delivered the previous day. There was no sign of life in the house, so we rang the doorbell, thinking maybe they overslept. We rang it again, and waited. Slowly the door opened, and our client's sleepy face appeared. She was obviously very surprised and confused to see us, and asked, "What are you doing here?" Just as surprised, we replied, "It's party time!" "Oh no," she said. "The party is next Saturday—not today!" With very red faces, we hastily made our retreat, while wondering how this could have happened. What was she thinking? Would flowers and rentals be delivered a week early? How could our fail-safe planning method go so wrong? Needless to say, our families and friends enjoyed "brunch" all weekend. We went back the following Saturday, this time on the right day, and did the graduation party all over again. We made sure that was the first, and LAST time, it ever happened!

Unfortunately, we have more of these catering nightmares to share, but, that's a whole other book.

Chapter 15

And Then We Wrote . . .

uring the past thirty years we have learned many "tips" that have saved both time and frustration. Though some of our advice is simply party "basics," you can never be too prepared to enjoy your own party.

The "to take list" has been a critical part of our Gourmet Gals & Guys planning and has accompanied us to every party for many years. We have adapted it here for a home "to do list." This simple concept is really a party bible which, if followed closely, will help you organize, plan, and implement your party from its inception to the departure of the last guest.

The "to do list" begins with the menu, but develops into a detailed horizontal outline. When you are through with the "to do list," the entire party is on a single page. The food from the menu is in the first column along with the time the dish should be placed in the oven, taken out of the refrigerator, or any other final step necessary to prepare the dish. Your individual notes about the dish, including necessary cookware, comprise the second column. Next, list the serving dishes and serving pieces for each and every item on the menu. Finally, garnishes and special touches for each dish are noted in the last column.

The first column helps you to remember all the menu items to be served, as there is inevitably a gelatin mold or some such dish in the refrigerator after the party is over. The first and second columns combined will assist you in judging both oven and refrigerator space required by identifying the pan size and amount of time the ovens will be in use. The third column assures that you have the necessary serving equipment available long before the party begins. The fourth column accommodates your creativity from the beginning of your menu planning and will remind you to implement the special touches during the last minute rush. A grocery list should be developed at the same time you are generating the "to do list" with as much of the food purchased and prepared in advance.

The universal worry of hostesses is, "How much?" No one likes to run out of food. If there was a special formula we could rely on, everyone would be more comfortable when entertaining. Unfortunately, there are as many variables when choosing amounts as there are food choices. In fact, some amounts depend on the menu. A rule of thumb, however, is to plan by ounces or cups. The more food selections, the fewer ounces of each particular dish per person.

For example, if meat is the only main course, plan to serve 8 ounces per guest, which allows for shrinkage or unusable ends. If combining meat and chicken on the same buffet, allow 5 ounces of meat and 5 ounces of usable chicken. You achieve the same total ounces per guest through a combination of items. Salads, vegetables, starches, and fruits will depend on how the item is prepared, but 1 cup per person is a general rule of thumb.

233

If there is no seating, plan to serve only finger foods. A buffet with more than two hot items becomes too time-consuming unless you have help. Therefore, the remaining food choices should be served cold or at room temperature. Always offer small plates rather than just napkins, even with a pick-up buffet, which allows guests to maneuver quickly away from the table. If there are no tables and chairs, serve foods that don't require a knife. The menu items can remain the same; simply prepare the food in smaller pieces that require only a fork.

The hors d'oeuvres buffet is the simplest way to entertain with a variety of dishes. A few tips to make it even easier are as follows:

- You probably have unusual serving pieces throughout the house holding other items. Turn a close eye to unusual containers that will hold food. This is the fun part of planning your party. One of our favorite hostesses designs her buffets around the serving pieces and then chooses the food.

- Most guests tend to hover in the kitchen at home parties — so why not throw in the sink? You can create a unique serving area by clearing the countertops and filling the sink with ice. Place shrimp with sauces, vegetables and dips, assorted cheeses, crab claws, caviar, fruits, or any food that is served cold decoratively into the ice. Find several unusual serving accessories like metal buckets or glass bowls that can withstand the cold, and don't forget extra greenery and flowers to enhance the serving area.

- Hot foods such as stews, chili, or soups can be served directly from the stove. Use a wonderful "worn" kettle

with an antique ladle, and surround the stove area with assorted breads and condiments.

- Place foods in different areas throughout the house.

- Place the bar in nontraffic areas away from the food. Accessible areas such as a terrace, patio, or porch are good choices for setting up the beverages.

- Chill the beverages at least 2 hours prior to party time. If short on ice chests, fill the washing machine with ice and chill beverages. You can even resort to the bathtub if necessary. One flick of the wrist and the melted ice goes down the drain.

- Provide three cocktail napkins and two beverage glasses per guest. One plate is not enough if serving from several different food areas — plan on two.

- The fork-only buffet is the easiest way to host a brunch, luncheon, or dinner party. Foods are the same as the seated dinner but with more variety. Serving more than one entree and an assortment of salads and vegetables creates a colorful, inviting table.

- Use water-based chafers, which are available at party rental stores, as food can burn in a candle-warmed chafer.

- Set up your buffet as follows: plates, cold foods, hot foods, napkins, and finally silverware.

For those who are more ambitious, the formal seated dinner is an exact science requiring more time, preparation, planning, and, of course, extra hands if serving more than ten guests. Choose the menu so that as many of the foods as possible can be prepared in advance. Always allow yourself an extra hour preparation time that you don't think you'll need. (Murphy's Law can come into play—if something is going to go wrong, you can bet it will be now!) For the brave at heart, we offer these words of advice:

- Plan the menu considering last minute cooking versus available oven space.

- Chill the plates for any salad or dessert that is served cold.

- Warm the plates for the entrees by wrapping them in an electric blanket one hour prior to serving, saving valuable oven space.

- Centerpieces should be low enough to permit guests to talk freely.

- The appearance of the plate is as important as the food. Color is important when choosing both menu items and plate garnishes.

Tips that apply to any size party in any setting are as follows:

- We often operate from a client's garage or laundry room for preparation and clean-up, as it keeps the "mess" of parties out of sight.

- Food isn't the only aspect of a great party—ambiance is half the formula for success.

- Control the temperature. Four hours before the party, lower the thermostat regardless of whether it's summer or winter. Sixty-eight degrees can soon become 80. Bodies radiate heat.

- Use indirect lighting, rheostats, and candles to set the mood.

- Play unobtrusive background music with the volume low enough for comfortable conversation.

- Relocate furniture in a room if it blocks traffic flow. Avoid bottlenecks.

- Outdoor parties after dark attract pesky critters. Light citronella candles and spray the yard with bug repellent an hour before the party starts.

- If guests come at dusk, remember they will leave when it's dark. Always light their way.

- Two to three pounds of ice per guest is a must during summer months.

- Plan your beverages as carefully as your menu. You should always offer nonalcoholic drinks, preferably a choice of two. When planning alcoholic beverages, consult with a liquor salesperson about the quantities.

The true mystique of entertaining, no matter where you live, is to project your own personality and to provide your guests with an aura of friendship, camaraderie, and sharing. We hope we have provided a source to stimulate your imagination, taste buds, and cooking talents to create magical hours for you and your guests.

Index